Activity-Based Management in Action

The Development, Unfolding, and Progression of ABC Management Systems

Edited by

Patrick L. Romano, CMA

A project carried out on behalf of the
Institute of Management Accountants
Montvale, New Jersey

This title is included as part of IMA's Research
Publication Service (RPS). Subscribers receive all
IMA publications issued during a 12-month period.
RPS is available through IMA @ $50 per year,
(201) 573-6278.

Published by

Institute of Management Accountants
10 Paragon Drive
Montvale, NJ 07645-1760

Claire Barth, Editor
Vision Art & Design Studios, Cover

Foreword

IMA is proud to add to the literature this anthology of ABC/ABM articles that appeared in the official magazine of the Institute of Management Accountants, *Management Accounting.* Editor Patrick L. Romano skillfully leads you through the ABC/ABM evolution, commenting along the way on the significance of each article. For an understanding of ABC/ABM, you are encouraged to read the beginning of each of the seven sections before reading the articles. Reading these parts first will give you a top-view perspective and allow you to appreciate the excitement this breakthrough costing methodology has invoked throughout corporate America.

Although ABC/ABM articles and books will continue to be written, particularly as to how ABC/ABM is used, they will be refinements of the ideas and concepts presented in this anthology. Stories about the use and power of ABC/ABM are certain to flood the literature as early implementations mature and documented success stories about them emerge. IMA's Statement on Management Accounting (SMA) No. 4T, "Implementing Activity-Based Costing," addresses the "how to," while future articles in *Management Accounting* will focus on "what to do" once ABC/ABM is implemented.

The Institute of Management Accountants is a not-for-profit educational organization devoted to developing a full corporate understanding of the importance of management accounting. Established in 1919, IMA helps corporations, institutions, and other organizations resolve accounting issues through meetings, research, educational programs, round tables, and several professional publications. With 90,000 members, IMA is the world's largest organization of management accountants and financial managers.

"ABC as a cross-functional management process can help organizations weed out spoilers within current processes and focus on profitable products and services," remarks Leo M. Loiselle, CPA, 1993-94 president of IMA. "ABC is also an important tool in developing baseline data for implementing business process redesign initiatives."

IMA has taken a leadership role in disseminating ABC/ABM and has established a Continuous Improvement Center (CIC) to help organizations become more competitive by improving the quality of their financial management systems. CIC provides assessments through benchmarking, offers forums, helps companies identify best practices, and provides a setting in which organizations can collaborate with one another.

IMA also has published the best-selling *Implementing Activity-Based Cost Management: Moving from Analysis to Action* and collaborated with CAM-I to issue *An ABC Manager's Primer: Straight Talk on Activity-Based Costing.*

IMA is a strong advocate of ABM, Loiselle says. "A properly designed ABC system measures costs of resources used for organizational activities. Once nonvalue-added activities are isolated and more accurate cost information becomes available, management can act to reduce waste, redundancy, and 'unused capacity' to improve profits and strengthen their competitive position."

This report, the introductions to each section, and the articles selected reflect the views of the editor and article authors and not necessarily those of the Institute of Management Accountants or its Committee on Research. ∎

Julian Freedman
Director of Research
Institute of Management Accountants

Preface

From about the mid-1980s, when early reports on activity-based costing (ABC) began to surface, management accounting practitioners have been provided with a new way to view cost accumulation and distribution. Many people at that time were eagerly seeking such a new way because traditional cost management systems increasingly were being criticized for their inability to provide the financial information necessary to manage the transition to the factory of the future. Thus, ABC was greeted with great enthusiasm early on.

At its inception ABC focused on improved costing of products and markets. This early focus appears to be giving way slowly to a new and broader vision, defined as activity-based management (ABM). The focus of ABM is on the management of activities and processes as the route to continuous improvement. Thus, ABC management systems appear to be unfolding and progressing to support all the firm's business processes better.

A number of articles in this book suggest even further progression—that cost concepts of the past, including fixed and variable costing and the effects of capacity costing, are being incorporated in new ABC systems to enhance managerial decision making. It appears that the power of the mind and of the computer will continue to revitalize management accounting and ABC systems. The new financial manager will use the computer to model the firm's business activities and processes. He or she will be part of the cross-functional team providing information to process owners to support activities and processes.

For almost 75 years, the Institute of Management Accountants (IMA) has placed itself on the cutting edge of research in accounting practice. The Institute's early leaders strongly encouraged personal research and the sharing of findings. New concepts, developments, and practices in cost accounting found their way into the Institute's periodicals. As in the past, the IMA continues to play a leading role in the dissemination of information on managerial accounting systems, through seminars, conferences, sponsorship of research projects on cost management, and its monthly magazine, *Management Accounting*.

This book on ABC management systems closely follows two prior publications on this subject, authorized by IMA's Committee on Research. They are: *Implementing Activity-Based Cost Management: Moving from Analysis to Action*, published in September 1992, and *An ABC Manager's Primer*, a project undertaken by the Consortium for Advanced Manufacturing-International and IMA, released in April 1993.

Activity-Based Management in Action is a collection of ABC articles from IMA's premier publication, *Management Accounting*. Almost 89% of the articles were published between 1991 and 1993. As such, they represent recent research reported by practitioners, consultants, and academics in a form convenient for use in both the continuing education of management accounting practitioners and the education of accounting students.

This anthology is divided into four parts: Introduction, Applications, Enhancements, and Integration. Each part is subdivided further into sections. The articles in each section support and amplify the theme identified for each part. This organization highlights the development, unfolding, and progression that ABC management systems have achieved over a very short period of time.

Sections 1 through 3 in Part 1 cover the introduction to ABC and the gradual migration of ABC systems from a product cost focus to the management of activities and processes—activity-based management. They expose the reader to the views of prominent leaders on the current status of ABC and, in the final section, place the reader in the middle of the dispute and controversy that have arisen over the benefits claimed for ABC management systems. Responses from IMA members, published in the Letters to the Editor column of the magazine, are included at the end of Section 3 to record the positions of many practitioners on both sides of this debate.

Sections 4 and 5, in Part 2, move us to the practice side of ABC. Authors suggest solutions to overcome organizational barriers so as to achieve successful ABC implementations. Reports on the outcomes of six ABC implementations, in different environments, follow in Section 5. In Section 6, Part 3, academics and practitioners report on the deficiencies of ABC systems. They propose enhancements to ABC to overcome these shortcomings, by incorporating traditional cost concepts. In the final part, Section 7 deals with the progression of ABC systems. First the ABC system is integrated into the financial reporting system and is used for external financial reporting. Then the reader is introduced to a new two-dimensional ABC design that supports both product costing and continuous improvement.

At the end of the book is a bibliography that expands the scope of ABC readings beyond those published in *Management Accounting*. In addition, the reader is introduced to IMA's Continuous Improvement Center (CIC). A new and major initiative by IMA, the Continuous Improvement Center is dedicated to the improvement of the financial function. The CIC will assist organizations to measure how well they are doing, to learn what others are doing, and to identify the best practices in financial management.

Patrick L. Romano

Acknowledgments

I would like to thank all at the Institute of Management Accountants who helped guide this work toward completion. I am especially grateful for the support and guidance provided by Julian Freedman, director of research; Senior Editor Claire Barth's editorial assistance; and the enthusiastic support given by the Committee on Research and its chairman, Dennis Neider.   ■

About the Author

Patrick L. Romano, CMA, CPA, was the director of research for IMA from 1985 through July 1992. In his earlier service with IMA he was an instructor in the IMA Professional Education Division as well as the director of conferences and seminars.

Mr. Romano was instrumental in implementing the IMA Bold Step research program. This program, from its earliest publication in 1987, *Management Accounting in the New Manufacturing Environment*, to its latest, *Implementing Activity-Based Cost Management: Moving from Analysis to Action*, focused on improving management accounting by identifying state-of-the-art techniques and showing how these techniques could be adapted to changing manufacturing and service technologies.

Patrick Romano developed the IMA professional education program course, "The Controller: Role and Techniques"; authored and coauthored articles that have appeared in *Management Accounting*, the *Financial Executive*, and other business journals; and served as technical editor of a 1982 IMA publication, *Increasing the Productivity of the Financial Manager Through Effective Use of Computer Technology*.

In industry, Mr. Romano served as vice president treasurer for an industrial products manufacturer and was chief financial officer for several publicly held companies in diversified service and real estate industries.

A member of the adjunct faculties of several local colleges and universities, Mr. Romano holds B.S. and MBA degrees in accounting and finance from New York University.   ■

Table of Contents

Part **1**

Section 1

Introduction to ABC

Three articles are presented in this first section to introduce ABC. The articles are arranged to indicate the unfolding of ABC into a more encompassing technique called activity-based management (ABM). ABC has progressed from its initial focus on computing costs of activities and processes and the outputs of activities, such as products and services. It now provides information for managing activities to achieve continuous improvement, increased productivity, and higher quality. With this brief description we now begin the journey into the world of ABC systems.

As Norm Raffish indicates in "How Much Does That Product Really Cost?", the first article,"It's not that traditional cost accounting doesn't work—it's that the world it was designed for is rapidly disappearing." This fact and the fact that burden-averaging and labor-based cost systems did not mirror the true economics of physical production and resource consumption were noted in the earlier writings of Professors Robert Kaplan and Robin Cooper of Harvard University.

Raffish describes the use of ABC as a more relevant method for costing products. He states that ABC focuses on the traceability of costs to products, based on the resources consumed by the activities needed to produce the individual products. To accomplish this goal you must analyze and define activities and isolate and measure cost drivers so you can determine product cost information as it most closely fits the reality of the manufacturing environment. The author provides a number of examples in his article to support the use and application of the ABC system.

Total cost management (TCM), described in the second article, "Activities: The Focal Point of Total Cost Management" by Michael Ostrenga, might easily be considered the precursor of what now is de-

fined as activity-based management (ABM), because total cost management (TCM) emphasizes the process view of activity management. Ostrenga indicates that TCM is a philosophy focused on the management of all company resources and the activities that consume those resources. It is a comprehensive approach, rooted in activity management, to improve the competitive position of a business.

TCM begins with process value analysis (PVA), a cost reduction and process improvement methodology. PVA focuses on identifying the resource-consuming activities within a process and the underlying drivers of cost. This analysis, done at the process level, targets nonvalue-added cost drivers for elimination while seeking optimization of those classified as value added. As Ostrenga emphasizes, PVA is the initial building block of TCM. It facilitates the development of activity-based costing, performance measurement, responsibility accounting, and investment management, while focusing on customer requirements, minimum cost and cycle time, and improved quality output.

The Raffish article noted that ABC identifies and computes costs for activities, processes, and the output of activities, such as products or services. TCM, as described by Ostrenga, emphasizes the process view of activity management.

In "Activity-Based Management," the third article, Peter B.B. Turney describes activity-based management. ABM provides information for managing activities using ABC data and other tools to achieve continuous improvement. ABM helps direct resources to activities that yield the greatest profit and helps improve the way work is carried out.

As Turney indicates, ABM has twin goals: (1) to improve the value received by the customer and (2) to improve profits by providing this value. Because these goals are reached by focusing on managing activities, Turney offers guidelines to practitioners for analyzing activities. First, target nonessential activities for elimination. Then focus on significant activities, the ones important to customers or to operating the business, which may provide the greatest opportunities for improvement. The next step includes benchmarking the activity against a similar activity in another company or another part of the organization. Comparing the activity to a benchmark of good practice helps determine the scope for improvement.

Finally, examine the links between activities so as to minimize time and duplication of work. Look at activities as links in a chain.

After you have completed the analysis of activities, you can address the causes of waste(cost drivers) so that waste is removed. Then finish with measuring the things an activity should be doing if it is contributing to the organization's success. These efforts, reports Turney, are as likely to improve quality as they are to reduce costs. ■

HOW MUCH DOES THAT PRODUCT REALLY CO$T?

Finding out may be as easy as ABC.

BY NORM RAFFISH

It's not that traditional cost accounting doesn't work—it's that the world it was designed for is rapidly disappearing. Product costs used to consist primarily of direct labor and material; today we have a manufacturing environment in which direct labor usually accounts for a ballpark figure of 5% to 15% of the costs and material accounts for 45% to 55%. That leaves us with a whopping 30% to 50% for overhead (see Figure 1). And the overhead is shifting from variable to fixed as a result of our investments in automation. Given this scenario, it's not difficult to imagine that our current cost accounting systems probably don't reflect the true costs of our products.

What clues do we have that this description is true? An article by Professor Robin Cooper of Harvard University in the *Harvard Business Review*, January-February 1989, was titled "You Need a New Cost System When...." The article describes several symptoms of problems with existing cost systems. Cooper says it may be time to redesign your cost system if:

- Functional managers want to drop seemingly profitable lines;
- Hard-to-make products show big profits;
- Departments have their own cost systems;
- You have a high-margin niche all to yourself;
- Competitors' prices are unrealistically low.

We need to recognize that our existing cost systems were meant primarily to value inventory and provide data for the profit and loss statements. They really were never designed to discriminate between product lines or products within those lines. Cost systems were meant to focus on "how much," not "why." It is understanding the "why," however, that permits management to focus on the issues that require action.

Photo by AFI/Jos Palmieri.

Will ABC help determine costs more accurately for products such as this circuit board?

INTERORGANIZATIONAL COST PERFORMANCE

Consider the concept of interorganizational cost (intercost) performance. How would your current cost systems deal with the cost of an engineering change or segregating the cost of quality? How would you assign those costs, if you knew them, to a specific product line or product? Just to focus on one example of the intercost problem, let's examine a production schedule change requested by Marketing to meet a customer's needs.

Normally, the various costs of expediting an order are borne by all the orders that pass through the production environment, through the standard technique of absorbing indirect costs into manufacturing overhead. Thus, the expedited order will appear to have a more favorable margin than it should. And, did anyone charge Engineering for total cost of the ECN? How much cost should have been assigned to the particular part or work order? In the long run, Manufacturing's operating results, when compared to budget, will look less favorable, and Marketing's performance actually may improve in the customer satisfaction area (see Figure 2). Do we really know the cost of that order, and did we capture or even understand the intercost effect on performance?

Two other points about traditional costing systems are worth mentioning before we move forward. The first deals with the identification of nonvalue-added activities. Current systems don't have any mechanisms to assist management in this critical area. It's difficult to put a continuous improvement program in place if you can't identify and quantify the nonvalue-added activities.

The second point is more fundamental to costing in general. Our systems today measure that segment of a product's life beginning at the time it enters production. The system is oblivious to the fact that 85% of the cost of a new product is committed after the design phase, and manufacturing can influence only about

10% to 15% or so of the cost (see Figure 3). We are not capturing and allocating research and development costs so that management can determine the true profitability of a product over its life.

Let's consider a different but not necessarily replacement approach. Does this imply two cost systems? Maybe. More on this subject when we discuss strategic versus tactical approaches to costing.

ACTIVITY-BASED COSTING

Activity-based costing (ABC) has been a concept waiting for the computer and a few innovative people. What is it? A good basic definition was developed by the Computer Aided Manufacturing-International (CAM-I) organization of Arlington, Texas, a nonprofit industry-sponsored consortium that works on contemporary industry problems. Its Cost Management System (CMS) project defines ABC as "the collection of financial and operation performance information tracing the significant activities of the firm to product costs."

CAM-I used cost management as an umbrella for many related issues. This broader definition encompasses activity-based costing, life cycle management, performance management, investment management, and cost planning and control. We will focus on ABC and its relationship to the intercost performance issues.

The three key areas of ABC are product cost differentiation, activities and their cost drivers, and identification of nonvalue-added cost improvement opportunities. ABC assigns product costs based on the activities that a product draws upon. An activity may be defined as a particular operation in the production cycle, or it could be defined as the entire material acquisition process. Activities use resources such as support labor, technology cells, or utilities. The agents that cause activities to happen are called cost drivers. An example of a cost driver is an engineering change order (ECO). The issuing of an ECO causes many activities to occur, such as release of the ECO documentation package, changes to the production schedule, acquisition of new material, changes to the process, and new quality instructions.

Figure 4A illustrates the basic ABC Logical Model. The Cost View indicates the general flow of costs. For example, the resources assigned to the inventory control activity will be directly traced or allocated to particular products based on some causal relationship. The Process View indicates the flow of information and transactions. As an example, the receipt of material on the dock triggers the inventory handling activities. In addition, information such as the number of moves, how many times an order was moved, and the cost per move can be obtained for performance analysis. An expanded example of this model is illustrated in Figure 4B.

The identification, measurement, and control of cost drivers is essential to ABC. Some cost drivers are very inefficient. They may have root causes that have been hidden from management's view for a long time. As an example, one root cause of having too much inventory may be the performance measurement that rewards the buyer for obtaining the lowest unit price of an item. If the buyer is procuring by the truckload to obtain his desired measurement, and the company needs only a few cases, then the result is predictable. One of the more severe and insidious of root causes stems from inappropriate or obsolete policies, procedures, and performance measurements.

Often policies and procedures have been overcome by events but remain in force through inattention to the new

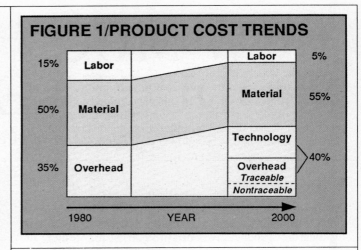

FIGURE 1/PRODUCT COST TRENDS

reality of the situation. For example, a vendor's goods might be certified as "source inspected," but, when they arrive, they are routinely moved to receiving inspection—because that is the procedure on the dock for all production goods. Then, of course, when the inspector sees the certification, he calls material handling and has the goods moved to Stores. This policy/procedure adds lead time to the process, causes the cost of a secondary material move, and has taken up the time of the inspector who should be inspecting material that needs his attention.

After we analyze and define activities and are able to isolate and measure their cost drivers, then we will be in a position to determine product cost information as it most closely fits the reality of the manufacturing environment.

Let's revisit the intercost issue to gain a better focus on the subject. We can assume that the engineering change referred to in Figure 2 was proposed and approved based on demonstrated need (the actual cost to propose, prepare, and deliver a complete ECO package will usually be far less than the impact of the change). That change, in this example, will affect Manufacturing and Marketing. Manufacturing will absorb the associated costs of the change into its budget and

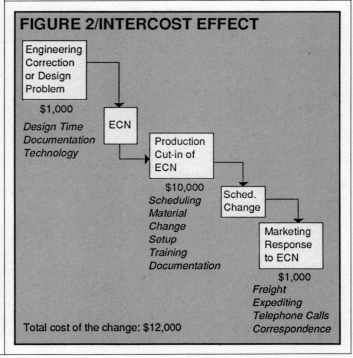

FIGURE 2/INTERCOST EFFECT

schedule. Marketing will absorb effects relating to changes in distribution costs and any customer ill will that may have been generated due to possible delays in the shipment. Using the concept of tracing or allocating the cost of activities to products, we can capture and evaluate true product costs as well as understand the intercost impact and its effect on performance measurement. In this case, understanding the root cause of the cost driver may lead us to discover that the product is of poor design and therefore needs constant engineering maintenance. This discovery could lead to redesigning the product or raising the selling price to cover the real product support costs.

How do you capture and allocate costs in an ABC system? It has been said that all you need is lots of cost pools. That statement is somewhat exaggerated, but there is some truth in it. Certainly in order to capture the necessary detail, new activity cost pools would be established. It is the direct cost

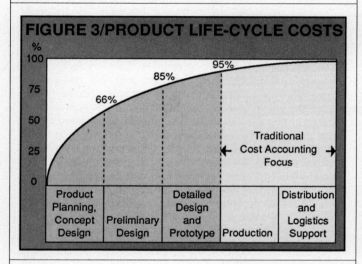

FIGURE 3/PRODUCT LIFE-CYCLE COSTS

tracing and allocation schemes that are critical, however. Traditionally we have assigned costs based on three volume-related criteria: direct labor (dollars or hours), material cost, and machine-hours. While these criteria still are valid for certain cost entities, cost assignment bases are needed for many overhead and indirect cost entities. Some of these new bases are number of setups, number of orders, number of times material is handled, and number of part numbers processed. Using such bases as a way to trace or allocate activity costs to a product offers a whole new perspective on product cost assignment.

As an example, the number of purchase orders or line items processed may be a much better way to assign material acquisition costs than the value of the material ordered. A work order may have one purchase order with $100,000 of material assigned to it. Another work order may have 10 purchase orders worth $75,000 assigned to it. Guess which one incurred the most acquisition costs. Under today's methods, guess which one was allocated the most cost.

REAL LIFE

Discussing new concepts can be interesting and even exciting, but if they don't work "in the field," they don't work.

A large industrial electronics firm was dissatisfied with the product costing information it was receiving, especially at the printed circuit board level. Management decided to try a new costing approach based on the work that CAM-I had done on ABC and activity-based performance analysis. In order not to disrupt the division or disturb the current financial systems, it chose a single department that fabricated printed circuit boards.

The division finance department coordinated the pilot project with support from Manufacturing Engineering. In its presentation to management, it explained why it felt the experiment was needed. The controller said that the current system did not provide accurate information for make/buy decisions or for investment opportunities and that the current decision-making process was using distorted information. The major deficiencies of the current system were the inability to recognize unnecessary (nonvalue-added) activities and the lack of adequate traceability of costs and of a way to quantify quality, throughput, and flexibility.

Project objectives as stated by management were:

- Provide a breakout of department costs into activity costs,
- Identify cost drivers and their causal relationships,
- Determine actual costs for each product line, and
- Provide a tool for better decision making.

The process began by defining the activities for the PCB shop based on its actual practices. In the main, most of the activities involved either preparation for production or the actual production of various product families. Next, a survey instrument was constructed. The primary purpose of the survey was to develop a database that defined what people really did and for which product line. For example, the survey disclosed that direct labor operators spent a far greater share of their time in material-handling tasks than had been recognized. In light of their pay scale, the delivery of material to the line is being reviewed for possible reorganization. Further, the analysis showed that support costs that had been allocated on a straight-line basis among products did in fact vary significantly by product family, especially as they related to the number of layers on a PC board.

Cost drivers were defined and quantified. Typical of the types of cost drivers were lack of technical supervision, chemical contamination, schedule change, excessive quality verification, time card audits, and Material Review Board activities. In all, more than 50 cost drivers were isolated. Some, of course, were meaningful while others generated little cost and were not tracked. The exercise of developing the activity

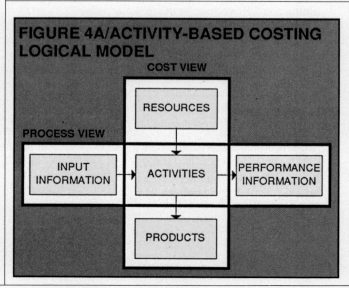

FIGURE 4A/ACTIVITY-BASED COSTING LOGICAL MODEL

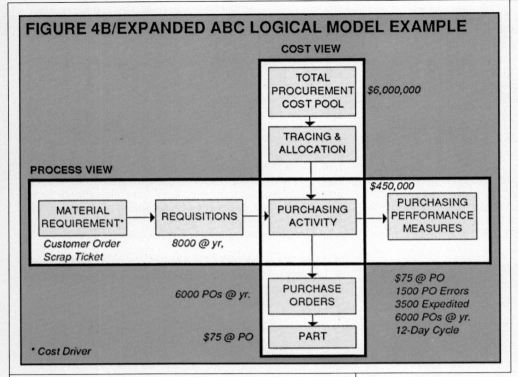

FIGURE 4B/EXPANDED ABC LOGICAL MODEL EXAMPLE

COST VIEW

TOTAL PROCUREMENT COST POOL — $6,000,000

TRACING & ALLOCATION

PROCESS VIEW

MATERIAL REQUIREMENT*
*Customer Order
Scrap Ticket*

→ REQUISITIONS
8000 @ yr,

→ PURCHASING ACTIVITY — $450,000

PURCHASING PERFORMANCE MEASURES

6000 POs @ yr.

PURCHASE ORDERS

$75 @ PO
1500 PO Errors
3500 Expedited
6000 POs @ yr.
12-Day Cycle

$75 @ PO → PART

* *Cost Driver*

---

the basis for the allocation.

WHAT NOW?

Activity-based costing is not a panacea for all the product cost accounting ills or shortcomings in manufacturing. It does not directly address the issues of life cycle costing or performance measurement, for example, although ABC will support those functions with valuable information. ABC is, however, a more relevant method for costing products than some older methods because it forces traceability of costs to products, based on the resources consumed by the activities needed to produce individual products. The key factors are activities and their associated cost drivers. If a product does not use an activity, it should not absorb any of its related costs.

The costing methods commonly used today, for example, may tie allocations of overhead to direct labor so that some products are being charged for resources they never used. Unless we change our allocation methods to recognize the shift in the character of overhead from variable toward fixed, as the use of technology increases, severe product cost distortion will only accelerate.

One final topic—will ABC necessitate another set of accounting records? At this stage of ABC's acceptance and development, many consider it an advanced analytical tool for management as opposed to an official set of records. It certainly may not yet be robust enough to replace our day-to-day systems. Each implementation of ABC at this point probably will be tailored to each user's objectives. There is not yet an "off the shelf" solution that has been accepted as the standard. In the last two years we have begun to see the emergence of commercially available software to assist in the implementation process.

Thus, although we currently may view ABC as a significant management tool for issues such as pricing schemes and product abandonment analysis rather than as a tactical accounting system, some firms are evaluating the impact of a conversion to ABC as the accounting system of record. As the ABC "body of knowledge" is expanded and codified, activity-based costing may well eventually replace our current cost accounting systems. ∎

and cost driver database was invaluable, however, for future and much larger application of ABC in the company.

In the final analysis, the percentage spread of overcosting to undercosting of the PC board product families ranged from a negative 100% to a positive 80%. The division now plans to expand the ABC activity to other departments.

A second example involves a large multidivisional consumer electronics manufacturer. In this case the manufacturer wanted to understand the impact of allocated costs on the two main product lines in one key division. One line (product line L) is older and has a moderately high labor content. The second line (product line A) is newer and uses more automation.

The initial figures indicated that the average base cost of the product line L (high labor) was about $350 a unit and that of product line A (high automation) was $240 a unit. Keep in mind that product line L was manufactured at about a 7:1 rate over product line A. This will explain the impact of shifting a small percentage of L's dollars to A.

The activity cost analysis showed several interesting points for management to consider. First, after cost based on activities was reallocated and the technology costs of product line A were isolated, the costs were restated to show product line L as $300 and product line A as $450. Second, because most of the technology costs were fixed or semivariable, as production in A was forecasted to increase the base unit cost would be reduced considerably, but in later years.

Third, product line L would have a longer profitable life than originally anticipated, and some price reductions would be in order so that it could remain competitive. Finally, the firm gained some valuable insights on activities and costs drivers with respect to automation. The current allocation schemes had no method for differentiating technology costs, such as the cost of industrial engineering support. The activity analysis revealed that the IE cost allocation for A versus L in actuality ran about 4:1. The current system had indicated that the ratio was about 1:8 because labor had been

Norm Raffish, CPIM, is a senior manager in the management consulting practice of Ernst & Young. Prior to joining the firm, he spent several years as a consultant and 12 years with the Xerox Corporation's Computer Services Division, engaged in industry and strategic product planning and the design and development of integrated manufacturing systems. He says that in 1991 the CAM-I CMS project will publish a new glossary on activity-based costing. It is hoped that this glossary will be the basis for a future common language in the area of ABC.

Activities: The Focal Point of Total Cost Management

Success depends on the firm's ability to manage activities.

BY MICHAEL R. OSTRENGA

Total cost management (TCM) is a business philosophy of managing all company resources and the activities that consume those resources. Managing costs in a TCM environment means focusing on activities and the events, circumstances, or conditions that cause or "drive" these cost-consuming activities.

It is important for management to understand that costs are not merely incurred, they are caused. When action is taken to reduce what causes the activities that consume resources, then a lasting reduction in costs will take place.

Based on our experience in applying the different principles of total cost management for several clients, we have verified that a central theme exists. That theme is "activities are the focal point of TCM."

This article is based on Ernst & Young's experience with large and small companies from discrete and process manufacturing. The large companies include an electronics manufacturer, a beverage processor, and a building supply company, all blue chip Fortune 500 companies. Companies with less than $50 million in revenue include a small sheet metal stamping company, a truck manufacturer, and a candy processor.

The specific project scope and business needs varied for each company and included:

■ Product costs that reflect the true resources consumed,

■ Process value analysis,
■ Cost reduction,
■ Improved performance measurements,
■ Responsibility accounting, and
■ Product line profitability.

Although the objectives for each company differed, when we analyzed their operations, the focus shifted inevitably to the effect activities and activity-consuming resources have on the economics of the business. In each case, although the *starting point* differed, the *focal point* didn't. It became apparent to us that activities were the focal point of total cost management.

The concepts discussed here are based on the application of TCM principles to the business needs of several of our client companies. I also will identify the role activity

Author Ostrenga presents process value analysis as an integrated foundation for activity-based costing.

7

management plays in the integration of these key TCM principles:

■ Process value analysis,
■ Activity-based process costing,
■ Activity-based product costing,
■ Responsibility accounting,
■ Performance measurements, and
■ Investment management.

PROCESS VALUE ANALYSIS

Process value analysis (PVA) is the initial building block of TCM and facilitates the development of performance measures, activity-based costing, responsibility accounting, and investment management. It focuses on meeting customer requirements, minimizing cost and cycle time, and improving the quality of output.

PVA relates activities to the events, circumstances, or conditions that create or "drive" the need for the activity and the resources consumed. These cost drivers are targeted for elimination/minimization if they relate to nonvalue added activities and optimization if they relate to value added.

PVA provides us with a better understanding of the cost relationship of processes and the underlying resource-consuming activities. As a result, our ability to manage resources and reduce the reliance on support costs is improved.

At one of our client companies, it became evident that the activity management and resultant cost reduction could be facilitated only by a reduction in the drivers or cause of resource commitment and not by the direct reduction in activities. This idea is a departure from much of the current literature that calls for the reduction of cost through activity management. Many articles fail to differentiate between activities and cost drivers and, whether it is intentional or not, obscure the need to reduce the driver of activities through process improvement to provide a meaningful and long-lasting cost reduction.

It's important to note, however, that a reduction in drivers, which results in a reduced dependency on activities, does not lower costs until the excess resources are reduced or redeployed into more productive areas.

The following project methodology enabled us to understand the client company's cost behavior and to position lasting improvements:

Process Definition

■ Document the process flow,
■ Identify the customer's internal and external requirements,
■ Define the outputs of each process step,
■ Determine process input requirements,
■ Compare customer requirements with outputs/inputs, and
■ Define the staffing levels (full-time equivalents) for each process.

Activity Analysis

■ Define activities within each process,
■ Identify activities as value added and nonvalue added using customer requirements,
■ Determine cycle time of each activity,
■ Calculate the cycle efficiency (value added time/total time) for each process, and
■ Cumulate cycle efficiency along business value chain.

Driver Analysis

■ Develop cause and effect—driver identification, and
■ Perform a Pareto analysis on the drivers and the activities they control.

Opportunity Improvement Planning

■ Develop perspective charts on value added/nonvalue added,
■ Develop an opportunity improvement plan to eliminate/minimize nonvalue added and optimize value added, and
■ Develop performance measures and improvement indicators to track opportunities.

ACTIVITY-BASED COSTING

There is a strong relationship between PVA and activity-based costing. Activities consume resources (cost) at a process level. Products consume activities in varying degrees based largely on their level of differentiation. Therefore, our ability to reduce nonvalue added activities and cost through process value analysis also reduces product costs because the activities consumed per given output as well as the cost per activity will be less. Furthermore, the cost drivers, uncovered by PVA, support the attachment of costs to the process and products.

According to activity-based costing theory, most support costs (nonmaterial costs) do not vary directly with labor volume but vary with product diversity and operation complexity. Thus, many existing product costs do not represent the true consumption of resources to produce them.

ACTIVITY-BASED PROCESS COSTING

Process control managers are responsible for and are held accountable for costs that are generated within their process area. These managers should have a cost management reporting system that provides them timely and accurate cost information to plan, control, and monitor the cost accounts for that process center.

Applying costs from outside the process or spreading costs from a corporate/plant level will not help the process manager correct a problem or know more about his process area. Yet, traditional cost information systems include allocated or noncontrollable costs in department reports that produce a "Pontius Pilate" syndrome among those responsible for managing a process. At the process level, managers should only see and be held accountable for controllable costs.

It's important to consider that the level of drivers identified in process value analysis may be at a lower level than the driver base used for activity-based costing. This occurs because the many different support costs at the process level could require an unmanageable number of cost pools and driver rates to show the same level of causal relationship. It may be appropriate to summarize costs into pools that have drivers that move in the same relative proportion. For example, setup, material handling to next sequence, and inspection all may be summarized into one pool having a common driver such as number of setups or number of work orders. This concept is called the surrogate driver method.[1]

One of our clients visualized controlling costs at the process level. The company was more interested in establishing better process costs that in turn could be related to process activities and controlled through responsibility accounting.

We demonstrated that, regardless of the traditional allocation of cost being used, the "economic" costs could be reduced through the focus on activities. These cost reductions would be realized at the process level. The effect of lower process costs would be verified by activity-based product costing, as product consumption of lower cost activities is shown.

This *process-cost* orientation is vital to the integration of PVA cost behavior identification to the realization of cost reduction through activity-based product costing. This concept has all but been lost in recent journals due to the activity-based costing emphasis on *product costs*.

Additionally, activity-based process costing provides a foundation for, and gives an organization important insights into, the interpretation of responsibility accounting.

ACTIVITY-BASED PRODUCT COSTING

Charging costs directly to products eliminates the need to allocate or assign costs. Costs that cannot be charged directly should be assigned to the product through activity-based costing.

In keeping with the philosophy that activities consume resources (process) and products consume activities, activity-based process costing becomes the precursor to product costing. Once the process costs are established, they become available for responsibility accounting and serve as the pool of costs to trace to products that consume the process activities.

Activity-based product costing methodology is similar to process costing. In process costing, financial accounts are associated with process activity pools through stage one drivers, and the costs in each process activity pool are summed and divided by stage two drivers or output measures to yield the activity-based costing rates. The costs within the pool represent those that are expected to move in the same direction and order of magnitude with a change in the "driver." The cost rates then are applied to products based on the identification of types and quantities of activities consumed by each product.

Our fieldwork has shown that activity-based product costing is sensitive to the ratio of overhead cost to total costs and the level at which product-focused processes enable direct charging.

One of our clients has a ratio of 80% material and 20% conversion cost at the plant level. With such a small amount of cost to reassign to products, the ability to demonstrate changes in product costs would seem to be limited. When we differentiated certain costs by product, however, significant cost changes were developed.

One significant area for improved costing was found in the assignment of storage costs. Because products and components had varying levels of volume and time in storage, the storage costs were segregated into transaction-related and storage-time related. The transaction-related costs were assigned to part numbers based on the number of times handled (received, issued, cycle counted), whereas, the costs related to storage time (depreciation, utilities, taxes) were assigned to part numbers based on the inventory turnover ratio.

This differentiation in storage costs proved enlightening from a product-cost perspective. It also pointed out the significance of cost and cycle-time relationships.

Other value-chain costs not typically considered product costs (research and development, marketing, accounting/finance, and so on) also were assigned to the product-cost level and added to the cost differentials.

Our focus was first to identify direct charge candidates, then to assign costs through driver rates, and finally to allocate any remaining costs. This method was followed in both the first and second stages of cost assignment. (See Figure 1.)

This company produced identical products in several plants. Thus, it gained a new product-cost perspective which in turn led to differentiated product plant costs and support for regional pricing decisions.

Another client had advanced to compact layouts with a product-focused process that eliminated resource contention for different product lines. In this environment, most support costs of the process were consumed by and were already being directly charged to the product. However, the significant cost of centralized purchasing, receiving, and material handling was still being allocated on an arbitrary labor-volume measure. Activity-

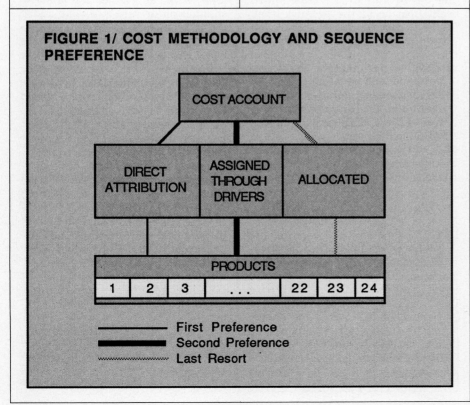

FIGURE 1/ COST METHODOLOGY AND SEQUENCE PREFERENCE

COST ACCOUNT

DIRECT ATTRIBUTION

ASSIGNED THROUGH DRIVERS

ALLOCATED

PRODUCTS

| 1 | 2 | 3 | ... | 22 | 23 | 24 |

——— First Preference
━━━ Second Preference
∿∿∿ Last Resort

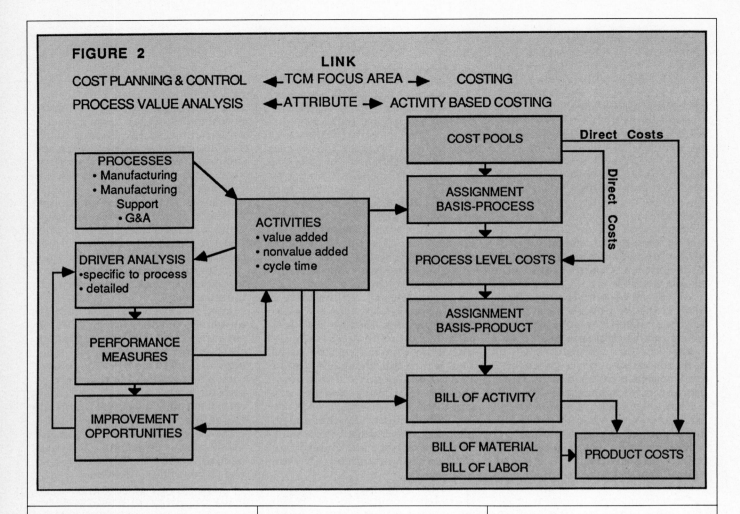

FIGURE 2

LINK

COST PLANNING & CONTROL ◄— TCM FOCUS AREA —► COSTING

PROCESS VALUE ANALYSIS ◄—ATTRIBUTE —► ACTIVITY BASED COSTING

PROCESSES
• Manufacturing
• Manufacturing
  Support
• G&A

ACTIVITIES
• value added
• nonvalue added
• cycle time

DRIVER ANALYSIS
•specific to process
• detailed

PERFORMANCE
MEASURES

IMPROVEMENT
OPPORTUNITIES

COST POOLS   Direct Costs

Direct Costs

ASSIGNMENT
BASIS-PROCESS

PROCESS LEVEL COSTS

ASSIGNMENT
BASIS-PRODUCT

BILL OF ACTIVITY

BILL OF MATERIAL
BILL OF LABOR

PRODUCT COSTS

based cost concepts were used to assign these additional "pervasive" support costs to product costs. The result was an improved cost and better insight into the material-acquisition cost related to raw material and components supporting each product.

Other situations, however, proved to have much more significant shifts in product costs where plant conversion costs were a higher percentage of total cost. Yet in all cases, the other value chain costs typically were allocated to products on sales, gross margin, or not associated with products at all. When applied through activity driver relationships, they have made a meaningful difference in the way costs were viewed.

In practice, a very powerful way to demonstrate the important connection between activity analysis and activity-based costing is to look at the value and nonvalue added costs concept (see Figure 2). To the degree we identify value added/ nonvalue added costs in each process activity pool, separate costing

rates can be developed to preserve the value added/nonvalue added identification at the product level. Table 1 represents a typical cost profile using Ernst & Young's process value analysis/activity-based costing linkage methodology.

This new way of looking at product cost provoked one of our clients to comment, "If my product cost is X% or Y$ too high to be competitive, I now know how to trace it back to the process through my bill of activities." And, conversely, because cost is created at the process

level and absorbed at the product level, it is easy to see the effect of changes on driver rates. The added distinction of value added and nonvalue added at the process level as well as product level helps reinforce the mind-set of opportunity in minimizing or eliminating nonvalue added and optimizing value added costs.

RESPONSIBILITY
ACCOUNTING

One of the foundations of cost management is the development of cost ownership through responsibility and accountability. Most companies fall victim to forcing costs incurred from manufacturing and administration support groups down to the department or process areas through inappropriate allocations. Typically, these allocations are on headcount or labor (salary) relationships. As we have discussed, not only do labor allocations distort the assignment of costs to products, but they also distort the cost of services

TABLE 1

	VA	NVA
Material	$X	$X
Labor	X	X
Overhead	X	X
	$X	$X
Opportunity Cost		X
Other Value Chain Costs	X	X
TOTAL	$X	$X

provided by support groups.

A chargeout methodology designed to relate the service costs to the underlying driver creating the need for service allows for an equitable distribution of cost. Thus, chargeout development is integrated with activity analysis and activity-based process costing. Activity analysis identifies the appropriate driver base, and activity-based process costing develops the cost of the output (product or service).

Structuring cost assignment in this fashion consistently supports the causal relationship with cost incurred and the driver-user requirements.

We can draw a further analogy here. In activity-based costing we saw how activities consume resources and products consume activities. In responsibility accounting, support service activities consume resources, and users consume support services.

Responsibility accounting is effective only when a sense of ownership has been established. In order to ensure this sense of ownership, costs deemed to be noncontrollable at a given level should be excluded. It is important to recognize that noncontrollable costs at a certain level are controllable elsewhere in the organization. For instance, while the head of a department may have "influence" over the amount of space his area consumes, it is difficult to imagine this person having control over real estate taxes or building depreciation. Yet many companies force down an allocated cost and "impose" responsibility on a department's expense statement.

One of our clients sought a responsibility accounting solution to cost control. When we designed this concept, we realized it was important to introduce costs to the responsibility center in which they are controlled. For example, typical department costs such as material handling and inspection were found to be controlled at the demand source. In this case, the source was the manufacturing operation activities, and its driver was the number of work orders.

When we recognized this cost behavior, the decision was made to establish budgetary and expense statements with flexible parameters that are based on activities

Traditional cost information systems may produce a 'Pontius Pilate syndrome.'

and cost driver relationships. We also decided to charge the cost to the manufacturing operations department as a user of the service and reflect the chargeout to the material handling and inspection department cost statements.

Relating the cost to the drivers establishes the driver as the measure of planned activity. Cost targets will be determined by sensitivity analysis performed on the effect of cost change as the activity level deviates from plan. These flexible targets recognize that plans will change. They also demonstrate to operating management that they cannot attain their targets by performing in ways that are counterproductive to the organization.

For managers held accountable for cost improvement, this philosophy of responsibility accounting should improve their attitude toward cost management. Businesses with this culture in place can be transformed from an organization of employees to an organization of "cost managers."

PERFORMANCE MEASUREMENT

Performance measurements traditionally have been financially oriented with an emphasis on short-term results. Short-term financial measures have been undermined by changes in technology, the advance of manufacturing process changes, and new ways to view the organization. Increased capital intensity and decreased touch labor costs have changed the way we must look at the business.

Traditional measures have become invalid measures of performance and often send misleading signals to management. Many of these measures are actually counterproductive because they modify behavior in such a way that leads to

increases in inventory, the creation of cost elsewhere in the value chain, increased levels of complexity, required resources, and quality problems.

Traditionally, companies produce significant amounts of data at higher levels of the organization. The amount of real relevant information for decision-making support should vary at different levels of management. Performance measurements should represent a mix of financial and nonfinancial operating measures consistent with the level of business responsibility. This structure will provide more meaningful information and a proactive support of the management of resources.

Our model suggests financial measures needed, for an overall reading of the firm's health must not be limited to any single measure such as ROI. Other considerations such as cash flow, earnings growth, capital employed, and so on round out the needs in financial measures.

As we view the middle management area, a pronounced increase in nonfinancial focus measures is required. These measures, although operational in nature, must still be integrated with the organization goals to ensure that management is moving toward the overall goals and does not suboptimize the organization while maximizing an individual area, department, or function.

Performance measures assist the cost reduction effort by focusing on the significant activity levels and measuring the drivers of activities. In concert with the continuous improvement philosophy, performance measures have baselines and targets established to measure the impact of change promoted through the operational improvements identified in process value analysis. The targeting of measures provides the necessary visibility to the status of nonvalue added elimination and value added optimization progress.

Performance measurements have a pervasive nature about them. As defined previously, total cost management is a business philosophy of managing resources and resource-consuming activities. Performance measurements position us for a better understanding of the economics of the business when activities and

An Overview of Total Cost Management

Total cost management has three major focus areas. These areas are cost planning and control, costing, and external regulations that must be supported by cost information. Each area consists of attributes that are critical to the overall focus area objective.

Cost Planning and Control. Cost planning provides operations management with prospective and historical cost and performance measurement information. The attributes of this focus area are process value analysis, responsibility accounting, performance measurements, and investment management.

Process value analysis is a cost reduction and process improvement methodology that focuses on identifying the resource-consuming activities within a process and the underlying "driver" of cost. The analysis is done at the process level (as opposed to product level), which represents the point of cost impact.

Responsibility accounting is the process by which actual cost information is reported against plans for those costs that are an individual's specific responsibility. These actual-to-plan comparisons are made at the level of cost impact (source)—not at the level of cost incurrence. For example, material handling costs are incurred at the support department level; however, the control and source of cost occur in the production department that demands the services.

Performance measurements measure the cost impact against a predetermined baseline. Measures are integrated vertically throughout the organization and horizontally along the value chain. Market, business, plant, and shop performance measurements should be consistent with the company's goals and critical success factors.

Investment management is the process by which management should relate investment decisions to strategic plans and operational goals while maintaining an acceptable return on investment. It uses the portfolio effect on the asset base and measures an estimate of improvements in quality, cycle time reduction, flexibility, and service through the elimination of waste (nonvalue added activities).

Costing. The second area of focus in total cost management is costing. Costing includes product valuation/profitability, pricing, product introductions, product discontinuances, and inventory valuation. Additionally, costing is necessary to support performance measurement and cost reduction opportunities through process value analysis. The costing focus area emphasizes the need to provide accurate and timely cost information in support of product and process costing.

Activity-based process costing and activity-based product costing are the two major attributes of costing. Activity-based process costing applies costs through a series of activity/driver bases. The process is made up of a series of activities directed at producing an output. Activity-based process costing is the precursor to activity-based product costing and helps facilitate performance measurements for responsibility accounting.

Activity-based product costing applies costs to products by developing cost pools within processes that represent costs that vary with a common activity/driver. An important distinction to note is that activities consume resources at the process level, while products consume activities. This allows us to integrate activity-based process and product costing by first costing the activity where incurred (process), and second, rolling up costed activities into products.

Activity-based product costing improves the tracing of costs to product where these costs typically were arbitrarily allocated in the past. Any costs that can be charged directly to products should be removed from the cost pools.

External Regulations. The regulatory focus area is directed toward providing the necessary financial and management reporting to meet the requirements of such external parties as the IRS and the SEC. Often, information required by these organizations differs significantly from information required for internal management purposes. (For example, allocations of overhead cost for financial purposes simply require a separation of costs deferred into inventory and those expensed through cost of sales). For internal management purposes, however, a much different distinction between causal relationships of cost and the effect of activities consumed by products for pricing, product introductions, discontinuances, and profitability measures is needed. ∎

---

resource patterns change. This was reinforced in our fieldwork.

Performance measurements provide an important building block in the process value analysis project. They set the baseline and measure the impact of changes in pursuit of continuous improvement. Performance measurements close the loop on activity-based process costing by relating the process cost to a measure of output producing "cost per" information.

Our client experience has shown that the comprehensiveness of measures can be demonstrated best by representing a balance between different categories such as:

- *Effectiveness.* Are we doing the right things—planned output/actual output?
- *Efficiency.* How well are we doing? What is the planned input per actual input?
- *Productivity.* How much output are we getting for a given input (or series of inputs)?
- *Utilization.* How are we using corporate resources such as inventory, asset turnover, etc.?

These measurement categories assist responsibility accounting programs by tying controllable cost measures to a more comprehensive view of managing resources.

INVESTMENT MANAGEMENT

Investment Management is a critical part of business strategy. Recognizing opportunities and earning an acceptable return is paramount for continued corporate health.

The investment strategy should be driven by specific product and process requirements as well as the company's strategy for dealing with technological change.

Investing and measuring return on individual assets is common but often shortsighted. The real value of an investment is the effect on the entire portfolio of assets. Consideration should be given to the synergy and integration of projects. The portfolio effect often proves that the total benefits outweigh the sum of the individual projects.

Typical cost and financial data such as ROI and ROA represent only one aspect of investment. Certain issues surrounding the use of ROI and ROA are subject to the accounting data. For instance, both the numerator and denominator of the equation is subject to certain accounting treatment on accruals, LIFO/FIFO inventory policy, and depreciation elections on assets. Consideration should be given to defining methodologies that demonstrate a better picture of the true *economics* of the business.

Improvements in quality, throughput, and other operational benefits are difficult to quantify but are real in terms of competitive posturing. These improvements should be included as estimates. It is better to make a fair representation than to ignore them altogether.

A company's cost management philosophy should provide visibility to cost reduction from new investment by focusing on the nonvalue added activities displaced and the improved efficiency of value added activities. All too often investment management focuses on the investment side of the equation and does little to follow the benefits. Our vision of cost management prescribes closing the loop by monitoring the change in activity-resource consumption through process value analysis. Figure 3 summarizes the role activities play in managing today's business through the principles of total cost management.

THE TRANSITION TO TCM

The first step to achieving total cost management is to assess the company's current environment, operations, philosophy, and organization. This assessment should identify the limitations of the current cost management system. It is important to have a sense of vision and a quest for continuous improvement through the management of resources in order to succeed.

We have developed a transition plan based on our experiences with clients (see Figure 4). Subsequent to the assesment, phase one begins with the process value analysis. The identification of cost behavior and activity/driver relationships through process value analysis then can be integrated with the performance measurements. Managers then can measure the impact of changes on activities and resources brought about through implementation of the operational improvement plan developed in process value analysis.

Phase two begins with the costing of activities at the process level where costs are incurred. Consequently, what efforts are made to reduce process costs will result in product cost savings when activity-based process and product costing are integrated.

Responsibility accounting can be built upon the phase one framework and the activity-based process costing work. Positioning responsibility accounting at this point takes full advantage of the understanding and differentiations of cost source (driver and demand source) and cost incurrence (expended activity resource). This will assist in placing the cost responsibility at the proper level of control in the value chain.

Phase two is completed with the incorporation of investment/asset management. The justification and tracking will be consistent with the operational improvement plan if the nonvalue added activities reduced or value added activities optimized are the focal point. Relating the investment of asset management to the responsibility area through established performance measures on the change in activities and the impact on process costs provides a solid basis on which to track the use of these resources after commitment.

Phase three produces a true picture of the total cost to provide products to the market. Using the insights gained in process value analysis and activity-based process costing, one can associate costs with products through:

■ Direct attribution,
■ Assignment through activities/

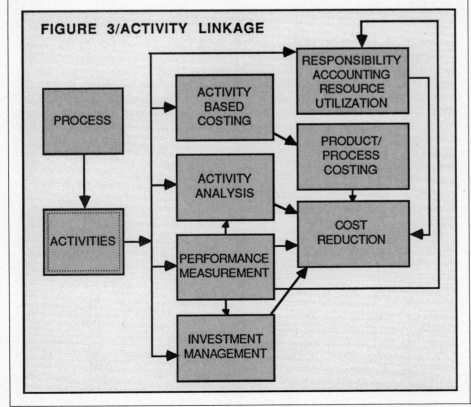

FIGURE 3/ACTIVITY LINKAGE

PROCESS

ACTIVITIES

ACTIVITY BASED COSTING

ACTIVITY ANALYSIS

PERFORMANCE MEASUREMENT

INVESTMENT MANAGEMENT

RESPONSIBILITY ACCOUNTING RESOURCE UTILIZATION

PRODUCT/ PROCESS COSTING

COST REDUCTION

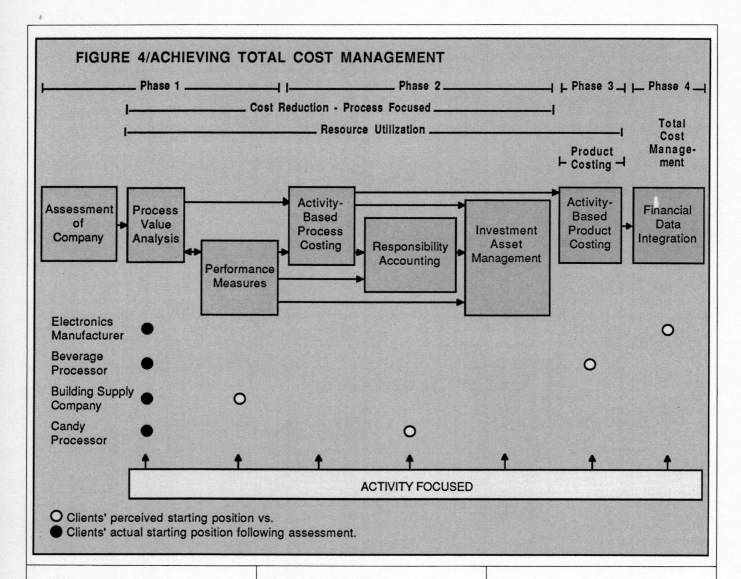

FIGURE 4/ACHIEVING TOTAL COST MANAGEMENT

Phase 1 — Phase 2 — Phase 3 — Phase 4

Cost Reduction - Process Focused

Resource Utilization

Product Costing

Total Cost Management

Assessment of Company → Process Value Analysis → Activity-Based Process Costing → Responsibility Accounting → Investment Asset Management → Activity-Based Product Costing → Financial Data Integration

Performance Measures

Electronics Manufacturer
Beverage Processor
Building Supply Company
Candy Processor

ACTIVITY FOCUSED

○ Clients' perceived starting position vs.
● Clients' actual starting position following assessment.

drivers, and

■ Allocation — last resort for remaining costs.

The costs associated with products in this fashion will reflect the resource input more accurately to produce different products.

Phase four, financial data integration and the use of activity information for both managerial and financial reporting, is still on the horizon. The advanced stages of research and continued development in practical applications with offline systems and models will help formulate the future needs for database definition and integration of total cost management into the financial data.

EQUATION FOR SUCCESS

Each total cost management principle positioned in this transition plan is strongly rooted in activity management.

Figure 4 illustrates the path to achieving total cost management. With most of our clients, the perceived starting position differed from the actual starting position after we assessed the needs of the company. While each project did not undertake a full PVA and performance measurement study, the work done in those areas was viewed as the critical foundation supporting the philosophy of managing company resources.

Many businesses still rely on managing by the summarized financial numbers. Yet the equation for success is a simple one: Cost is caused, cost is incurred. The only effective way to reduce cost is to manage resource-consuming activities through its driver relationships. Reducing cost alone won't have a lasting effect. If, however, the *cause* is removed, the savings are long term. Activities are at the

focal point of our ability to create excellence in our businesses. It's vital to take a fresh perspective to help transform our businesses into an improved competitive position through total cost management and its focal point — activities. ■

Michael R. Ostrenga is a senior manager and director for Ernst & Young's Cost Management and Manufacturing Industry consulting services for Wisconsin. He is a member of NAA's Milwaukee Chapter, through which this article was submitted.

[1] Robin Cooper and Robert S. Kaplan, "How Cost Accounting Distorts Product Cost," MANAGEMENT ACCOUNTING®, April 1988.

| Is this article of interest to you? If so, circle appropriate number on Reader Service Card. | Yes 58 | No 59 |

ACTIVITY-BASED MANAGEMENT

ABM puts ABC information to work.

This article is adapted with permission from Peter B.B. Turney, Common Cents: The ABC Performance Breakthrough, *Cost Technology, Portland, Ore., 1992.*

BY PETER B.B. TURNEY

To achieve continuous improvement, you must be informed. You need accurate and timely information about the work done (the activities) and the objects of that work (the products and the customers). That is what activity-based costing (ABC) is all about.[1]

But gaining good-quality information is only half the battle. The real key to success is putting ABC information to work to identify appropriate strategies, improve product design, and remove waste from operating activities.

Take the case of Stockham Valve and Fittings. Stockham used ABC to:

■ Match parts to the lowest-cost processes,
■ Pick new parts patterns to reduce subsequent manufacturing cost,
■ Initiate equipment modifications to reduce cost,
■ Increase the price of products that were priced below ABC cost, and
■ Drop unprofitable products from marketing's price sheet and the production schedule.

Using ABC to improve a business is called *activity-based management*

Peter B.B. Turney (standing, second from left) with the National Semiconductor ABM project team.

(ABM). It guides efforts to adapt business strategies to meet competitive pressures as well as to improve business operations.

THE LINK TO ABC

ABM and ABC are made for each other. ABC supplies the information, and ABM uses this information in various analyses designed to yield continuous improvement (see Figure 1).

The ABC model in Figure 1 has two parts, each of which plays a critical role in ABM. The first part is the cost assignment view. It reflects the need to assign the cost of resources to activities and the cost of activities to cost objects (such as customers and products) in order to analyze critical

decisions. These decisions include pricing, product sourcing, product design decisions, and setting priorities for improvement efforts.

The second part of the ABC model is the process view. It reflects the need for a new category of information about activity performance. This information shows what causes work (cost drivers) and how well it is done (performance measures). It helps identify improvement opportunities and ways to improve.

Cost drivers are factors that determine the work load and effort required to perform an activity. They tell you *why* an activity is performed and *how much effort* must be expended to carry out the work. For example, the occurrence of a large number of defects is a cost driver that can increase the effort needed to carry out an activity.

Performance measures describe the work done and the results achieved in an activity. They tell *how well* an activity is performed.

ABC information enables ABM to guide the continuous improvement process. It helps direct resources to activities that yield the greatest profitability and helps improve the way the work is carried out.

ACTIVITY-BASED MANAGEMENT

ABM aims at two goals, both common to any company. The first is to improve the value received by customers. The second is to improve profits by providing this value. These goals are reached by focusing on managing activities.

Meeting these goals starts with a simple realization—customers have very simple wants. They want products and services that fit a specific need. They want quality. They want service. They want an affordable price. They want to be delighted. *And they want it now!*

Meeting customer wants is one thing. Meeting them profitably is quite another. It's not enough to tell stockholders that your products have the highest quality in the industry or that customers consistently rate you highest in customer satisfaction. You also must provide an adequate return on stockholder investment. There's really no conflict here. In the long run, your profitability is important to your customers because they want you around for the long haul (which you won't be if you're unprofitable).

It's important to realize, too, that managing activities is *not* a custodial task. Rather, it's a process of relentless and continuous improvement of all aspects of your business—it involves an ongoing search for opportunities to improve. That search, in turn, involves a careful and methodical study of activities. Which activities should be performed? And how should those activities be carried out?

Let's address these questions by looking at some examples of improving strategic position and capability.

Improving Strategic Position. Activities are determined by strategic choices. A successful business deploys resources to those activities that yield the highest strategic benefit.

For example, a hospital makes a strategic decision to be a certified trauma center. This deliberate choice determines the activities and resources needed. A trauma center requires a different set of medical activities and resources than do other types of medical services.

To find out what is needed, the hospital must analyze ABC information about the link between its strategy and the activities and resources needed to put the strategy into place. These analyses can guide strategic decisions prior to implementation as well as help evaluate their ongoing effectiveness.

As another example, Armistead Insurance Company used ABC to refine the strategy of a computer data services unit that performed data analysis for fast-food franchisers. Unfortunate-

ly the operation was unprofitable, and the existing cost system provided few insights as to why.

ABC showed that Armistead customers differed in cost and profitability. Small customers were found to be unprofitable because of the high cost of acquiring and installing a new system for each of them. The result—Armistead raised prices for small franchisers and started a program to reduce the cost of acquiring new customers.[2]

Improving Strategic Capability. The key to implementing any strategy successfully is to improve what matters to your customer. This idea is not new, but it has never been more important than now.

What does matter to your customer? That's going to vary from business to business and from activity to activity within the business.

For example, Ford Motor Company says "Quality Is Job One." What Ford means is that good quality is the most important consideration for its customers, but what does "quality" *mean* to its customers? Ford needs to analyze information about quality. Is it low faults on delivery or doors closing with a satisfying clunk? If it is faults on delivery, what is the defect rate? What has been the trend on this key performance measure? Which activities were responsible for the defects? How much cost is associated with this "poor quality"?

ABC can supply much of this information. It points out the cost of poor quality by revealing activity centers

filled with detection and correction activities. Information on cost drivers and performance measures reveals opportunities for improvement and helps monitor progress. The impact of poor quality on product cost is revealed in each product's bill of activities. (This last piece of information is important because quality can vary significantly from product to product.)

Dayton Extruded Plastics is a case in point. It was widely believed at Dayton that scrap was "free." For one thing, very little material was lost. Scrapped extrusions were ground into powder and fed back to the extruders as raw material. For another, the existing cost system "confirmed" that scrap cost nothing—only good extrusions carried cost.

Implementing an ABC system brought Dayton Extruded Plastics face to face with the reality of scrap. Dayton managers found it was expensive to run extruders just to produce scrap (including the cost of extra capacity). Many costly activities (such as inspecting, checking line work, and handling returns from customers) also were associated with detecting and correcting quality problems. And grinding up reject extrusions required additional equipment and resources.

Improving activity performance has three steps:

- Analyze activities to identify opportunities for improvement.
- Dig for drivers—look for factors that cause waste (the cost drivers).
- Measure the things an activity

FIGURE 1/HOW ABM USES ABC INFORMATION

This figure is based on a chart developed by Norm Raffish and Peter B.B. Turney for *The CAM-I Glossary of Activity Based Management,* Computer Aided Manufacturing-International, Arlington, Texas, 1991.

should be doing well if it is contributing to the organization's success and the profitable servicing of its customers.

ANALYZE ACTIVITIES

Understanding why work is done, and how well it's done, is the key to eliminating waste and also can strengthen strategic position, as many organizations can testify. Here are some analysis guidelines to follow:

1. *Identify nonessential activities*. If an activity is not essential, it's reasonable to ask, "Why do we do it?" If we ask why, it's an easy step to the next question, "How do we get rid of it?"

Activities with value fall into one of two categories. In the first, an activity has value if it's essential to the customer. Polishing a precision optic, for example, has value because the customer wants outstanding optical performance.

In the second, an activity has value if it's essential to the functioning of the organization. Preparing financial statements is not of immediate concern to customers, but it does satisfy an organizational need: Financial statements must be prepared to satisfy stockholders, bankers, and regulators.

All other activities are nonvalue added. They are activities that are judged nonessential, and they are candidates for elimination. Expediting products is an example of a nonvalue-added activity. Customers don't care if products are expedited or not. They just want to receive the product by a certain time. Therefore, expediting really doesn't add any value for the customer. It can be eliminated without customers even noticing, if order and manufacturing lead times are reduced. Reducing lead times, in turn, permits reduced batch sizes and increased flexibility.

2. *Analyze significant activities*. A typical business can have 200 to 300 activities. There simply isn't the time (or resources) to analyze all of them at once.

The key, then, is to focus on significant activities—the ones important to customers or operating the business. Moreover, these are the activities that provide the greatest opportunities for improvement. In fact, I've yet to visit a business that didn't fit Pareto's rule: 80% of what you care about is deter-

WHAT IS CUSTOMER VALUE?

Customer value is about what customers get (the realization) and what they give up to get it (the sacrifice). Subtract sacrifice from realization and you have customer value.

Realization comes in a bundle. Included in the bundle are the features of the product or service. For a car, features include interior space, engine size, type of transmission, front, rear, or all-wheel drive, and so on. For a checking account, features include electronic bill paying, access to automatic teller machines, and 24-hour verification of your account balance.

But realization goes well beyond features. Whether buying cars or checking services, customers value good quality and service. In some cases, quality is the primary purchase consideration. In all cases, quality af-

fects the cost of using the product or service.

Customers also buy future costs when they buy a product or service. Future costs are incurred to use and service a car. Fees are incurred for services associated with a checking account. Some products (such as nuclear fuel) also have disposal costs.

There's no realization without sacrifice. Many products and services require time and effort, both in initial purchase and in learning how to use them. It takes time, for example, to master a new software program.[1]

[1]This discussion of customer value is based on definitions found in M. Stahl and G. Bound, editors, *Competing Globally Through Customer Value: The Management of Strategic Suprasystems*, Greenwood Publishing Group, Inc., Westport, Conn., 1991.

Parts for vinyl window systems emerge from an extruder at the Springboro, Ohio, plant of Dayton Extruded Plastics.

mined by 20% of what you do.

You can test this easily for yourself. Pick a department in your company. Then rank its activities in descending order of cost. You'll likely find that 20% of the activities cause 80% of the cost—and those activities are the ones worth analyzing.

3. *Compare activities to the best practices*. An activity should bear comparison to a similar activity in another company or another part of the organization. Just because an activ-

ity is value added doesn't mean it's efficient or that its work is of good quality.

Comparing an activity to a benchmark of good practice helps determine the scope for improvement. Xerox, for example, has an extensive benchmarking program. Activities are rated on such factors as quality, lead time, flexibility, cost, and customer satisfaction. Each activity is rated against an identified best practice. In the case of distribution, for example, the best practice was the mail-order distributor, L.L. Bean.[3]

As another example, you may determine that taking customer orders is an essential activity. You find that it is being done manually. The best practice, however, uses electronic data interchange, costs less per transaction, has a lower error rate, and provides faster service. Clearly there's room for improvement over manual order taking.

4. *Examine the links between activities.* Activities work together in a chain to meet common goals. The links of this chain must be constructed so as to minimize time and duplication of work.

The product design process illustrates what can be accomplished. In the traditional approach, design activities are performed serially. Product designers prepare the product specifications without consulting production. When the design is finished, production tries to manufacture the product (often with difficulty). Not surprisingly, this approach is repetitive, time consuming, and costly.

Concurrent engineering is a better way to go. In this approach, activities are performed in parallel. Product design, manufacturing, marketing, and procurement work together toward a common goal. There's less repetition and duplication, and better quality products get to the customer faster.

Studying product or transaction flows also can reveal delay and repetition. Ideally, work should proceed in an uninterrupted, continuous flow. Each activity should process a transaction only once.

For example, a study in Pacific Bell's customer payment center found that 25% of the center's work was devoted to processing 0.1% of the payments. More than one-third of all payments were processed twice and, in some cases, several times.

To improve this situation, a new work flow was proposed to change the way payments were processed. Individual work cells would process each type of payment. The emphasis was on processing each payment only once, in a continuous flow. It was estimated that these changes would reduce resource requirements by 25%.[4]

DIG FOR DRIVERS

Identifying nonessential and poor performing activities is the first step to improvement. The second step is to look for things that require you to perform nonessential activities or to perform below par. These things are the cost drivers.

For example, let's say you identified moving the product as nonessential. The customer doesn't care if the product is moved from one process to another because that activity doesn't affect what's received. So moving the product is a nonvalue-added activity.

But how do you eliminate the activity? You can't, not while there is distance between the two processes. Failure to move the product would result in piles of inventory at the end of the first process and no work for the second process.

The distance between the two processes—the plant layout—is the moving activity's cost driver. If you reorganize the plant to place the two processes next to each other, the cost driver is eliminated. It's no longer necessary to move the products over a distance.

Understanding and managing cost drivers is crucial to improvement. Simply understanding that waste exists doesn't result in automatic removal of that waste. Only when the causes of waste are addressed (the cost drivers) can the waste be removed.

MEASURE WHAT MATTERS

Activity and cost driver analysis is periodic. But activity performance goes on day in and day out. How do you ensure that ongoing efforts will focus successfully (and collectively) on what matters to the organization?

The answer is to develop a performance measurement system that fosters improvement in the right areas. Such a measurement system has three elements:[5]

1. *Determine the mission.* The first step is to determine what matters to the company. Generally this step results in a statement of mission—the key objectives considered important to profitably meeting customer needs.

Zytec Corporation, for example, wrote a mission statement that focused on six objectives directed toward meeting customer needs:

- Improve total quality commitment.
- Reduce total cycle time.
- Improve Zytec's service to customers.
- Improve profitability and financial stability.
- Improve housekeeping and safety.
- Increase employee involvement.

These objectives defined what was important to the success of the company as a whole. They articulated a vision of how the company should focus its improvement efforts.[6]

Partly as a result of this approach to performance measurement, Zytec's improvement program was extremely successful. Major improvements were seen in all areas of the mission statement.

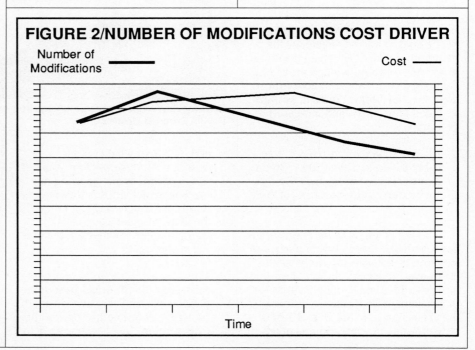

FIGURE 2/NUMBER OF MODIFICATIONS COST DRIVER

Number of Modifications

Cost

Time

2. *Communicate the objectives.* After specifying what matters, the next step is communicating it to the people in the organization. Everybody should understand the importance of the company's mission and how each objective relates to his or her activity. With this understanding comes the possibility of a collective focus on a common goal.

3. *Develop the measures.* The final step is to develop performance measures for each activity. These measures should signify how each activity contributes to the overall mission. They also coordinate and motivate the efforts of the activity, and they provide facts about activity performance that direct improvement efforts.

Zytec accomplished this step by identifying improvement targets for the coming year for all activities associated with each of the six objectives. For example, the automatic insertion activity identified its total quality commitment as "improve yields by 2%." It set its cycle time target as "reduce average cycle times by 5%."[7]

As another example, the Oscilloscope Group at Tektronix found ABC a fertile source of performance measures. Cost drivers were plotted against the cost of related activities over time. The intent was to prepare large charts of these graphs and to display them in the activity area. The idea was to draw people's attention to the relationship between the cost driver's quantity and the resources dedicated to the activities.

Figure 2 shows such a chart for a cost driver—number of modifications. The number of modifications was a count of engineering changes made to products. It was believed that this cost driver affected several activities, including engineering and bill-of-materials maintenance.

Before any resources could be redeployed, a number of questions had to be addressed. Should a new product introduction have "surge capacity"? (Usually many modifications were associated with a new product.) What was the impact of the engineers' learning to handle modifications with less time and fewer resources? How should the company deal with the concern of some engineers that the analysis might result in layoffs?

Despite these questions, the measurement exercise was believed worthwhile. The graphs stimulated a lot of discussion about managing activities and about use of resources, which resulted in positive changes—the goal of ABM.

ACTIVITY-BASED COST REDUCTION

The best way to reduce cost—one of several focal points of ABM—is to change the way activities are used or performed (managing the activities first), then to redeploy the resources freed by the improvement.

In contrast, conventional approaches to cost cutting favor across-the-board solutions. Such efforts work in the short run but usually fail in the long run because resources—often staff—are eliminated without regard to the underlying work.

The following five guidelines show how to reduce cost by managing activities:

1. *Reduce time and effort.* A key element of improvement is reducing the time and effort needed to perform an activity. This reduction comes from process or product improvement.

   For example, the time to set up a machine can be reduced by improving training, eliminating conflicts in employee assignments, and placing tools and dies in convenient locations. Practicing the setup routine can create the manufacturing version of a "Grand Prix pit stop team." Reductions of 90% in setup time are not unusual.

   Setup time also can be reduced by changing the product design. Engineers at Dayton Extruded Plastics, for example, changed the specifications for the vinyl weatherizing material used in extruded window frames. This change eliminated the need to add a weather-resistant coating to the frame. As a result, setup time was reduced because a simpler die could be used and a second extruder wasn't required.

   Reductions in time and effort may come not from the activity in question but from the preceding activity. For example, the defect rate of parts received by a machining activity is a cost driver for that activity. Improving quality in the preceding activity reduces the quantity of this cost driver and the effort required by machining.

2. *Eliminate unnecessary activities.* Some activities are candidates for elimination because they aren't valued by customers or aren't essential to running the organization. It is possible, for example, to eliminate material handling activities through changes to the processes or products. Steps can be taken to ensure that all incoming materials and parts are fit for use. The parts can be delivered directly to the shop floor as needed. Changes can be requested in the vendor's production process to improve quality and increase responsiveness. And parts that cause quality problems can be redesigned to eliminate those problems.

   Once these changes have been made, it is no longer necessary to inspect parts when they are delivered or to place the parts on the shelf in the stockroom. Eliminating these activities reduces overall cost and the cost of products that no longer use those

DOES IMPROVED QUALITY REDUCE COST?

It used to be a common belief that improved quality meant higher cost. This seemed reasonable. Doesn't improved quality mean more inspectors, more rework, more costly warranties, and the like?

How wrong we were. It's poor quality that costs money (and loses customers). Poor quality is doing the job more than once. It's wasting materials. It's having costly systems to keep track of defective parts. It's paying salaries for hordes of inspectors. It's incurring the cost of warranties and customer returns. And it's suffering the anger of disgruntled customers.

Improving quality is a sure way to reduce cost. Do it right the first time.

Work on reducing cost drivers that cause errors (such as frequent schedule changes, excessive process variability, or poor product design).

Paradoxically, reducing cost the activity-based way almost always improves quality. Eliminating unnecessary work, for example, reduces opportunities to "get it wrong" and tightens the linkages between activities.

ABM fits well with any quality improvement program. It encourages the actions that improve quality and directs attention to quality improvements with the greatest cost reduction potential.

activities.

Stockham Valve and Fittings, for example, used ABC to identify process changes that would eliminate scrap, rework, and other activities associated with poor quality. Stockham also used ABC to identify a group of products that had potential for cost reduction. Among the changes was an improvement to the tooling on one product. This single change eliminated several manufacturing operations and related setup, moving, and scheduling activities. Prior to this change, the product's ABC cost exceeded its selling price. Now it is competitive again.

3. *Select low-cost activities.* Designers of products and processes often have choices among competing activities. They can reduce cost by picking the lowest-cost activity.

A designer of an electronics product, for instance, may be able to specify the type of activity required for inserting components into circuit boards. Components such as resistors, diodes, and integrated circuits (ICs) may be inserted either manually or automatically. There also may be an option to place the components on the boards using surface mount equipment.

Each of these activities is associated with a different set of resources. Manual insertion is predominantly a direct-labor activity. Automatic insertion, however, requires equipment, software, setup for each batch of circuit boards that receives components, and additional process engineering and training. Each type of automatic insertion or placement also differs in resources required.

Because each of these activities has a different cost, the designer's selection has an important impact on costs. At Hewlett-Packard's Roseville Network Division, for example, the ABC system showed that manual insertion cost about three times more than automatic insertion.[8]

Process designers face similar choices. For example, a part designed for machine insertion also might be inserted manually. A process designer may choose to have the part inserted manually because a drop in the batch size makes it uneconomical to program and set up an insertion machine.

National Semiconductor Corporation used ABC to identify a lower-cost way of documenting product specifications. The current approach was to prepare the specifications manually, which cost in excess of $320,000 per year; it took about 12 weeks to complete the documentation for a single product.

The solution was to acquire a personal computer and to automate data analysis and reporting functions. This change reduced activity cycle time to three weeks, improved productivity by 75%, and eliminated order backlogs.

4. *Share activities whenever possible.* If a customer has unique needs, it's necessary to perform activities specific to that customer. If customers have common needs, it's wasteful not to service those needs with the same activities.

For instance, product designers can use common parts in new product designs. A common part is one that is used in several products to perform the same function (such as a gasket used in several car models). The only parts that need to be unique are those that add product differentiating functions valued by customers.

The activities associated with common parts—such as part number maintenance, scheduling, and vendor relations—are shared by all products that use them. This sharing increases the volume of parts served each time an activity is carried out, thus reducing the cost per part.

This insight was recognized by the Oscilloscope Group of Tektronix. The Group introduced an ABC system that used the number of different parts as an activity driver.[9] This driver then assigned the cost of procurement activities to the parts.

The result was an increase in the reported cost of unique (and therefore low volume) parts and a reduction in the cost of common parts. The engineers responded over a three-year period by redesigning portable oscilloscopes to reduce part counts in these products from 3,500 to 2,500.[10]

Process designers also can cut costs by combining products into work cells. Products can be combined when they have similar designs (members of a product family) and when the manufacturing process is sufficiently flexible to handle any differences. Cost is reduced because the products in the cell share activities such as supervision, testing, training, scheduling, material handling, storage, and documentation.

5. *Redeploy unused resources.* In the final analysis, cost can be reduced only if resources are redeployed.

Reducing the work load of an activity does not, by itself, reduce the equipment or number of people dedicated to that activity. Management must make a conscious decision to deal with the freed resources—by growing the business to take up the slack, redeploying the resources to other activities, or removing them from the company.

ABC can be used to calculate the type and amount of unused or underused resources. Resource plans based on this information then become the basis for redeployment.

The efforts described in this article are as likely to improve quality as they are to reduce cost. Remember, activity and quality management go hand-in-hand in any improvement program a company sets up. ∎

Peter B.B. Turney is Tektronix professor of cost management at Portland State University and chief executive officer of Cost Technology, Portland, Ore. He can be reached at (503) 292-5690.

[1] This article uses industry standard terminology. See Norm Raffish and Peter B.B. Turney, *The CAM-I Glossary of Activity-Based Management,* Computer Aided Manufacturing-International, Arlington, Texas, 1991.
[2] J.L. Colley, Jr., R.A. Gary, IV, J.C. Reid, and R.C. Simpson, III, "Data Services, Inc. (B)," UVA-OM-582, University of Virginia, Charlottesville, Va.
[3] *Competitive Benchmarking: What It Is and What It Can Do For You,* Xerox Corporate Quality Office, Stamford, Conn., 1984.
[4] H. Thomas Johnson, Gail J. Fults, and Paul Jackson, "Activity Management and Performance Measurement in a Service Organization," in Peter B.B. Turney, editor, *Performance Excellence in Manufacturing and Service Organizations,* American Accounting Association, Sarasota, Fla., 1990.
[5] Howard M. Armitage and Anthony A. Atkinson, "The Choice of Productivity Measures in Organizations," in Robert S. Kaplan, editor, *Measures for Manufacturing Excellence,* Harvard Business School Press, Boston, Mass., 1990.
[6] Robin Cooper and Peter B.B. Turney, "Zytec Corporation (B)," 190-066, Harvard Business School Press, Boston, Mass., 1989.
[7] For an extensive discussion of performance measurement issues, see Robert W. Hall, H. Thomas Johnson, and Peter B.B. Turney, *Measuring Up: Charting Pathways to Manufacturing Excellence,* Dow-Jones Irwin, Homewood, Ill., 1990.
[8] Robin Cooper and Peter B.B. Turney, "Hewlett-Packard: The Roseville Network Division," 189-117, Harvard Business School Press, Boston, Mass., 1989.
[9] In the past, activity drivers sometimes have been referred to as cost drivers, a usage inconsistent with industry standard terminology. See *The CAM-I Glossary of Activity-Based Management,* op. cit.
[10] Robin Cooper and Peter B.B. Turney, "Tektronix: The Portable Instrument Division," 188-142, 143, 144, Harvard Business School Press, Boston, Mass., 1988.

The Current Status of ABC

The second section of the introduction undertakes the task of providing answers to the questions that have been raised consistently since early descriptions of ABC appeared in management accounting literature. They are:

- What is the current status of ABC practice in the business world today?
- In spite of all the success stories reported and written about in prestigious journals, can evidence be provided to show that such systems have been implemented successfully?

The authors of both articles in this section, leaders in research and ABC implementations, provide responses that reduce the void indicated by the preceding questions.

In the first article, Alfred King, a former managing director of IMA, puts a series of wide-ranging questions to Professors Robert Kaplan and Robin Cooper, pioneers in the ABC field. The authors respond by tracing the development of their work from early ABC systems to manage the mix of products and customers to their present systems, which focus management attention on setting priorities for continuous improvement efforts. They reveal that ABC and continuous improvement programs not only are compatible but work extremely well together. Certainly ABC, they say, has enhanced the communication as to what the underlying economics of the firm are. ABC information has eliminated much conflict and misunderstanding — all managers in the firm are reading from the same hymnbook.

Elaborating on some of their latest insights, the authors concede that their old way of defining costs as variable in the long run was wrong, and a better way to express this phenomenon is to say that in the long run resource spending (acquiring the capacity to perform activities) will tend to follow resource usage (use of resources acquired). The link between spending and usage is excess capacity. Further, they say, you should charge to products and customers the capacity that actually is used. The remainder is an idle capacity cost of the period. By following this concept you reduce the fluctuations in unit cost, because capacity is divided by capacity usage and not total capacity.

The authors conclude that management accountants now have the tools (ABC) to communicate with all the managers in the business and should be able to develop, at "least cost," customized systems that will pay off for the firm.

The second article, "From ABC to ABM," was written by the authors of an IMA-sponsored research study, *Implementing Activity-Based Cost Managment: Moving from Analysis to Action,*" published in 1992. The article reveals their findings and the results of this study. IMA embarked on the study because few success stories of bottom-line improvement had surfaced. IMA wanted to know whether there were real problems with the tools, concepts, or implementation of ABC systems or whether companies were unwilling to disclose this information because they feel it gives them a competitive advantage. The desire was for real-life examples and case studies from which executive management and the management community could learn. The authors — Robin Cooper, Robert Kaplan, Lawrence Maisel, Eileen Morrissey, and Ronald Oehm — have provided detailed information on ABC implementation by outlining the theory and practice of ABC implementation and by discussing eight actual case study sites.

The authors indicate that ABC models can be developed with a relatively modest commitment of financial, personnel, and time resources. The team identifies the activities performed and the organization resources used, estimates the cost of performing these activities, and then links the activity costs to outputs — products, customers, projects, and so on — that benefit from the activities consumed. This part of the work can be considered a restructuring of, and mapping of, the organization resources from functional categories (departments, cost centers) to related resources, activities, and business processes. Managers generally were pleasantly surprised at how useful this information was. The ABC model information was treated as a management information system and not as part of the firm's accounting system.

What did the study reveal? A number of important conclusions resulted, in spite of the fact that five of the eight firms made no significant change in action or decision as a result of ABC. The conclusions are:

- ABC is a management process. The cross-functional view of the processes enabled managers to manage the activities and business processes better.
- ABC benefitted strategic and operational decisions and also stimulated process improvements and activity management.
- ABC information, by itself, does not lead to improved profits and operating performance. A conscious change process must be instituted by the company to gain improved results. ∎

THE CURRENT STATUS OF ACTIVITY-BASED COSTING:
AN INTERVIEW WITH ROBIN COOPER AND ROBERT S. KAPLAN

Where is ABC on the path to total implementation?

BY ALFRED M. KING, CMA

Robin Cooper and Robert S. Kaplan have been pioneers in the field of activity-based costing (ABC) and have written numerous articles on the subject over the past five years. Prentice-Hall has recently published their latest textbook, Design of Cost Management Systems: Text, Cases, and Readings. *In this interview with Alfred King, senior vice president of Valuation Research Corporation and formerly a managing director of IMA, they review the background of ABC, some of the effects it has had on business, ways in which its focus has changed, and its future prospects.*

Q **After five years of experience with activity-based costing, you have had real-world practice with a number of companies. What are some of the major types of decisions which you feel can be made more knowledgeably with cost management systems that rely upon activity-based costing principles?**

RC: Most of the early benefits we observed related to managing the mix of products and customers. A well-designed ABC system provides managers with a better understanding of the way profits are generated at both the product and the customer level. Managers can take advantage of this understanding and increase profitability by getting rid of unprofitable customers and products or transforming them into profitable ones and attempting to sell more to the profitable ones.

RSK: We certainly started our work with a focus on managing product and customer mix, and that continues to be an important strategic application of ABC. In the last few years, however, we have seen the numbers coming from the activity-based cost analysis being used in conjunction with process improvements. By measuring the costs of business processes such as purchasing, taking a sales order, moving materials, and inspection, people in some companies for the first time have seen how costly some of these activities are. Now they are directing their improvement efforts to reducing the cost of performing many of these activities. Even better, they are attempting to understand some of the fundamental drivers of these activities and perhaps eliminate the need to perform some activities entirely.

Some people feel that companies are trying to move into a JIT environment anyway and that they don't need activity-based costing to do so. These people fail to realize that many opportunities exist to apply continuous improvement activities. Without a financial model, many efforts may get directed to areas where there is not a lot of spending and where the gains from improvement are not that high. So developing an activity-based cost model *first* helps managers to set priorities. It lets them see where most of the dollars are being spent, what the fundamental drivers of those processes are, and where, if you can make changes, they can get big payoffs.

So ABC has turned out to be helpful for both focusing managerial attention and setting priorities for continuous improvement efforts. After the fact, ABC provides validation about the savings from successful cost reduction programs. What are the real cost sav-

Robin Cooper

Robert S. Kaplan

ings from reducing setup time or inspection activities or from shortening material-handling distances? We have found that activity-based costing and continuous improvement programs work extremely well together and are highly compatible.

ABC also promotes improved design for manufacturability programs. The ABC analysis reveals that complex and unique product designs can lead to high manufacturing and support expenses. Several companies, particularly those with relatively short product life cycles, are using results from the activity-based costing analysis to influence design decisions of their engineers.

RC: When product life cycles are really short, you don't have enough time to correct a poorly designed product before it is replaced by a new one. ABC gives these firms, which are selling their design skill as much as their products, the ability to fine tune that skill, to become proficient at designing low-cost, high-quality products that meet their customers' needs.

Q**What are some of the significant decisions or actions you have seen in the companies you have worked with? In other words, what are some of the real "bottom line" dollars-and-cents results that companies have achieved with this kind of ABC analysis? What have been some of the appropriate actions that companies have taken?**

RSK: We have seen firms eliminate some of their low-volume customers from whom they can't get price increases. Sometimes they are able to put surcharges on small orders. We are seeing ABC provide the *climate* for these improvement activities. It is still early, though. Most firms haven't yet gotten large benefits that are easy to measure because it is still early in the process.

ABC is not just getting the numbers. For an ABC program to be successful, organizations have to get people to buy into the actions, and that takes time. Then they have to implement the actions, and that takes time. Then they have to take the next stage of action, either to use the excess capacity that has been created or to manage the excess capacity out of the system. To go from an ABC analysis to bottom line profit improvement requires a whole set of linked steps.

RC: It's important to realize that ABC triggers actions but by itself does not cause savings to occur. If the ABC system is well designed it adds to managerial intuition, enabling people to put energy where previously they may not have put it. The new actions are really a mixture of the economic insights provided by the activity-based system, plus managerial intuition.

> *ABC triggers actions but by itself does not cause savings to occur.*

RSK: I have asked managers to attempt to quantify the hard, tangible benefits. In two companies that have had activity-based cost systems for several years, I didn't get a dollars-and-cents answer. The managers said that the activity-based cost information provided a much better language for everybody to use in their everyday discussions. Everybody now was talking from the same page. Before, there was tremendous conflict. Manufacturing people blamed the cost accounting system, and the cost accounting people became defensive, saying "you don't understand the system," and the marketing people were not even part of the discussion.

Now everybody agrees on what the underlying economics of the firm are. The managers I interviewed said this agreement has been tremendously helpful to them as they go ahead and try to manage for the medium to long term. Everybody is reading from the same page and not squabbling about the underlying economics of their business.

RC: Some of the benefits will be almost impossible to identify. For example, a well-designed ABC system will warn against a strategy of introducing custom products with a selling price below reported ABC cost. However, because the firm never introduces a large number of custom products, the detrimental effects of adopting such a strategy are never observed. ABC has had a profound but invisible effect on the profitability of the firm.

Q**You mentioned in your presentation, and in a recent article in *Harvard Business Re-**view, that there is a difference between usage of resources and spending on resources. Would you elaborate on that distinction?**

RC: The distinction between resource usage and resource spending is the latest insight in the development of ABC theory. Fundamentally, you can think of spending as acquiring the capacity to perform activities. If you hire an inspector who can perform 5,000 inspections a month, you have created a capacity, on which you are spending money, to perform 5,000 inspections. Usage, on the other hand, has to do with how many inspections that inspector actually performs. Let's say in this month, the inspector performs only 4,000 inspections. ABC calculates the expense of the activity actually performed. If each inspection costs, say, $5, and we have used up 4,000 of them, we used $20,000 of inspection resources. But we are spending at a $25,000 level. Therefore, this month we had excess capacity of $5,000 for the inspection activity. By carefully identifying usage versus spending, ABC allows managers to see both how much of available resources they are using and the economics of excess capacity.

RSK: Basically, products and services are continually using resources. The supply of resources, machines, and people, however, comes in lumpy amounts. We used to say that all costs are variable in the long run, not realizing that is the wrong way to think about it. The correct way of expressing this phenomenon is to say that in the long run spending on resources will tend to follow their usage. If you want to find out where spending will be in the future, you would be better off looking at usage today and modeling usage in the future. You may not change spending in the short run, but eventually, if management acts, spending will come into alignment with usage.

Cost systems can model resource usage, but except for a very few types of resources they can't model spending. The only exceptions are those resources acquired from outside the firm, such as material and energy, for which, if you don't use the resource, you don't have to pay. But for resources acquired and controlled internally, spending tends to be fixed in the short run. It is effectively independent of usage. Over time, as usage changes, the spending will align with it, at least if managers are paying attention.

We can't predict spending because that is a managerial decision. We can predict resource usage. We can show managers where spending likely will change based on changes in resources being used. If excess capacity exists and they don't want to get rid of that capacity, managers can use it to generate more throughput, thus earning more revenues without increasing spending. So the resource usage model turns out to be critically important. It should be a good predictor of future spending.

Q Putting it a different way, if you cut your usage of resources but don't reduce your spending on people and other overhead elements, then in the short run you will not have any improvement in bottom line profitability. Is that a fair way of putting it?

RSK: Absolutely. In effect, your *products* will cost less because they are using fewer resources, but you will have a lot more excess capacity that is not being used by existing products or customers.

Q In your recent joint textbook, *Design of Cost Management Systems*, you have a chapter on capacity costing. You have some very interesting concepts on what you believe is the most appropriate method of calculating capacity cost.

RSK: At first we thought that the cost of excess capacity was a side issue to ABC but one that we still needed to get straight. We now realize that excess capacity costing is not a side issue—it's a central issue. Excess capacity provides the link between resource usage and resource spending. Spending on capacity-type resources gives you a supply of available time or available number of transactions that can be handled. If you don't use all that capacity, you should charge to the products and customers only the portion of the capacity that actually is used. The remaining amount, which is not used, is considered part of the cost of being in business for that period or, specifically, the cost of unused or idle capacity. Many companies make the mistake of taking their total spending on resources and dividing by actual output. By doing that, the unit cost of product output fluctuates significantly,

Authors Cooper and Kaplan plan next joint project.

period by period, depending upon volume fluctuations. That makes the whole picture difficult to interpret.

RC: Activity-based costing changes our view of capacity. In a traditional unit-based system, capacity is defined by the volume of production—the number of units produced. In ABC, capacity is defined as the ability to perform activities, therefore, every activity identified in ABC has the potential of going into an excess capacity position. A well-designed ABC system should identify the practical capacity to perform each activity and use that capacity to generate the costs of performing the activity.

Q There has been a lot of emphasis on cost management for manufacturing organizations. An even larger part of our gross national product is devoted to service operations of one sort or another. Bring us up to date on where activity-based costing stands in this major arena.

RSK: Banks, particularly the money center banks, have been doing some-

thing like activity-based costing for 20 years. That work continues, and it is migrating out to more and more banks. The recent trend in banks is to get out of their "factory," which is where they do transactions processing, and to look at their customer profitability. This focus mirrors some of the issues that we are seeing in manufacturing companies. In our book we wrote a case that describes the early development of a large bank's customer profitability report. As in manufacturing companies, the bank is using the customer profitability analysis to share its economics with its customers, trying to change customers' behavior, perhaps by repricing some of the services it is providing or getting the customers to use its service in different ways. The customer profitability application in the bank is very similar to what we find in manufacturing companies.

We are starting to work with insurance companies to examine their cost structures. We have been successful in understanding the operating expenses of insurance companies, again by type of product as well as by type of customer. We are working with a telecommunications company to look at the cost and use of the network. Other applications are with airline companies, looking at flight route profitability, and airline information systems departments, examining the reservation systems and the billing systems. ABC is migrating very naturally to all of these service organizations.

Q People in service organizations, in the broad sense, shouldn't hesitate to look at activity-based costing as a technique and a tool for continuous improvement.

RSK: Service companies have exactly the same set of issues as manufacturing concerns in analyzing their operating expenses, in finding out what activities are being performed by their resources, and in learning which products, services, and customers are demanding those activities. This information enables them to take actions to transform losses into profits and increase the profits from existing services and customers even further.

RC: The fascinating aspect of service industries is that the definition of their "product" is somewhat plastic. In manufacturing you have a widget that you can kick around, and therefore everybody accepts the product as a widget. The resources consumed by widgets tend to be fairly consistent over time. When you look at the products in service companies, the customer defines to a much greater extent the resources that are consumed.

In a service business, when you view products as consuming activities, you can partition the "standard products" in numerous ways. For example, a passbook savings account that is used once a month and has a balance of more than $5,000 differs greatly from one that is being used continuously and has near-zero balances. In an ABC analysis those two accounts, even though they are the same standard passbook product on the surface, can be treated as very different products.

Q Let's switch gears. How does activity-based costing help justify the major investments that companies are making in continuous improvement, such as design for manufacturability, total quality control, JIT, and other techniques?

RSK: With the hierarchical model of

operating cost expenses that Robin developed, we now see that a lot of support resources are going to perform batch and product-sustaining types of activities. We never focused on these kinds of activities before. When we look at where the continuous improvement activities—including total quality management, just-in-time, and design for manufacturability—are being applied, they are revealed, under an activity-based cost analysis, to be batch and product-sustaining activities. The reason why there is so much interest in working on those activities is that we spent 40 or 50 years studying and improving the unit-level activities of direct labor time, machine hour time, and material content of products.

The distinction between resource consumption and resource spending is the latest insight in the development of ABC theory.

We probably have obtained most of the benefits from trying to improve activities that are performed each time we make a unit of a product. We have *not* focused on the activities necessary to produce a batch of a product such as setting up a machine, moving materials, writing purchase orders, or handling customer orders; or to do product-sustaining activities such as designing products, initiating engineering change notices, and the like. The ABC hierarchical model signals the tremendous buckets of opportunity in batch and product-sustaining activities that can be improved by Kaizen or continuous improvement activities.

RC: We can see this effect by revisiting the capacity, spending, and resource usage issues we talked about earlier. ABC allows you to take snapshots at regular intervals to see how well the JIT, DFM (design for manufacturing), and TQC programs have reduced resource usage. This resource usage decrease should be well captured by the ABC analysis. Simultaneously, ABC identifies excess capac-

ity. It tells how well the firm has managed to find alternative uses for the resources that now have been freed up. Thus it shows how effectively companies are implementing continuous improvement and whether they have successfully achieved bottom line benefits from their efforts by reducing the spending on resources to the now lower demands for resources.

Q You have been working in activity-based costing about five years. Where do you think we will be over the next five years in the cost-management ABC area?

RSK: One direction will be to attack corporate and general overhead to find out the activities performed by corporate overhead resources and what the drivers of those activities are. I suspect that many of those activities are done not for individual products or individual customers but for regions or lines of business.

A second direction will be to look more closely at the research and development activity, the resources going into R&D, and what types of activities are being performed there. If we can monitor R&D and help that whole product and technology management activity, we should be able to develop improved financial measures for product and process development.

RC: I see activity-based systems being applied to understand the life cycle cost of a product. ABC can capture the introduction phases of a product—all the chaos required to educate the customer, make prototypes of new products, and so on. All those costs will be captured. As the product matures, these early costs disappear to be replaced by straight manufacturing costs. The improved insights on total life cycle costs will allow us to begin thinking about better design methods and how to market and price products so that over their lives they can be more profitable.

RSK: We also will understand better how to link the information from an activity-based cost analysis to performance measures. We must target the areas where improvements are necessary and provide feedback on how well people are doing. We can improve those critically important measures.

RC: Many firms today are pointed in the right direction: reduce defects, reduce cycle time, improve design. Rapidly those firms are going to reach a point at which there is a tradeoff between introducing new products quickly versus a decrease in cycle time. I think at that point ABC can play a critical role and help healthy firms to manage those tradeoffs.

A lot of people today are preaching that you don't need cost information—that all you need to know is in which direction to jump. I think that is a shallow analysis. Perhaps there are times when a cost/benefit tradeoff is so obvious you don't need to run the financial numbers. Once you get rid of those glaring inefficiencies, however, the financial numbers will be very important to guide companies' efforts.

RSK: In the 1980s, there was a lot of slack rope in organizations that had not been managing their processes well. Now that they have made continuous improvements, the rope is starting to get tight. When the slack is reduced, companies will need an economic model—based on financial numbers—to help them understand the nature of the tradeoffs needed.

Q **As you are designing an ABC system, is there any conflict between an emphasis on performance measurement and an emphasis on product costing?**

RSK: There is no conflict. If you are interested mostly in understanding products and customer profitability, then you can design a comparatively simple ABC system to give you the major insights on product and customer profitability. If you want to go inside processes, improve them, and make

them more efficient—in effect, the activity management story—then companies need to understand activities at a more detailed level. They have to do a deeper and more comprehensive analysis of the underlying activities.

RC: We have learned during the last few years that the appropriate way to design an ABC system depends on what you want the system to do. You can't use a cookie cutter approach to ABC, even in the same firm. One division may need a customer orientation, another division a product orientation, and a third a cost reduction orientation, while a fourth might have a product design orientation. All of these systems will be different. Not only will the ABCs differ across the facilities, but within the same facility over time they have got to evolve and adapt to changing conditions.

Q **Let me wrap up this interview with a final question on cost management and ABC. What is the most important role ahead for the management accountant in this exciting process?**

RSK: Increasingly, the financial person will create value in the organization because he or she really understands the operations and is able to develop a customized system that has the highest payoff at the least cost for that organization. That role will require continual involvement in management-level activities and an understanding of the critical success factors in the business, the technology of the business, the nature of the outside product, and customer markets. Systems must be kept appropriate and up to date for that environment to meet management objectives. It's a more challenging—perhaps a more frightening—task. Certainly it is going to be a much more exciting and interesting time for management accountants.

We now have the tools the management accountant can use to provide a common language for managers in operations, in engineering, in product design, and in marketing, to talk about the economics of their business. This requires that the management accountant be involved with all those groups, making sure that everybody is reading from the same page and fully understands the economics of the business. The management accountant is not a decision maker by herself or himself but is in a position to provide information to focus management's attention

so that management will make the decisions that will increase value.

RC: In the really successful implementations we see the ABC system owned by everybody. It has become a *business system*, not an accounting or financial system. That moves the management accountant's role from being a record keeper on the sidelines to being one of the active players. One of the implications is that the modern management accountant has to have a very broad business education. It is good for the profession to make the management accountant more of a generalist.

RSK: To reinforce that, some new accreditation standards recently were passed for business schools in general and accounting departments in particular. If you look closely you will see that there is now a requirement that accounting students get some exposure to operations and technology management. This is part of the recognition that accountants have to *understand* the businesses in which they are operating.

Q **If they do, will they be able to play on the top management team?**

RSK: We hope that they eventually *become* top management! ∎

Robert S. Kaplan is the Arthur Lowes Dickinson Professor of Accounting at the Harvard Business School and a professor of industrial administration at Carnegie-Mellon University. He received a Ph.D. in operations research from Cornell University. He is the author of more than 70 papers in accounting and management journals. Among his books is Relevance Lost: The Rise and Fall of Management Accounting *(Harvard Business School Press, 1987), written with Thomas Johnson.*

Robin Cooper is an associate professor at the Harvard Business School. He earned both his MBA and his DBA from the School. In 1990 he received the first Innovations in Accounting Education Award from the American Accounting Association in recognition of his course development efforts in product costing. He is the author of numerous articles.

Is this article of interest to you? If so, circle appropriate number on Reader Service Card.

	Yes	No
	52	53

From ABC to ABM

Does activity-based management automatically follow from an activity-based costing project?

BY ROBIN COOPER, ROBERT S. KAPLAN, LAWRENCE S. MAISEL, EILEEN MORRISSEY, AND RONALD M. OEHM

"ABC has built our confidence during negotiations. Today we don't crumble when confronted by a customer demanding price improvements ... ABC also made us more aggressive in pursuing new business—we're aggressive on bids for products that we believe our competitors are not pricing correctly."

This controller was describing the impact of an ABC project at his division.[1] But what has the situation been in regard to activity-based costing and activity-based management (ABM) at most organizations?

There has been little systematic evidence as to the design of actual ABC systems and the circumstances that would lead companies to initiate an ABC project. Few success stories of bottom-line improvement have surfaced. Is the silence because companies are unwilling to disclose information, or are there real problems with the implementation of ABC and ABM systems?

The IMA Committee on Research, together with Robert S. Kaplan, Robin Cooper, Lawrence Maisel, and the management consulting division of KPMG Peat Marwick, decided to find out what has happened when companies have carried out an ABC project.[2] Their study examined, analyzed, and synthesized the actual experiences of eight companies that implemented activity-based cost systems.

The experiences of the companies showed that activity-based cost models can be developed using a "generally accepted" set of practices with a relatively modest commitment of financial, personnel, and time resources. In developing an ABC model, the project team first identifies the activities performed by the organization's resources and estimates the costs of performing the activities. The activity costs then are linked to the organizational outputs—products, services, customers, projects, and organizational units—that benefit from the activities performed.

CASE SITES AND SCOPE

The case sites included five manufacturing organizations, a financial services company, the finance department of a large energy company, and a distribution company (see sidebar, p. 56). None of the eight sites developed a complete model of all organizational expenses in its initial effort, but, in aggregate, the eight sites included models of manufacturing operating expenses, marketing and selling expenses, distribution expenses, and general corporate overhead expenses.

All five manufacturing organizations analyzed production expenses to obtain the expenses of organizational activities and the costs of individual products. Two of the manufacturing companies also analyzed marketing and selling expenses to obtain measures of customer and market segment profitability. All the manufacturing companies emphasized the role that activity costing and activity analysis should take to stimulate operating process improvements. The companies explicitly recognized the linkage of ABC to their formal quality initiatives. The model designs typically included specific activities and activity centers to collect information on quality-related expenses.

The studies done at the financial services company and the finance department of the energy company showed how activity-based cost management can be extended to an organization's general and administrative expenses. The study at the distribution company developed an activity-based cost model of product distribution and customer service expenses.

In summary, the eight sites illustrate how activity-based cost management encompasses all aspects of a company's value-added chain: (1) purchasing and procurement, (2) operations, (3) marketing and selling, (4) distribution, and (5) general and administrative expenses.

Jos. Palmieri/AFI

Could ABM help your company be among the chosen—those that report a success story of bottom-line improvement?

ACTIVITY AND BUSINESS PROCESS ANALYSIS

The implementing companies found that one of the first benefits from the ABC analysis was the restructuring and mapping of the organization's expenses from functional categories and departments to show how they related to the activities and business processes. In each study, senior managers reported that this information revealed for the first time the costs of the activities their units were performing. They expected to use this information to make decisions on outsourcing activities, eliminating activities, or, most common, improving the efficiency with which activities were performed.

The general usefulness of activity and business process costs came as somewhat of a surprise to managers. Apparently these managers had believed erroneously that ABC was only a product costing system. Before conducting the ABC project, they had not appreciated how useful it would be to be able to identify the activities performed by support resources and to determine the costs incurred to perform these activities.

Contributing to the insights from the activity analysis were the several types of activity classifications used by the sites. Most used some form of the activity-based cost hierarchy in which activities are classified as unit, batch, product-sustaining, or facility-sustaining. Several of the sites attempted to perform a value classification for activities, but most found this process difficult and controversial.

COST DRIVER ANALYSIS

Identifying and measuring cost drivers proved to be the hardest part of the implementation. One company excluded two important expense categories from the initial study because it lacked information about how individual products and services used these resources. Other companies reported that even when they used surrogate cost drivers they had to perform extensive programming to access existing corporate databases and also considerable manual data collection.

Williams Brothers Metals, however, which initially expected difficulty in collecting cost driver information, found that almost all of the desired information was accessible on machine-readable databases. A key project member recalled the cost driver analysis. He said, "When we started, we didn't know what was available in the systems. Designing cost drivers was a big deal. You really need to have good systems in place before you start an activity-based management project."

PRODUCTS AND CUSTOMERS

All the sites drove their organizational expenses from activities to individual products, customers, or other cost objects. The manufacturing companies generally found, as expected, that low-volume, complex products tended to be much more expensive than the existing standard cost system had shown. The ABC models provided a "bill-of-activity costs" that enabled managers to see the costs of procurement, inventory carrying and management, materials handling, inspection, shipment, and setup for individual products. This information was expected to lead to changes in the production scheduling, design, mix, and pricing for an organization's products.

For example, the automotive division of Slade Manufacturing started immediately to rationalize its products and customers to reduce complexity and enhance profitability. It instituted price increases on other products that yielded $1.2 million in additional revenues. The division also was using its more accurate product costing data strategically. It deliberately refused to accede to an important customer's request for a significant price reduction for the last three years of an existing contract. The division enjoyed higher prices for the two years until the products were transferred away, it freed up capacity to develop and bid for profitable next-generation products that would be produced when the existing products left, and it locked a major competitor into committing a significant part of its capacity to an unprofitable contract.

The two companies that produced customer profitability reports also found the typical ABC pattern, with several customers shown to be highly profitable, most customers at or near breakeven profitability, and a few customers highly unprofitable. For example, large-volume customers with whom one company had been doing business for many years were quite profitable. Newly acquired customers or small customers, for whom generous credit terms and extensive sales and technical support were provided, were unprofitable.

TABLE 1/MODEL DEVELOPMENT

Site	Duration[2]	FTEs[3]	Role for Outside Consultants[1]		
			Facilitate[4]	Analysis[5]	Create Change[6]
AMD	4	2.5	3	3	0
ARCO ALASKA	2	2.5	3	4	1
WILLIAMS BROTHERS	8	2.0	3	3	0
STEWARD	3	0.25	5	5	0
KRAFT	6	2.5	3	1	0
MONARCH	6	1.5-2.0	3	3	0
FARRALL	6	2.0	3	3	0
SLADE	4	2.0	4	4	3

[1] The role for outside consultants is coded on a scale from 0 to 5:
   "0": zero involvement in a particular task,
   "1": low involvement,
   "3": medium involvement, and
   "5": active involvement.
[2] Duration is the estimated time, in months, to estimate and analyze the organization's first ABC model.
[3] FTEs represents the Full-Time-Equivalent company people involved in the ABC project over its duration. Several of the companies, particularly Steward, used outside consultants extensively to help in the model development process, which reduced the required commitment for internal people.
[4] Facilitate includes initial training and awareness seminars, and design of ABC model.
[5] Analysis includes interpretation and presentation of results and development and presentation of recommended actions.
[6] Create Change involves spurring the organization into action, developing an agenda for and facilitating organizational commitment, decision making, and action.

The other company identified several market segments that were only marginally profitable. Mass merchandisers purchased very low-margin products and likely never could become high-profit contributors. The international and original equipment manufacturer (OEM) markets, with modest sales, were at or below break even. The project sponsor indicated that "since the ABC implementation, we have developed and initiated an exit strategy for the OEM market and have held off any attempt to grow our international market. The ABC data put certain decisions on the table. We now had data to support our discussions."

Similar findings occurred for Steward, a financial services company. Its product profitability model showed that only two products—equity securities and high-yield securities—were profitable. The remaining securities were breakeven or showed significant losses. Based on these results, the company cut back on one product line, international, almost immediately and reorganized its product responsibilities to increase the focus on profit improvement. A second ABC model, of account executive (AE) profitability, showed that AE support costs were much higher than previously believed. The director and head of the equity department indicated, "The ABC study revealed the average breakeven point for an AE was $325,000 in gross commissions. This was a much higher number than we had assumed. Based on these results, unprofitable AEs who do not fall into a special category [new hire, important link to other product lines, or special/unique trades] may be asked to leave. By looking at the activity expenses associated with each AE, I have better insight into the avoidable expenses if an AE leaves."

At Williams Brothers Metals, the distribution company, the analysis indicated that the products shipped as mill direct were the most profitable. Such shipments incurred almost no inventory and materials handling costs. This finding, however, caused management to question the competitive advantage of its distribution business if the most profitable products bypassed most internal processes.

PROJECT RESOURCES

With one exception, each of the sites had its own project team do the bulk of the model development (see Table 1), which includ-

THE EIGHT CASE STUDY SITES

The eight case studies occurred in quite different settings:

Production and Marketing Cost Analysis—Manufacturing Companies
   Farrall Corporation: two plants of a manufacturer of water filters and housings;
   Monarch Mirror Door Company: two plants of a private $70 million manufacturer;
   Advanced Micro Devices: the Malaysian assembly and test facility for a $1 billion semiconductor company;
   Slade Manufacturing Inc.: Hudson Automotive Parts Company: Youngstown plant of a $120 million automotive components division of a $700 million manufacturer;
   KRAFT USA: two processing plants of a very large food company.

General & Administrative Cost Analysis—for Service Organizations
   Steward & Company: a regional institutional brokerage company;
   ARCO Alaska, Inc.: controller's department (175 employees).

Distribution Cost Analysis
   Williams Brothers Metals: a privately held metal fabrication and distribution company.

Note: In some cases, company name and industry are disguised.

ed interviews, formal and informal data collection, and running the model. Senior financial people played a critical role at all the sites. With the exception of the financial services company, where the motivation for the project came from the company CEO, the motivation and sponsorship at the other sites began and was maintained in a finance group. Most of the teams, however, drew upon people other than those from the finance group—the main contributors came from Management Information Services (MIS) and Operations. Four sites used senior management project steering committees—these sites were the ones where subsequent management actions were most noticeable.

At most of the sites, outside consultants played a facilitating role, providing initial training and awareness seminars and helping the project team

structure the interviews. They transferred the hard data from the company's databases and the soft data from management interviews and estimates into a PC-based activity-based software model and assisted in analyzing and preparing reports and presentations for the project sponsor and senior management. Most of the day-to-day work, however, was performed by the internally staffed project teams.

The average time for a project was about four months. Elapsed time ranged from two months at ARCO Alaska (because of the limited scope of the project and the restricted availability of two summer interns who did the data collection and model development) to about eight months for companies at which the scope of the projects extended beyond initial expectations. The companies committed about 2.0 full-time employees (FTEs) during the duration of the project, plus assistance from outside (or internal) consultants to prepare and train people in the organization and help in the analysis and report presentation tasks.

All the sites used a PC-based software package that had been developed specifically for activity-based cost analysis. None of the companies tried to use a mainframe computer or existing cost accounting package to develop the ABC model. Data on expenses, product characteristics, and cost drivers were derived, when available, from existing databases on the company's systems and downloaded to the PC-based ABC software package. Data not available in machine-readable form were entered manually.

Companies continued to run all their existing financial systems in parallel with their new ABC models. Some observers have questioned whether managers would find credible the numbers created "outside" the official financial reporting system. This hypothetical concern never was expressed in any of the interviews conducted at the eight sites. If anything, managers found the numbers generated from the activity-based analysis more credible and relevant than the numbers generated from the official costing system. No site considered or intended the activity-based model to be a replacement for the organization's financial transaction system. At all eight cases, this system continued to function as before and was expected to remain in the future. *The activity-based model was treated as a management information system, not as part of the accounting system* (see sidebar on this page).

ACTIONS AND DELAYS

Several of the companies already had taken action based on the insights gained from the ABC analysis. These actions included repricing, de-emphasizing, eliminating, and reorganizing certain product lines, services, or market segments. They also included process improvements to reduce the cost of key business activities and processes. But many of the companies had yet to act on the findings, even when the ABC analysis indicated that significant numbers of products, customers, or processes were much more expensive than the traditional cost accounting systems had been reporting.

In part, the delay could be attributed to the recency of the activity-based cost management approach in the chosen companies. For most of the sites, the estimation of the ABC model was not completed until mid-1991. Because of the time frame of the research study, these sites were visited while the ABC model still was undergoing final estimation or, at best, shortly after the final estimates had occurred. Senior management either had not been briefed completely on the findings or had had insufficient time to establish profit priorities for taking action.

Given the radical change in thinking required by activity-based cost management, and the extended length of time for any new management decision and action to occur, the study may have captured companies at too early a stage to judge the efficacy of improved management actions based on the newly gathered ABC information.

But a more fundamental cause of the delays in taking action may have been inadequate preparation of the organization for changes in thinking and decision making. Delays like those at many of the sites, in moving from a fully estimated and analyzed ABC model to actions that improve profits, should concern corporate sponsors and finance managers who wish to have the output from their ABC models used productively.

The most successful projects occurred when a specific *target* for change was identified early in the project, during the analysis stage. The target was the person or group whose decisions were expected to change as a consequence of the information revealed by the activity-based model. Also helpful was having a *sponsor* for the action stage, a senior person who wanted change to occur and who could authorize the actions to be taken by the target person or group.

Many companies do not have an explicit game plan for making the transition from generating information in the ABC analysis stage to having line managers make decisions in an action stage. The game plan should include identifying, early in the project, both the sponsor and the target for the changes that are expected in the action stage. Otherwise, companies could find that their ABC project keeps cycling within the analysis stage. In this pattern, the finance sponsor is following what could be called a *"Field-of-Dreams"* strategy: "If I build it [the ABC model], the line managers will come [and take action]." Unfortunately, the Field-of-Dreams strategy usually proceeds with the project team being asked to refine the model,

WHAT WAS REVEALED BY THE STUDY?

Among the principal findings from the study are the following:

- Activity-based cost management is more than a system. It is a management process. Managers at each company understood that the ABC information enabled them to manage activities and business processes by providing a cross-functional, integrated view of the firm.
- ABC management benefits both strategic and operational decisions. Companies were using the information to make major decisions on product lines, market segments, and customer relationships, as well as to stimulate process improvements and activity management.
- An ABC model can supplement and coexist with traditional financial systems. Companies continued to operate their existing financial systems while developing and interpreting ABC models.
- ABC information, by itself, does not invoke actions and decisions leading to improved profits and operating performance. Management must institute a conscious process of organizational change and implementation if the organization is to receive benefits from the improved insights resulting from an ABC analysis.

re-estimate it on new data (e.g., this year's actuals, next year's budget), and develop new models for different organizational sites.

The danger of this pattern is that after several years of refinement, re-estimation, and extension—but no managerial decisions or actions—the ABC project is viewed as the concern of the finance group only. It is not thought of as an initiative that has to be addressed, accepted, internalized, and acted upon by operating managers.

Sponsors and project managers of the analysis stage must recognize that a comprehensive ABC model is not an end in its own right. No organization ever made more money merely because it had a more accurate understanding of its economics. Only when understanding is translated into action is the potential for profit improvement unleashed. ∎

Robin Cooper, DBA, is professor of management at the Peter Drucker Center at the Claremont Graduate School in Claremont, Calif.

Robert S. Kaplan, Ph.D., is the Arthur Lowes Dickinson Professor of Accounting at the Harvard Business School.

Lawrence Maisel, CPA, is the managing director of Maisel Consulting Group, a firm specializing in profit improvement, business process redesign, and performance measurements using activity-based management. Prior to forming Maisel Consulting Group, he was the national director for KPMG Peat Marwick's Financial Management Consulting practice.

Eileen Morrissey, CPA, is currently a senior manager in Price Waterhouse's national manufacturing management consulting practice, specializing in activity-based costing.

Ronald M. Oehm serves as partner-in-charge of KPMG Peat Marwick's management consulting business, serving clients in manufacturing and technology industries.

[1]This company is the one called Slade Manufacturing, Inc., in the research study. The name has been disguised.
[2]The research study referred to in this article is *Implementing Activity-Based Cost Management: Moving from Analysis to Action*, published by the IMA.

Section 3

Controversy: Are ABC Systems Effective Management Tools?

The purpose of this final section of the introduction is to present disparate views about ABC systems as effective management tools—the views of advocates, detractors, and doubters. Can ABC systems replace traditional accounting systems? Improved product costing aside, have ABC systems been oversold? Could it be that the foundation for those arguments slowly is being undermined by the breakthroughs being reported for ABC systems? Admittedly, the 1950s top-down, traditional cost system attempted to control operations through dollarized costs, manipulated worker behavior, and negated worker empowerment. It may have contributed to reduced productivity and the decline of manufacturing capability and capacity. But what about the new, evolving ABC management systems that mirror manufacturing processes, are focused on the customer, target processes for improvement, and have continual "bottom-up" involvement by accountants, engineers, and production people?

Three respected researchers, in the articles that follow, involve themselves in this healthy debate. Following these articles will be found responses to the H. Thomas Johnson article from *Management Accounting* readers, published in the Letters to the Editor column. These responses, mainly from ABC practitioners, can be useful in evaluating the strengths and weaknesses of ABC systems.

In the first article, "The New Cost/Management Accounting: More Questions Than Answers," William Ferrara is troubled and has difficulty believing

that his discipline, cost/management accounting, seems to be so out-of-date and out-of-touch. Further, he is troubled because the costs developed by traditional accounting systems are not adequate to meet the new manufacturing environment of the '90s. He explores a number of basic issues, namely, market-driven versus engineering-driven standards and the movement toward actual cost systems, and renews the absorption costing/direct costing debate. He indicates that target costs established from competitive market prices usually are well below currently achievable costs developed through engineering standards (standard costs), which encourage Japanese workers to work toward continual improvement. He finds this externally imposed standard intriguing and different from that described in current textbooks. He is disappointed that little or nothing has been said about how direct costing, or cost-volume-profit analysis, is affected by the ABC system.

Another issue explored is the definition and use of the term "cost driver." He refers to Professor John Shanks's writings as the first to clarify the concept of cost drivers and to make a solid case that volume is not the only cost driver. The latter idea is a possible reason for the diminution of importance of direct costing, because direct costing centers on the distinction between fixed and variable costs and output volume as the supreme driver. Today, of course, there are many kinds of drivers, among them resource drivers, activity drivers, and batch-based, product-sustaining, and other drivers. All can be defined clearly but do contribute to the confusion about the term "driver."

Among the many concluding thoughts that Ferrara leaves us with is that some products are in different stages of their life cycle and can't be mandated to meet a specific profit requirement during every year of their life.

H. Thomas Johnson has put on his boxing gloves in "It's Time to Stop Overselling Activity-Based Concepts." He is ready to meet all challenges to his assertion that ABC does not drive companies to change their fundamental views about how to organize work efficiently to satisfy customers. The point Johnson makes is that the firm must "discover and adapt competitive ways of organizing work, not how to be more profitable by shifting product mix." Indeed, he feels compelled to make known that ABC should be "redirected and slowed down, if not stopped altogether."

What annoys Johnson is his belief that management accounting information is used to control people's work and "accounting targets" are used to control operations, a trend that began in the 1950s. He feels that this trend resulted only in changing people's behavior to "control cost by manipulating processes and, thereby, neglect customers, employees, suppliers, and society in general." In this light he sees ABC as simply "reconfiguring existing accounting information." Hence his distrust of the value provided by ABC.

Johnson advocates that management accounting gain understanding of the new "customer-focused, process-oriented management thinking." You must begin with the customer-focused mission statement and then have everyone in the organization systematically improve the processes they control. "Focus on reducing variation and lead time in the work itself, and costs will take care of themselves." You need to control processes, not people, says Johnson.

In the final article in this section, "In Defense of Activity-Based Cost Management," Robert Kaplan defends ABC. His current research focuses on developing new management accounting systems for the rapidly changing environment of manufacturing and service organizations.

Kaplan defines an activity-based cost model as a system "designed to inform management about the economics of the past, current, and future operations." It is an economic road map of the organization. He supports organizations that adopt the "lean production paradigm," which includes programs such as JIT, TQM, DFM, and other acronyms, with organized learning and improvement activities. Furthermore, he sees no conflict between improvement programs, which provide information on quality and process time, and activity-based cost management, which provides information on the cost of activities and business processes. Companies active in process improvement and customer satisfaction programs should be able to see their improvements realized when the next ABC model is estimated.

Can ABC systems replace traditional accounting systems?

Kaplan indicates that "an economic or financial model is needed to show whether the operating improvements have been exploited through lower expenses and higher revenues or whether the improvements created unused capacity and customer services that were not valued in the marketplace." Thus while ABC models do not provide measures of quality and process time as improvement programs do, they complement those programs by indicating the quantity and cost of resources used in processes.

With regard to total customer satisfaction Kaplan feels that a company should not adhere blindly to this concept because some customers make great and costly demands and don't want to pay the cost of satisfying these demands. A customer-based ABC model, he states, can help management decide whether a particular customer's needs should be satisfied. Marketing efforts then can be better spent on gaining new customers, rather than serving unprofitable ones. ■

The New Cost/Management Accounting
MORE QUESTIONS THAN ANSWERS

Is the management accounting system as hopeless as the critics say?

BY WILLIAM L. FERRARA

Certificate of Merit, 1989-90

Even the most casual observer of the accounting scene could not possibly be unaware of the avalanche of criticism during the past five or so years concerning the "current state of cost/management accounting." Hardly a day goes by without our receiving another paper on the subject, or a solicitation to attend a costly meeting where the "new and better" systems will be discussed.

Those of us who have spent a great portion of our lives studying, teaching, consulting, and working with cost/management accounting are both pleased and troubled by the attention focused on us and our discipline. We are pleased because it's always been obvious to us that our discipline is worthy of greater attention. On the other hand, we are troubled because we have difficulty believing that we are so out-of-date and in need of so much retraining.

There is no doubt that many changes have occurred in the economic environment since the late 19th century development of cost accounting. Nonetheless, it seemed as if the subject matter of cost/management accounting had evolved naturally and logically by the 1970s into a full-blown management accounting scheme based on standard costing, flexible budgeting, cost-volume-profit analysis, variance analysis, capital budgeting, and goal congruence, along with the behavioral impact of various accounting measurements. Our literature and our textbooks seemed loaded with meaningful materials on management accounting for planning, control, and decision making.

By the early 1980s educators were in a position to visualize offering elementary, intermediate, and advanced cost/management accounting courses like those offered for many years in financial accounting. Then, seemingly almost overnight, the criticism started.

One part of the criticism stressed something many of us had long recognized—that direct labor had decreased and fixed costs had increased so that direct materials and perhaps energy were the only variable costs of consequence left in many manufacturing firms. This preponderance of fixed costs and the diminished direct labor placed greater emphasis on fixed cost assignments to products via measures of activity other than direct labor.

Another part of the criticism is related to the "new" manufacturing environment, encompassing robotics, flexible manufacturing systems, just-in-time systems, and the challenge to U.S. producers from the "new" manufacturing ideologies and techniques coming from Japan. In my opinion, the real issue was and still is the significant increase in worldwide competition, coupled with the new manufacturing ideologies and techniques. As a number of U.S. firms and industries began to lose market share, "old-fashioned" cost accounting and pricing strategies based thereon were considered a significant part of the problem. It was difficult to argue with someone who suggested that cost accounting systems based on a manufacturing environment related to the early 1900s were not adequate for the new environment, especially the 1990s.

There are indeed problems, but they have not been ad-

AP/Wide World.

Computers revolutionized manufacturing. Above, one of the calculators of U.S. Navy, Dahlgren, Va.

dressed as they should be. Part of the difficulty seems to be a lack of knowledge concerning cost/management accounting history, and another part is due to the fact that at least some of the "experts" seem unaware of each other. I would like here to bring together diverse and apparently incomplete points of view in order to identify questions to be resolved and the kind of research needed to resolve those questions.

BASIC ISSUES

*M*arket-Driven vs. Engineering-Driven Standards. An article on Japanese management accounting in the *Harvard Business Review* (July-August 1988), by Toshiro Hiromoto, truly brings home the difference between market-driven and engineering-driven standards. Hiromoto says, "[Japanese companies] establish target costs from estimates of a competitive market price. These target costs are usually well below currently achievable costs, which are based on standard technologies and processes. Managers then set benchmarks to measure incremental progress toward meeting the target cost objectives." He continues: "In general, Japanese management accounting does not stress optimizing within existing constraints. Rather, it encourages employees to make continual improvements by tightening those constraints."

The difference between what Hiromoto is suggesting and procedures described in current textbooks is immense. The approach he outlines also appears different from methods endorsed by some recent articles and conferences, which stress measuring costs right and finding the true product cost.[1] Hiromoto says of Japanese management accountants, "It is more important, they argue, to have an overhead allocation system (and other aspects of management accounting) that motivates employees to work in harmony with the company's long-term goals than to pinpoint production costs. Japanese managers want their accounting systems to help create a competitive future, not quantify the performance of their organizations at this moment."

The difference between market-driven and engineering-driven standards is illustrated in Figure 1.

Those of us who have been in management accounting for some time can identify readily with engineering-driven standards and the concentration on variances between standard and actual costs. Nonetheless, how easy it is to be intrigued by the utility of a market-driven (externally imposed) standard and its concentration on variances between actual and allowable costs.

The Movement Toward Actual Cost Systems. Allowable cost is appealing also because it is not considered the ultimate goal. When the allowable cost is achieved it then is tightened by a monthly cost reduction rate. What we

have here is a continuous learning or experience curve that we try to make happen. Hiromoto explains, "In subsequent years, the actual cost of the previous period becomes the starting point for further tightening, thereby creating a cost reduction dynamic for as long as the model remains in production."[2]

After all these years of pushing for a standard cost system, we now have an eloquent argument for an actual cost system. But is this any different than old Satchel Paige looking over his shoulder or our old football coach saying that you've got to strive to get better or you're bound to get worse? Fortunately, as indicated by Hiromoto, some U.S. firms have adopted approaches similar to what he has seen in Japan.

The Old Absorption Costing/Direct Costing Controversy. As we peruse the literature on the purported new activity-based costing, we cannot help but get the impression that what we are working with is another version (perhaps refined) of absorption costing. The stress is on allocating or assigning manufacturing, marketing, and even administrative costs to products so as to calculate a "true product cost" or to "measure costs right."[3] Little or nothing is said about how direct costing or cost-volume-profit analysis is affected by the new activity-based costing system. This omission is unfortunate because we appear to be turning our backs on something that has come to be a central feature of cost/management accounting methodology, and few, if any, seem to have noticed or are concerned.

What we have here is a wonderful opportunity for research, which has been virtually ignored. From the late 1950s until at least the early 1970s, many practitioners were extolling in the literature the benefits of direct costing, contribution reporting, and cost-volume-profit analysis.[4] Firms such as Westinghouse, Armstrong, Dresser Industries, and Johnson and Johnson were readily identified as users of the direct costing philosophy. Even a number of firms in the steel industry were involved.[5]

Direct costing obviously was not a subject confined to academic circles. Furthermore, the practitioner discussions did not deal only with manufacturing costs but considered all costs, including manufacturing, marketing, and administrative costs. Similarly, the practitioners did not concentrate on variable costs and contribution margins to the exclusion of an appropriate role for fixed costs in internal management reporting.[6]

An Opportunity for Research. All of the above commentary provides a great incentive for research. A number of companies identified as early users of direct costing should be the subject of case studies that could cover the period virtually from the end of World War II to date. Appropriate questions would be:

■ Why did the companies move toward direct

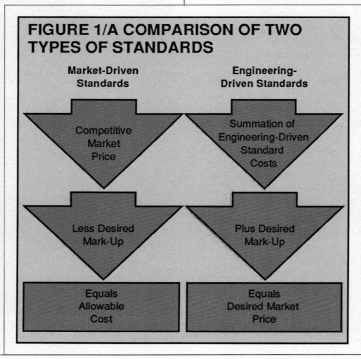

FIGURE 1/A COMPARISON OF TWO TYPES OF STANDARDS

Market-Driven Standards

Competitive Market Price

Less Desired Mark-Up

Equals Allowable Cost

Engineering-Driven Standards

Summation of Engineering-Driven Standard Costs

Plus Desired Mark-Up

Equals Desired Market Price

costing in the 1950s and 1960s?

- What changes have occurred since they adopted direct costing; to what extent have they refined it or moved away from it and why?
- Have they moved toward the new activity-based costing systems? Why or why not?

As a part of these case studies, many of the participants actually involved in installing the early direct costing systems, as well as their successors, could be interviewed. They are still with us, even though they are retired in some instances. Similarly, the involved public accounting partners and high level officials of consulting firms and their successors could be interviewed. It is a shame—if not a tragedy—that this kind of research has not been taken on. The case for the new cost/management accounting is, and will be, woefully inadequate until such research is accomplished and until that research is integrated adequately into the case for the new systems.

After or even while the above recommended case study research is continuing, other appropriate research methodologies should be considered. Simulations and experiments contrasting the old and the new systems should provide some very interesting results. Similarly, appropriately constructed data banks, based on industrial organization-sponsored questionnaires, also should yield interesting results.

SOME COMMENT ON CORPORATE STRATEGY

Much has been written in recent years about corporate strategy, and articles on activity-based costing have referred often to corporate strategy. Hiromoto also commented on corporate strategy. In his case, however, the comments seem more complete and more profound:

"The secret of Japanese management accounting: integrate it into corporate strategy."

"Japanese managers seem to worry less about whether an overhead allocation scheme reflects the precise demands each product makes on corporate resources than about how the system affects the cost-reduction priorities of middle

---

TABLE 1/COST DRIVERS — STRUCTURAL VS. EXECUTIONAL*

Structural Cost Drivers

Strategic choices underlying the firm's economic structure that drive cost position for any given product group.

Scale — How big an investment to make in manufacturing, in R&D, and in marketing resources?

Scope — What degree of vertical integration to have? Horizontal integration is more related to scale

Experience — How many times in the past has the firm already done what it is doing again?

Technology — What process technologies to use at each step of the firm's value chain?

Complexity — How wide a line of products or services to offer to customers?

Executional Cost Drivers

Those determinants of a firm's cost position that hinge on its ability to "execute" successfully.

- Work force involvement — "participation" (the concept of work force commitment to continual improvement);'
- Total quality management (beliefs and achievement regarding product quality);
- Capacity utilization (the choices as to scale or plant construction);
- Plant layout efficiency (efficiency of the layout against current norms);
- Product configuration (effectiveness of the design or formulation);
- Exploitation of linkages with suppliers and/or customers, per the firm's value chain.

* Adapted from John K. Shank, "Strategic Cost Management: New Wine, or Just New Bottles," Journal of Management Accounting Research, Fall 1989, pp. 56,57.

---

managers and shop floor workers. As a result, they sometimes use allocation techniques that executives in the United States might dismiss as simplistic or even misguided."

Before the reader gets carried away with Hiromoto's commentary, it would be appropriate to refer to U.S. literature of the 1960s, which makes essentially the same point:

"The idea of a desired behavior pattern being the induced behavior pattern can be referred to in terms of whether or not an individual responsibility report or responsibility technique yields the 'desired inclination.' The existence of desired inclination is measured in terms of the extent to which induced behavior is consistent with the goals of the organization as a whole."[7]

Robert Anthony referred to "desired inclination" as "goal congruence" in the sense that a control system "should be structured so that the goals of people in the organization are, so far as feasible, consistent with the goals of the organization as a whole."[8] Charles Horngren referred to the same concept as "harmony of objectives."[9]

One way to summarize these thoughts on corporate strategy would be to say that the advocates of the new cost/management accounting have forgotten or at least have slighted accounting research of a behavioral nature, whereas the Japanese may have used "behavioral impact" as the core of their system. These summary thoughts may be a bit simplistic, however. In this regard, the following commentary on cost drivers and life cycle costing should be helpful.

COST DRIVERS

The words "cost drivers" have become almost commonplace in the literature on the new cost/management accounting. Nevertheless, these words typically are defined and used very poorly. In fact, in most instances, the words "cost drivers" have been simplistically substituted for the old words "measure of activity" in the context of what causes costs and how the costs should be allocated or assigned to products.

In the accounting literature, only John Shank seems to have given operational meaning to the term. In particular, he used Daniel Riley's distinction between structural and executional cost drivers.[10] The differences between these two categories, as well as an illustrative list of drivers in each category, are shown in Table 1.

Shank says that structural cost drivers underlie the "economic structure that drives cost position for any given product group." The specific structural cost drivers he lists are scale, scope, experience, technology, and complexity. Shank says that the executional cost drivers "are those determinants of a firm's cost position which hinge on its ability to 'execute' successfully." He also suggests that for structural cost drivers "more is not always better," whereas for executional cost drivers "more is always better."

In a certain sense the structural cost drivers can be related to the design phase of a product's life cycle, whereas the executional cost drivers can be related to the implementation or post-design phase. In total, both groups of cost drivers encompass what is now known as cost management, which in the old days was partitioned into cost reduction and cost control. The distinction between cost reduction and cost control also is related or analogous to the distinction between the design and post-design phases of a product's life cycle.

The above commentary on the new concept of cost drivers and on some of our older concepts is intended to facilitate thinking about the old and its relationship to the new. In my opinion, Shank was the first truly to clarify the concept of cost drivers and make a solid case that volume was not the only cost driver. In fact, Shank may have identified a reason for a diminution in the importance of direct costing, which is centered on the distinction between fixed and variable costs and output volume as the supreme cost driver. When the notion of cost drivers is integrated fully into cost/management accounting, the fixed vs. variable cost distinction may turn out to be considerably less important than it has been.

At this point, it should be obvious to the reader that I also am trying to understand and make some sense out of the new cost/management accounting. We must continue to observe and take part in ongoing developments in regard to corporate strategy and the very related concept of cost drivers. As the active participants in new developments continue their efforts, they will clarify the difference between, and the need for a difference between, the old and the new cost/management accounting. The earlier suggested case study research on direct costing certainly should be a part of this process. Another part of the process should relate to work force involvement as an executional cost driver.

Hiromoto and his Japanese colleagues should be encouraged to give us specific case study information on human resources policies and practices as well as other data relative to those Japanese firms that have been successful in generating work force involvement. Securing similar case study information for U.S. firms that also have been successful in this regard should be an active research objective. Those of us who have observed too many labor/management confrontations have a certain amount of difficulty foreseeing simultaneous achievement of a diminishing cost function and work force involvement.

LIFE CYCLE COSTING

Like cost drivers and corporate strategy, life cycle costing is another set of buzz words that is difficult to describe precisely. Nonetheless, we hear these words too often to ignore how they might fit into the new cost/management accounting. Related words and concepts are: stages in a product's life cycle, portfolios of products, and strategic positioning.

One version of life cycle costing is to consider the summation of a purchaser's costs from the point of initial purchase to the point of ultimate disposition of the product by the purchaser "n" years down the road. This version can yield a corporate marketing strategy designed to convince a purchaser to buy a product because of its cost effectiveness over its entire life.

Another version of life cycle costing is to consider cost factors during each stage of a product's life cycle, that is, de-

As manufacturing moved to automation human labor became less and less a cost factor. Above, Mark III computer at Harvard.

sign, introduction, and the intended "star" and "cash cow" stages. During each stage the cost management problems are generally distinct. As we pursue the notion of stages in the life cycle, the concept of portfolios of products naturally emerges, along with the idea that a desirable portfolio should be balanced in the sense of being a combination of products in different stages of their life cycles. Thus, a company could easily be applying different cost management policies simultaneously but for different product lines that are in different stages of their life cycles.

The earlier distinction between market-driven and engineering-driven standards could easily fit the idea of products in different stages of their life cycles. Market-driven standards might fit products in their design and introductory phases. As products move toward star and cash cow phases, and if the life cycle lasts long enough and production standards are achievable, engineering-driven standards might fit.

On the other hand, if product life cycles are shorter than they used to be and production runs are smaller, engineering standards may no longer be as relevant as they were in the day of Henry Ford. In these days products just may not last long enough to achieve the standardization necessary for engineering standards.

Somewhat related is the concept of strategic positioning, which involves how a firm chooses to compete. A firm might choose to compete by having cost leadership or product differentiation. As stated by Shank, "For a firm following a cost leadership strategy in a mature, commodity business, carefully engineered product standards are likely to be a very important, ongoing management control tool. But, for a firm following a product differentiation strategy in a market-driven, rapidly growing, fast-changing business, carefully engineered standard manufacturing costs may well be much less important." Given that the typical firm is involved with numerous product lines, both of the above approaches to strategic positioning may apply in the same firm at the same time.

Obviously, much research remains to be done concerning how a firm should integrate corporate strategy, cost driver analysis, and life cycle costing into its cost/management accounting system. At this stage all we can do is ask questions and monitor the progress of the various firms, consultants, and researchers involved in the integration efforts. However, as we move toward this integration, it may be useful to keep the following in mind:

- Accounting analyses are rarely, if ever, exact—all they can do is give a "feel" for the financial dimensions of various activities and opportunities. The intuition and gut feel of a sharp and creative person or group is generally all important for making decisions based on such analyses.
- The anticipated behavioral impact of alternative accounting performance measurements always must be considered.
- Do not allow regulatory requirements (including external reporting) to dictate the method of accounting analyses.
- Let's focus on results for families or portfolios of interrelated activities. The families can and will change over time and for some analyses should include suppliers and customers. Be careful with analyses concerning individual members of the family—make sure total systems effects are considered in some reasonable manner.
- Continuity and sustainability of families or systems of interrelated activities is consistent with the idea that *not all*

product lines (activities) should be required to meet the same minimum profit requirements (performance standards) during each and every year of their lives. How can products in different stages of their life cycles be forced to meet the same minimum standard each year? The result would be an unbalanced portfolio made up solely of mature products and a system of activities without much sustainability.

- Year-to-year profitability mandates relate more to portfolios of products than to individual products. Generally, only portfolios should have a mandate for a year-to-year positive bottom line.

Much yet remains to be done by way of research, especially of a case study nature, in order to put together an adequate statement on the new cost/management accounting. Market-driven vs. engineering-driven standards plus the movement toward actual cost systems and activity-based costing will probably be a part of the new system. Not much will be accomplished, however, unless the new system is properly integrated with most, if not all of the aspects of corporate strategy, cost driver analysis, and life cycle costing. ∎

William L. Ferrara, Ph.D., is the David M. Beights Professor of Accounting at Stetson University, De Land, Florida. Previously he taught at Penn State University for 27 years. He is editor of the Journal of Management Accounting Research, *a publication of the American Accounting Association.*
Dr. Ferrara has been a national officer of the NAA and has served as a member of the Board of Regents of the Institute of Certified Management Accountants. He is a member of the Daytona Beach Area Chapter, through which this article was submitted. Readers who would like more information should contact the author at Stetson University, School of Business, De Land, FL 32720.

---

[1] See for example the following two articles: Robin Cooper and Robert S. Kaplan, "How Cost Accounting Distorts Product Costs," MANAGEMENT ACCOUNTING®, April 1988; and "Measure Costs Right: Make the Right Decisions," *Harvard Business Review*, September-October 1988.
Also see the advertising piece for the December 8-9, 1989, conference on "Activity Based Costing" sponsored by The Manufacturing Institute. The conference subtitle was "Find Your True Product Cost."
[2] See "How Milliken Stays On Top," by J.D. Edwards, C.D. Heagy, and H.W. Rakes, *Journal of Accountancy*, April 1989, for a U.S. firm with a similar philosophy.
[3] See the two articles by Cooper and Kaplan, cited in note 1.
[4] See for example: Robert Beyer, *Profitability Accounting for Planning and Control*, The Ronald Press Company, 1963; second edition with Donald Trawicki, 1972; National Association of Accountants, *Current Application of Direct Costing*, Research Report 37, 1961; National Association of Accountants, *Information for Marketing Management*, 1971; Sanford Simon, *Managing Marketing Profitability*, American Management Association, 1969.
[5] See the list of participating companies for the study *Current Application of Direct Costing*, mentioned in note 4. Also see the articles "Profit Planning" by Marshall Evans, *Harvard Business Review*, July-August 1959, and "Sequential Profit Measurement—Optimum Profit" by William Langenberg, *NAA Bulletin*, June 1964.
[6] See for example Chapter 7 on "Measuring Segment Profitability" in Beyer and Trawicki, mentioned in note 4.
[7] William L. Ferrara, "Responsibility Reporting vs. Direct Costing—Is There a Conflict?", MANAGEMENT ACCOUNTING®, June 1967.
[8] Robert N. Anthony, *Management Accounting*, 3rd edition, Richard D. Irwin Inc., Homewood, Ill., 1964.
[9] Charles Horngren, "Choosing Accounting Practices for Reporting to Management," *NAA Bulletin*, September 1962.
[10] John K. Shank, "Strategic Cost Management: New Wine, or Just New Bottles," *Journal of Management Accounting Research*, Fall 1989; Daniel Riley, "Competitive Cost Based Investment Strategies for Industrial Companies," *Manufacturing Issues*, Booz, Allen, Hamilton, New York, 1987.

Is this article of interest to you? If so, circle	**Yes**	**No**
appropriate number on Reader Service Card.	72	73

IT'S TIME TO STOP ACTIVITY-BASED

Start focusing on total

BY H. THOMAS JOHNSON

Activity-based" is a phrase managers hear almost as frequently, and with similar connotations, as the phrase "world-class." Have problems with profitability? Try activity-based costing. Difficulty competing? Try activity-based management. Those activity-based panaceas, along with activity-based information and activity-based thinking, are recommended to any company striving to achieve world-class status as a profitable competitor.

Where did the activity-based juggernaut get started, and how reliable are the claims made on its behalf? As someone who helped put the activity-based concept in motion, I feel compelled to warn people that I believe it has gone too far. It should be redirected and slowed down, if not stopped altogether.

To understand the scope and limitations of activity-based concepts, it is necessary to know something about their origins and history. Many erroneous "histories" of activity-based concepts have appeared in the cost management literature, often written by people who are selling some type of activity-based product—such as consulting services, seminars, or software. If flawed historical accounts go undetected, users of currently popular activity-based products run a high chance of repeating past mistakes. Indeed, few users of these activity-based panaceas seem to understand how activity-based tools condemn them to repeat errors of the past.

Robert A. Seltsam

Some companies use posters, like this one, to remind employees of their goals toward customer satisfaction.

OVERSELLING CONCEPTS

customer satisfaction instead.

HOW IT ALL BEGAN

There are two paths that lead to present-day activity-based pursuits. Both paths come out of the business world, not the academic world. A few management accountants in the academic world, notably Gordon Shillinglaw at Columbia and George Staubus at Berkeley, had articulated activity-based concepts by the early 1960s. However, the activity concepts they enunciated seem not to have influenced other academic thinking (until very recently), nor do they appear to have influenced the two paths of activity-based development in business.

The older path, which is activity cost analysis, begins in the early 1960s at General Electric, where finance and control people were seeking better information for managing indirect costs. GE accountants 30 years ago may have been the first people to use the term "activity" to describe work that causes costs. The other path to present-day activity-based cost management, popularly known as ABC, seems to originate independently of GE's activity cost developments. ABC derives from the efforts of several companies and consultants in the 1970s and early 1980s to improve the quality of product cost accounting information.

Seen in retrospect, both activity cost analysis and ABC resulted from attempts to improve the usefulness of accounting information for making decisions affecting work-force productivity and product mix. Both paths led managers toward more profitable, or less costly, ways to do "business as usual." Neither path led companies toward new thinking about how to make business more competitive in the global economy. I will come back to this point later because today one frequently hears the claim that activity-based cost management tools help companies achieve long-term profitability and competitiveness in the global economy. I believe anyone who understands the original purpose and nature of activity-based tools realizes the absurdity of that claim.

ACTIVITY COST ANALYSIS AT GE

In 1963, General Electric appointed a team from the controller's department to study and recommend ways to stop chronic growth of indirect costs. The team noted that most indirect costs are triggered by "upstream" decisions made long before the cost is incurred. For example, engineering decisions made during the design of a product ultimately trigger myriad indirect costs for parts ordering, machine changeovers, parts stocking, and customer service calls. Those "downstream" costs, when incurred, however, are never traced back to engineering decisions, nor are engineers ever informed about the downstream cost consequences of their decisions. The company's accounting and budgeting systems focused attention primarily on the costs incurred in each department, not on decisions in other departments that caused the costs.

To get better control of indirect costs, GE's 1963 study team proposed a novel technique to control the *activities* that cause those costs.[1] The technique traces each indirect activity in the company to one output of a particular department, such as engineering, marketing, or manufacturing engineering.

The engineering department, for example, produces outputs such as "new drawings," "old drawings," "requisitions to make components," "requisitions to buy components," "parts list items for products," and "manufacturing change orders." Those outputs cause other departments to engage in activities such as parts ordering, production standards setting, tooling, receiving, stockkeeping, quality control, and internal transportation. To identify linkages between engineering's outputs and other departments' activities, you interview supervisors and workers in the other departments to find out just what it is they do that is triggered by output of the engineering department. Interviewing the supervisor of the manufacturing department may reveal, for instance, that a high percentage of his or her department's activity is tooling, triggered by manufacturing change orders that come from the engineering department.

The goal of this analysis is to determine the approximate percentage of time each employee spends in a month or a year on indirect activities such as tooling or parts ordering (or whatever) and to trace the primary cause of each activity to an output of one department. For example, after interviewing all supervisors to determine the percentage of company time spent on tooling (not all tooling may be done just in the manufacturing department), it may be decided that "manufacturing change orders" from the engineering department is the single most important cause of tooling. GE in the 1960s referred to causes of activities as "key controlling parameters." "Cost driver" or "activity driver" would be terms people are more likely to use today in similar contexts.

GE introduced cost information into this activity analysis by tallying costs of each activity in every department of the business for an interval of time, such as a month or a year. Costs were estimated by multiplying the time devoted to each activity by an appropriate average rate for labor or machines and adding estimates of related costs for resources other than labor and machinery. These other costs would include utilities, rents, and any other costs deemed appropriate. Then GE collected information about the quantity or count of each activity driver, such as the number of new drawings, number of old drawings, number of purchase orders, number of manufacturing operations, and so forth. These counts were estimates that covered the same time interval as that used to compile costs of activities.

With the information about activity costs and "driver" counts, one can estimate the activity cost per unit of each *activity driver*. Thus, if one year sees the engineering department generate 10,000 "new drawings" (an activity driver) when the cost of "drafting" (an activity driven by new drawings) is $950,000, then the average cost generated in the drafting activity by each new drawing is $95.00.

Similarly, one can estimate the cost of other *activities* that "new drawings" generate, such as *inspection* at $15 per new drawing, *data processing* at $25 per new drawing, $80 per new drawing for *quality control* activity, $20 for *stockkeeping*, and $40 for *parts ordering*. With $95 for *drafting*, the total cost of all activity triggered by the activity driver "new drawings" is $275.

These cost data tell managers, in effect, to manage indirect costs by controlling drivers of activity and by controlling the activities that drivers

trigger. With such information, product design people in the engineering department ostensibly can judge more effectively the impact on indirect costs of decisions to initiate "new drawings" as opposed to using existing "old drawings." Design engineers presumably can make better decisions about their own work if they know that the total downstream cost of introducing a new product with a new drawing is, for example, $275 and the cost of introducing the same product by modifying an old drawing is $60—because of less inspection, less new parts ordering, less drafting, less production engineering, and so forth. Moreover, information on costs of activity drivers presumably gives supervisors of indirect activities a better understanding of the forces that cause their costs. Supervisors in charge of parts ordering or inspection, for example, can point to the impact of engineers' new drawings on costs in their own departments.

GE modified and perfected this activity-based cost management technique over the years by developing standardized lists of activities known as "activity dictionaries" and by creating efficient interviewing techniques for collecting activity and activity driver information. The principle, however, always remained the same: Costs reported in accounting-based budget reports are too aggregated to be man-

aged directly; only causes (drivers or activities) of resource consumption can be managed.

ACTIVITY-BASED PRODUCT COSTING

An interesting twist that GE might have added to this technique is to use activity driver information to estimate product costs. If a company knows the annual count of activity drivers triggered by each product line, it can sum up the total costs of each driver to get the cost of the product line. This is exactly the procedure advocated by architects of ABC product costing systems since the 1970s.

In fact, Peter Drucker foreshadowed the procedure in a 1963 *Harvard Business Review* article that warned of the dangers in using traditional product cost accounting information to guide marketing decisions.[2] The considerable information processing required by this procedure for costing products was scarcely feasible, however, before the advent of modern PC-based spreadsheet software. GE seems never to have taken the additional steps to compile product cost information from its activity-based cost management information.

Today's best known "solution" to the problem, cost-driver activity-based

FOCUS ON PEOPLE —NOT COSTS

BY SUSAN JAYSON

Why has American industry lost the competitive edge? According to Tom Johnson, it's because companies have routinely ignored customers, quality, and employee training while focusing their goals on costs and financial returns. While many companies now are trying to become world-class competitors by making major changes in the way they measure and manage costs and in the evaluation of short- and long-term performance, the real path to competitiveness, Professor Johnson says, requires a complete transformation in thinking. Recently we spoke with Professor Johnson about the issues raised in his new book and the challenges management accountants now face.

According to your new book, Relevance Regained: From Top-Down Control to Bottom-Up Empowerment, *published by The Free Press, companies should abandon their obsession with results-oriented accounting data*

Tom Johnson

and make total customer satisfaction their goal. How can companies achieve this objective?

Companies should focus on goals that matter, not goals that count. What matters in business is to create fulfilling jobs and survive by profitably satisfying customers' wants (without harming society or the environment). That is the message, as I see it, in W. Edwards Deming's famous "chain reaction" from his book *Out of the Crisis*. Of course, survival requires that receipts from consumers at least equal what is paid to all employees and suppliers, including suppliers of equity capital. The accounting system helps a company track receipts and payments. But focusing its goals on accounting results—revenue, cost, and profit—only diminishes a company's chances for survival.

Accounting goals direct attention to effects, not root causes. Survival requires astute management of root causes. In today's global economy that means optimizing a system of stable processes that is capable of profitably exceeding customer expectations. To optimize their systems, companies must listen to the "voice of the customer" and the "voice of the process." Accounting systems are deaf to both voices—they cannot tell you if a customer is satisfied or if a costing (ABC), was eventually codified by Harvard Business School professor Robin Cooper. Cost-driver ABC, as Cooper articulated it, was developed during the 1970s and early 1980s in consulting firms such as Bain & Co. and Boston Consulting Group and in companies such as Schrader Bellows, John Deere, Union Pacific, and—if we stretch the definitions a bit—perhaps at Caterpillar and Hewlett-Packard. The chief impetus driving the development of ABC in those companies was the search for better product cost information to guide pricing and product mix decisions.

The current attention many businesses pay to activity-based product costing reflects a desire to improve the cost information they use to evaluate and plan either pricing strategies or product and customer mix decisions. Businesses use information about the financial consequences of intended actions as a guide for planning and to choose among alternatives. Cost information serves in many planning and decision-support roles, such as estimating profit margins of products and product lines, preparing departmental cost budgets, and charging administrative services to production departments. To perform these tasks, companies presumably need reliable cost information.

ABC tools reduce distortions in the cost accounting information businesses typically use to plan and make marketing decisions. Indeed, as you realize, accounting systems provide poor information to evaluate modern manufacturers' product costs.[3] Such systems properly match costs against revenues at a macro level in financial statements, but they systematically distort costs at the micro level of individual products. The distortion arises because of the way manufacturing cost accountants traditionally allocate overhead to products: more or less in proportion to output volume, using cost drivers (i.e., allocation denominators) such as direct labor hours, machine hours, or material dollars. Allocating overhead with such drivers provides reliable product cost information only if we assume all overhead costs are triggered by or vary in proportion to units of output. However, the fastest growing overhead costs in American manufacturing companies after the 1950s were caused by drivers that are triggered by batches put into production and by number of product lines, not by units of output.[4]

By using drivers triggered by units of output (e.g., direct labor hours or machine hours) to allocate overhead triggered by batches and product lines, companies systematically *undercost* the low-volume products that have tended to cause most overhead growth in recent years, and they systematically *overcost* high-volume products that tend not to cause overhead to grow. These systematic distortions tend to cancel out at the macro level and, therefore, do not affect income and asset totals reported in financial statements. But they give a misleading picture of an individual product's margins, as many American and European manufacturers discovered in the 1970s and 1980s when, using financial cost accounting information to measure product costs, they erroneously assumed they could improve their company's profitability by abandoning *overcosted* commodity-type product lines and by proliferating *undercosted* varieties of newer "high-tech" lines. In fact, that strategy usually depressed earnings and, in several cases, generated a "death spiral" that led companies to the edge of bankruptcy.[5]

Recognition of problems with traditional product cost accounting grew during the 1970s. Activity-based costing began to appear in the late 1970s as a solution to the distortions inherent in product cost accounting information.[6] Advocates of ABC tell companies, in effect, to cost products differently for financial reporting information than for planning and decision-support information. For financial reporting, they recommend companies continue allocating overhead

process is stable and capable.

In other words, accounting systems focus attention on an end result but do not specify the means to achieve that end. To achieve the accounting targets mandated by top management, subordinates are left to manipulate processes in any way they see fit. The long-term result is unstable processes, unhappy customers, and loss of jobs. I think that result describes most large American companies in the last 30 years.

Before 1960, however, most American businesses did not use accounting goals to control operations. They did not routinely ignore customers, quality, and employee training while focusing their goals on costs and financial returns. They seemed to understand, intuitively, that positive financial outcomes resulted from listening to, not coercing, people.

Only leaders at the top can change a company's goals. As Dr. Deming has said many times, what American business needs more than anything is a transformation in management thinking from top down. *Relevance Regained* shows how traditional accounting-driven attitudes about control prevent managers from making that transformation.

Should management accounting systems be eliminated? If so, how will this affect the management accounting profession?

I don't advocate eliminating management accounting, only the use of accounting information to control people's work. Businesses used accounting targets to control operations for the first time in the 1950s. Eventually these accounting controls prompted people to control cost by manipulating processes and, thereby, neglect customers, employees, suppliers, and society in general.

If companies cease using accounting to control work, management accountants will not be put out of business. They always will develop budgets and other reports that describe and anticipate the financial consequences of management plans, they will assist efforts to plan and track cash flows, and they will help companies design better financial scorecards and more relevant information systems. Moreover, management accountants can do much to introduce companies to target costing and process control costing—two advanced nonaccounting procedures for estimating the financial consequences of plans and operations.

How can management accountants support the goal of total customer satisfaction?

Management accountants can do two things to support the goal of total customer satisfaction. First, they can gain a thorough understanding, through reading and seminars, of the new customer-focused, process-oriented management thinking. By transforming their own thinking, management accountants can play a leadership role in helping everyone in the organization understand how bottom-up, real-time information from customers and processes will replace top-down accounting control information. Second, management accountants can begin to apply the new thinking in their own particular work. They must identify their own internal customers' expectations, map accounting processes, track lead times in their work, and initiate efforts to improve customer satisfaction continuously by removing constraints that cause variation, delay, and excess. Management accountants in several companies—Harley-Davidson and Hewlett-Packard are two that come to mind—have improved their work immeasurably by replacing "scale economy and large batch" mind sets with "lot-size-of-one" thinking.

using the volume-sensitive drivers they have used since the early years of this century. For more reliable planning and decision-support information, however, proponents of ABC tell companies to trace costs to both volume-sensitive and nonvolume-sensitive driver pools. ABC estimates costs of products by adding up costs of the actual drivers that each product consumes.

Simple in concept, ABC was a practical impossibility until the advent of low-cost microchip technologies (and MRP-style databases) in the 1970s made it economical to collect and compile large amounts of nonvolume-sensitive cost driver information. In principle, a two-stage approach is used in ABC product costing. The thrust of the design, as codified originally by Robin Cooper, is to identify a relatively small set of both volume-sensitive and non-volume-sensitive overhead cost drivers (say six to twelve) and to trace indirect costs to each driver. Then the company determines the percentage of the drivers consumed by each product or service. The result is an estimate of the indirect costs of each product based on nonvolume-sensitive drivers such as engineering change notices (ECNs), setups, and inspections, as well as the traditional volume-sensitive drivers such as direct labor hours and material dollars.

The "drivers" referred to here resemble both the "activity drivers" and the "activities" found in GE's early cross-functional activity cost analysis. In the ABC literature, the word "activity" often is used synonymously with "driver," although *activity* is the word that has stuck to describe the nonvolume-sensitive driver-based product costing technique.

This activity-based cost-driver information is considered by many to be appropriate for marketing decisions. Presumably it helps marketing managers evaluate the cost of standard products and the profitability of product mix. With reliable product margin information, managers in tough competitive situations supposedly "know when to hold and know when to fold."

Indeed, in any company turning out a wide array of products that consume resources in diverse ways, activity-based data cost products more reliably than does traditional cost accounting information. Moreover, information about costs of drivers, such as the cost of a purchase order, can be an efficient and very effective way of differentiating unit, batch, and product-level costs among products. This can provide useful information for preparing income statements.[7]

MEANWHILE, BACK TO THE FUTURE

The activity-based cost management tools that developed along the two paths described above are accounting tools designed to improve accounting information. Improved accounting information undoubtedly was a great help to companies seeking lower costs and higher profits under competitive con-

Why can't activity-based costing make U.S. companies competitive?

Activity-based costing, as that concept was expressed by General Electric accountants in the early 1960s and by other cost accountants in the early 1980s, improves the clarity and reliability of cost accounting information by using the work that causes resource-consuming activity as a basis for allocating indirect costs. Some activity-based afficionados say this is "tracing," not allocating, but I fail to see the difference. My point is that activity-based costing simply reconfigures existing *accounting* information. You see that in the popular ABC software products on the market today. I don't know any ABC software that doesn't begin with numbers from the accounting system. Accounting information *of any stripe*, activity-based or otherwise, cannot tell you if customers are satisfied or if processes are stable and capable. It is deaf to the voices companies must hear if they are to succeed in the global economy.

Moreover, activity-based accounting invariably impairs companies' long-term performance if managers use this "better" cost information to direct marketing strategies or to make operating decisions. In almost every ABC story I have heard, the "better" information has told managers to economize on constraints such as setup time, sales order processing time, or machine processing time by producing longer runs and by delivering larger batches to customers at less frequent intervals. Sadly, companies often find too late that this activity-based cost information has prompted them to pursue "less costly" and "higher margin" opportunities that global competitors would not have pursued in the first place. I call that "rearranging deck chairs on the Titanic."

The answer, I believe, is to discard the idea that activity-based information has value in managing operations. People who believe that activity-based information opens doors to world-class performance simply do not understand how businesses succeed in the global economy. Instead of wasting time compiling "cross-functional activity information," everyone in companies should begin to map customer-focused processes and participate in team-oriented improvement of processes and systems.

What happens when companies implement such improvement programs as TQM and JIT but maintain traditional, hierarchical financial controls?

By leaving top-down hierarchical accounting controls in place, top managers implicitly encourage actions that impair process lead times and flexibility. For example, consider what happens when top-down pressure to "cover fixed overhead costs" is applied to a department where workers, trained in JIT, have reduced changeover times and linked previously decoupled processes into continuous flows that fill customer orders on customer terms. To gratify top management's short-run need to "cover costs," employees boost end-of-period production, knowing that their actions will impair costs, quality, and service in the long run. This has to be demoralizing. So why do it? I should think it would be better to stop sending monthly variance reports down to operating personnel and, instead, pressure *top management* to "cover unabsorbed overhead cost" either by creating new revenue streams or by redeploying (*not* laying off) "fixed overhead" resources. That implies, of course, having top managers who understand customers and processes.

Here's another example. Consider what happens when top-down merit pay systems survive in departments where workers are engaged in "TQM-style" process improvement efforts. Comditions that existed up to the 1970s.

Unfortunately, the decade of the 1970s ushered in a new competitive environment—call it the global economy—in which accounting information is not capable of guiding companies toward competitiveness and long-term profitability. Accounting information cannot speak to the sources of competitiveness and profitability in today's global economy.[8]

The underlying basis of business competition today is information technology. Whereas ability to tap economic opportunities in energy-based technology drove competitiveness before the 1950s, it is the ability to tap opportunities in information technology that drives competition today. In a practical sense, that means the customer is now in charge. Information technology empowers the customer with choice, thus making it necessary for companies to listen to and respond quickly to change in the voice of the customer. No accounting system ever told anyone if a customer were satisfied or if a process were in control or capable of satisfying customer expectations.

Even activity-based reconstructions of accounting information cannot transmit the voice of the customer or the voice of the process. This fact was evident in GE's early technique for activity-based cost analysis, which anticipated and accomplished virtually everything that consultants or company personnel claim for activity-based cost management systems today. Knowing that this technique received wide use in GE during the 1970s and 1980s should cause one to question the power of activity-based costing tools to reverse declining competitiveness in American companies.

General Electric, certainly one of America's best-managed companies in any era, faced severe problems coping with Japanese import competition in the 1970s and early 1980s. Widespread application of modern activity-based cost management tools from as far back as the early 1960s did not avert declining competitiveness at GE during and after the 1970s. Nor, one supposes, did it avert declining competitiveness in countless clients of consulting firms that licensed and used GE's activity cost analysis techniques for the mid-1970s.

There is no reason, however, why activity cost analysis tools would have led GE or any other American company down the path it had to follow after 1975 to compete with Japanese competitors such as Toshiba, Toyota, and Hitachi. *These activity-based cost management tools did not generate process maps, had no customer focus, and did not lead to bottom-up ideas for generating continuous process improvement.* Their activity-based information identified causes of costs far better than traditional cost accounting and budget tools did. For that reason, this activity information undoubtedly improved many companies' efforts to cut costs. But never could it have prompted actions that improve competitiveness by increasing responsiveness to customers and flexibility in processes.

Activity analysis of the type espoused by GE in the 1960s, and manifest in virtually all modes of activity cost management promoted today, focuses attention on changing the amount of activity (or work) a company does for a given amount of revenue. It does not focus people's attention on changing how work is done, nor does it explicitly and systematically link activity with satisfaction of customer wants. It simply links activity with activity drivers and says: Reduce the amount of activity (hence, cost) for a given amount of revenue by reducing or "economizing" on activity drivers. For example, sales orders drive countless activities throughout a company. So, to reduce costs, reduce the activity (and cost) that goes with handling sales orders by reducing the number of orders—presumably by eliminating orders that generate below-average revenue. Similarly, with factory-floor setups, another major driver of activity, to reduce activity costs, reduce the number of setups by eliminating or-

petition to win at someone else's expense, the *sine qua non* of most merit pay schemes, kills the cooperative teamwork that is essential to process improvements aimed at optimizing the system. So why do we do it? The reason, I believe, is that most top managers do not understand what Dr. Deming means when he says "the job of management is to optimize the system."

The root problem is that our traditional hierarchical financial controls reflect the belief of most American managers that they optimize the whole by driving each part to maximize its own individual advantage. That belief and the financial controls that reinforce it weaken the cooperation that is required if a business is to succeed in the global economy.

What are the consequences of remote-control management?

Remote-control management (using top-down accounting information to control business operations) deterred American businesses from understanding the new time-intensive, people-oriented, and resource-conserving management methods used by leading Japanese manufacturers, especially Toyota, after the 1960s. American-style remote-control managers of the 1960s, 1970s, and 1980s lost sight of customers, processes, and people as they single mindedly pursued financial goals for their own sake. I believe an urgent national priority should be to replace remote-control management thinking in business and government with the win/win quality philosophy that Dr. Deming espouses.

If managers followed "bottom-up empowerment" instead of "top-down control," what would be the effect on the factory floor?

The change really affects all personnel in the organization, not just those on the factory floor. The basic change is a transforma-

tion in how everyone thinks about work. Bottom-up empowerment, in my view, occurs when someone can say "I know how my work, the work of those I depend on, and the work of those who depend on me really combine to make a difference for our ultimate customers." This happens when everyone's work is guided by and aligned to a common vision that company leaders shape and project by their own example. One sees signs of this alignment where employers are capturing data on charts and sketching maps of the processes and systems in which they work. Such signs suggest that people have begun to understand customer expectations, variation and its consequences, and continuous improvement.

How and when should traditional financial and accounting measures be used?

Companies will compile traditional financial and accounting measures to report results, as always. The public will continue to demand scorecard information, to compare companies and to evaluate an individual company's performance over time. Top managers will continue to need financial and accounting scorecards to fulfill their fiduciary responsibilities. But every effort should be made to resist the temptation to use scorecard information as targets to drive people's actions.

Companies also should compile nonaccounting financial information to predict the financial consequences of planned activities and current operations. Planning budgets clearly fall under this heading. So does target costing, a mode of planning that focuses attention on market price, a cost that matters to customers. And "process control costing" is a little-known nonaccounting approach to evaluating the financial consequences of operations that I discuss in *Relevance Regained.*

ders below a certain size.

The logic in this strategy is impeccable if cutting costs and raising margins is your main objective. But the strategy may be a road to disaster if customers really want frequent delivery of small lots, not large shipments at infrequent intervals. If customers really want frequent delivery of small lots, and someone else can meet their needs at an acceptable price that is below your costs, then you might want to ask if activity analysis is really pointing you in the direction you should be moving to be competitive. To satisfy customers, you probably should change the way you do work so that you can efficiently handle *more* activity drivers (e.g., sales orders or setups) per dollar of revenue, not less. But to compete on smaller-sized and customized orders means you probably must reduce the lead time of processes involved in major activities such as order processing, parts ordering, stocking, and component assembly. No activity analysis I know will point you in that direction.

Instead of activity analysis, companies seeking the pathway to competitiveness need to map and improve customer-focused processes. Indeed, there is almost no similarity between the process analysis discussed today by quality management experts and the activity analysis discussed by cost

Companies need to map and improve customer-focused processes.

management authorities.

Process information identifies a customer, a supplier, and a mechanism to transform a supplier's inputs into customer-directed output. Cross-functional activity information simply shows where and how much time (or cost) a company devotes to a broad class of work, such as engineering, maintenance, order acquisition, or budgeting. While that information can be revealing, and usually is not available from cost accounting information, it does not show how work is done or how well it contributes to customer satisfaction. *Like the management accounting information it is designed to supplant, cross-functional activity cost information tracks results, not processes.* It is a tool that greatly improves cost-focused management practices of the past, but it is not a tool for managing competitive operations in the global economy.

Indeed, activity-based analysis does

not create an environment for learning about problems, nor does it invite people to identify and remove constraints that create delay, excess, and variation. Unlike process information, activity information usually is compiled and monitored by central staff personnel or outside consultants, not by company personnel who actually do the work. Process information always is compiled and monitored by the people in the process.

Cross-functional activity analysis, by contrast, tends to be top-down and not customer oriented. It does not reveal how the work of an individual or the work of a team of people contributes to customer satisfaction. Hence, activity data do not motivate continuous process improvement.

Most proposals for using activity-based cost management information to "improve operations" invariably fail to fulfill the customer-focused imperatives of global management. These proposals usually recommend building to scale or working for speed to cut costs by producing output. Too often, activity-based cost recommendations aim at economizing on an "activity driver" by producing output customers probably don't want in the first place. Such recommendations, so often associated with activity-based management, usually reflect and reinforce a top-down authoritarian management

---

In your book, you state that business schools have focused on the wrong customer. How should business schools become more responsive to their real customer?

Business schools should focus both their professional training and their academic research on society's managed organizations, such as businesses, not-for-profit institutions, government agencies, and so forth. Managed organizations play a dominant role in our lives, yet business schools focus almost no attention on developing a theory to explain their existence and their operations. Since the 1950s, business schools have focused most of their research and teaching on issues raised by theories borrowed from economics and psychology, even though economists and psychologists for the most part did not develop their theories to explain managed organizations. Economic theories of market behavior and psychological theories of human behavior focus attention on the individual, not on cooperative group activity. Economists and psychologists have a pretty clear idea how their research connects with the real world, but business scholars steeped in those theories are, in my opinion, unplugged from reality.

What business schools must do is generate theories that account for and explain behavior in society's managed organizations. To do this, they must overcome their long-standing resistance to field research in managed organizations. And they must be open to nontraditional bodies of theory, such as W. Edwards Deming's theory of profound knowledge. Testing the hypotheses suggested by Deming's theory could keep legions of scholars occupied for decades to come, yet I see almost no evidence of such work in our graduate schools of business. Most business school research (and teaching) aims at satisfying the expectations of the business schools' primary customer for the last 30 years—editors

of so-called "tier one" scholarly journals. Business schools will not be an important catalyst for change until there is a profound shift in that aim or in the vision of those editors.

What has been the reaction to your ideas from practitioners and academe?

Very, very positive, judging from reactions to presentations I have given in the past year and to prepublication reviews of *Relevance Regained*. The only negative reactions, so far, have come from a few top executives of Fortune 100 companies and from a few business school deans—which is hardly surprising. But the strong support for these ideas that I have received from countless professors, accountants, financial controllers, quality mavens, production managers, marketers, and even top executives (mostly of small and medium-sized companies) suggests I may have articulated some widely held but seldom-uttered doubts about the way we have done business in this country for the past few decades.

Are you hopeful that U.S. companies can change their focus from cost accounting targets to customer responsiveness?

They must if they are to survive and create fulfilling jobs for our citizens. A top-down focus that puts costs ahead of people eventually kills innovation and impairs a global organization's ability to learn and adapt to environmental change. Based on what biologists tell us about natural selection, that does not seem to be a viable formula for long-term survival. Moreover, focusing on costs ahead of people probably implies an endless downward spiral of layoffs and compensation reductions until every employee in our society is paid at the lowest common global denominator. Let's pray that if we ever reach that point it will be when minimum style that is antithetical to the bottom-up process management style companies must adopt in the global economy. Activity-based management typifies the results-driven, "ends justifies the means" value system that is decried by Edwards Deming, Masaaki Imai, and other quality gurus and is being eloquently attacked today by GE's Chairman John F. Welch.[9]

To achieve competitive and profitable operations in a customer-driven global economy, companies must give customers what they want, not *persuade* them to purchase what the company now produces at lowest cost. If customers favor frequent delivery of small lots, or if they favor smaller-sized products, then companies must respond accordingly—*even when it initially costs more.* The long-run global imperative, of course, is to find ways to reduce costs (primarily by removing constraints that cause delay, excess, and variation) of producing what the customer wants in the form the customer wants it.

Ironically, companies that continually improve customer-focused processes eventually discover that their process improvements eliminate most of the "overhead activity" that, by causing distortions in product costs, prompted the development of ABC tools in the first place! Many cost management authorities describe this

"overhead activity" by referring to the "Pareto relationship," named for the relationship between population and income discovered in the late 19th Century by economist Vilfredo Pareto. These cost management experts say that ABC usually helps managers discover that 20 or so percent of a company's products, or revenue, generates 80 or so percent of their overhead activity—the Pareto 80:20 relationship.

While I don't dispute the existence of this skewed relationship between work and results in most American businesses today, I would challenge the suggestion that ABC cost information will help one achieve a more balanced relationship. ABC advocates tell companies, in effect, not to change the way they orchestrate work—just create better information to identify products that require a lot of work for little revenue and shift production away from those dogs and cats toward more "big hitters." This short-term cost-cutting or margin-enhancing strategy, however, usually leads to decisions that impair competitiveness in the long term.

Instead of wasting time designing ABC systems to locate "hidden profits" on products that customers probably don't want anyway, companies should begin taking steps to eliminate delay, excess, and variation from processes. Soon they will discover, I believe, that

better orchestration of work will lead to closer correlation between effort and results *everywhere.* At the limit, one percent of effort will always generate one percent of results, and so on. In that world, only two forces drive product costs—time (and the price of time) and material. In that world you don't need ABC or any other system to cost products—you just need to know the time it takes to do something, the price of that time, and the price of any material consumed to get the job done.

WRAP-UP

Activity-based cost driver information overcomes distortions inherent in traditional cost accounting information. Driver-based ABC tools restore relevance to product cost information and thereby help companies avoid costly marketing blunders in the short term. Activity-based information, however, does not help companies achieve continuous improvement of globally competitive operations.[10] Until a company changes the way it thinks about customers, people, and work, it undoubtedly will use activity-based information simply to improve how it does business as usual—that is, seeking economies of scale and speed in decoupled processes. Using activity-based cost information to improve business as usual only helps companies commit "relevance lost" all over again!

Activity-based prescriptions for improved competitiveness usually entail steps that lead to selling more or doing less of what should not be sold or done in the first place. Indeed, activity-based cost information does nothing to change old remote-control, top-down management behavior. Simply because improved cost information becomes available, a company does not change its commitment to mass-produce output at high speed, to control costs by encouraging people to manipulate processes, and to persuade customers to buy output the company has produced to cover its costs. American businesses will not become long-term global competitors until they change the way managers think. No cost information, not even activity-based cost management information, will do that.

I do not believe better product cost information itself could have prevented most American manufacturers from losing long-term market share and profitability in the 1970s and 1980s. It might have been enough to sustain market share and profitability if com-

worldwide productivity levels are high enough to support a humanly decent standard of living.

What do you hope publication of Relevance Regained *will accomplish?*

I hope the book will move management accounting and business discourse away from discussions of how to improve cost and management accounting systems, which was the focus of discussions triggered by the book *Relevance Lost* I co-authored with Robert S. Kaplan in 1987, to discussions of the behavior one should expect of people in successful global businesses. Discussions of desired business behavior automatically should prompt consideration of the transformation in thinking that Dr. Deming refers to as the most important job facing American business people. ∎

DEMING'S MESSAGE FOR MANAGEMENT ACCOUNTANTS

When did you first hear the name W. Edwards Deming? For many of you, it probably was in the famous 1980 NBC-TV documentary, "If Japan Can, Why Can't We?" Later in the decade articles about Dr. Deming appeared, and in 1986 his book *Out of the Crisis* presented the full scope of his thinking to the general public. The last few years have brought a flood of popular literature—books, articles, and videotapes—about "the man who discovered quality" (see books and articles in the list of recommended reading at the end of this article).

Dr. Deming's message, especially as he has expressed it recently in his "system of profound knowledge," addresses many issues germane to management accounting. For Dr. Deming, a key issue facing American business is for top managers to adopt new thinking, a new "paradigm" if you will. However, the widely held idea that accounting targets (including activity-based accounting targets) should be used to control people's work prevents managers from adopting this new thinking and putting it to work in companies. Underlying traditional management accounting controls is a flawed understanding of the role that people and work play in business. Dr. Deming's articulation of that role is especially pertinent to management accountants.

To Dr. Deming, work is a *process*. Humans transform output they receive from suppliers into output they supply to customers. Processes in a business form a *system* of *interdependent* (i.e., cooperative, not competitive) components that have an *aim*, which in business is to exceed customer expectations profitably. Management's job is to *optimize the system* by ensuring that its components cooperate, not compete. In this regard, a company earns the required long-term rate of return—a condition necessary for survival—by optimizing the system, not by maximizing returns to individual components of the system. To optimize the system, managers must understand

W. Edwards Deming

theory, especially the *theory of variation* and its corollary, the need to *control processes, not people*. The theory provides a basis for knowing when and when not to take action to improve outcomes. Without a theory that connects means and ends, a singleminded focus on results invariably prompts interventions that create instability in processes and, ultimately, declining performance.

In American business, top managers "manage by the numbers" without coherent theory. They encourage employees and suppliers to manipulate processes in order to achieve accounting goals. This thinking lies behind most of our accounting-based control and reward systems. Workers, individually or in groups, are driven to compete in the belief that the whole will be greater if each part tries to maximize its individual contribution to the whole. The result, according to Dr. Deming, is to destroy everyone's joy in work, to generate fear, and to suppress learning and innovation. The alterna-

tive is to focus on enhancing the talents and opportunities of people—customers, suppliers, employees, society—by substituting win/win cooperation for win/lose competition.

I believe management accountants must adopt and promote the transformation in management thinking that Dr. Deming advocates. They should be among the first people in a company to learn and to teach others that the customer-focused theory of variation, not accounting, is the "language of business" in the global economy. More than ever before, today's managers require quantitative data, if not accounting control data. As Dr. Deming so often says, "In God we trust; all others must supply data." With their skills in data analysis and statistics, management accountants can help pioneer the development of the real-time customer-focused and process-focused information systems that turn companies into genuine "learning organizations."

Where should management accountants start this journey? I would suggest following three paths simultaneously. First, begin at once to read everything you can about the Deming philosophy. The list of books and articles on the next page is not meant to be inclusive—just enough to get you started. Second, attend one of Dr. Deming's four-day seminars at your earliest convenience. For information on those seminars (and more) contact Quality Enhancement Seminars, Inc. in Los Angeles at (310) 824-9623. If you can't attend one of the live seminars, ask QES for information about satellite telecasts that may be scheduled for your area, or check into videotapes. Finally, get involved with a Deming Study/User Group in your area. Efforts are under way to create a national network of such groups, but there is nothing to report at the moment. In the meantime, contact a local chapter of American Society for Quality Control (ASQC) or Association for Quality and Participation (AQP) for more information—now. ∎

H. Thomas Johnson

petitors, especially from Japan, had not changed fundamental assumptions about how to organize work to satisfy

customers. That is the point—how to discover and adopt competitive ways of organizing work, not how to be

more profitable by shifting product mix in companies that continue to follow traditional remote-control management practices. While ABC gives companies a better "rack and stack" of their overhead costs, it does not drive them to change their fundamental views about how to organize work to satisfy customers efficiently.

Moreover, the answer to competitiveness is not to do the activity analysis that leads up to calculating ABC product costs. I have heard some companies say that going through the activity analysis it takes to calculate activity-based driver costs has helped them improve their operations. I have no doubt this is true, especially given the chaotic state of decoupled operations in most American companies when they first wake up to the need to improve. One-time savings—sometimes referred to as "low-hanging fruit"—await any rational attempt to analyze work. But something more is needed for the continuous improvement in output of customer-focused processes.

Instead of beginning with activity-based information, begin at the beginning—by articulating a customer-focused mission statement and then encouraging everyone to help map and systematically improve the processes in which they work. If your goal is competitive operations, don't waste time gathering data and compiling information in order to cost work you shouldn't be doing anyway. Focus on reducing variation and lead time in the work itself, and costs will take care of themselves. Do ABC if you think you must. But don't fool yourself into thinking that activity-based concepts will help you become a global competitor. For that, get busy with the improvement process! ∎

H. Thomas Johnson is the Retzlaff Professor of Quality Management at Portland State University. He is the coauthor with Robert S. Kaplan of Relevance Lost: The Rise and Fall of Management Accounting. *Dr. Johnson is a member of the IMA's Portland Chapter and can be reached at (503) 725-4771.*

[1] General Electric, "Lower Business Costs: A Method for Evaluating Indirect Effort" (ENS-A-179A, July 1964).
[2] Peter F. Drucker, "Managing for Business Effectiveness," *Harvard Business Review*, May-June 1963, pp. 59-62.
[3] H. Thomas Johnson and Robert S. Kaplan, *Relevance Lost: The Rise and Fall of Management Accounting*, Harvard Business School Press, Boston, Mass., 1987, ch. 8; Robin Cooper and Robert S. Kaplan, "Measure Costs Right: Make the Right Decisions," *Harvard Business Review*, September-October 1988, pp. 96-103.

RECOMMENDED READINGS

(in suggested order)

BOOKS
Nancy R. Mann, *The Keys to Excellence: The Story of the Deming Philosophy,* Prestwick Books, Los Angeles, 1987.

Mary Walton, *The Deming Management Method,* Dodd, Mead, New York, 1986.

Henry R. Neave, *The Deming Dimension,* SPC Press, Knoxville, Tenn., 1990.

W. Edwards Deming, *Out of the Crisis,* Massachusetts Institute of Technology, Cambridge, 1986.

William W. Scherkenbach, *The Deming Route to Quality and Productivity: Roadmaps and Roadblocks,* CEEPRESS, Washington, 1986.

William W. Scherkenbach, *Deming's Road to Continual Improvement,* SPC Press, Knoxville, Tenn., 1991.

Mary Walton, *Deming Management at Work,* G.P. Putnam's Sons, New York, 1990.

ARTICLES
Brian L. Joiner and Peter R. Scholtes, "Total Quality Leadership Vs. Management by Control," Joiner Associates Inc., Madison, Wis., 1985 (available from Joiner Associates).

Brian L. Joiner and Marie A. Gaudard, "Variation, Management, and W. Edwards Deming," *Quality Progress*, December 1990, pp. 29-37.

Peter R. Scholtes and Heero Hacquebord, "Beginning the Quality Transformation," *Quality Progress*. Part I, July 1988, pp. 28-33; Part II, August 1988, pp. 44-48. ∎

[4] The distinction between unit, batch, and product-level cost drivers, articulated originally by Robin Cooper of Harvard Business School, is the conceptual foundation that supports modern activity-based product costing. The definitive statement of this distinction is found in Robin Cooper, "Cost Classification in Unit-Based and Activity-Based Manufacturing Cost Systems," *Journal of Cost Management*, fall 1990, pp. 4-14.
[5] For a detailed example, see the story of "margin retreat" by SKF Bearings in George Stalk, "Time-The Next Source of Competitive Advantage," *Harvard Business Review*, July-August 1988, p. 43; also see Robin Cooper, "Schrader Bellows," Harvard Business School Case, number 6-186-050 et al., 1985.
[6] Robin Cooper, "The Two-Stage Procedure in Cost Accounting: Part One," *Journal of Cost Management*, summer 1987, pp. 43-51; Johnson and Kaplan, *Relevance Lost*, ch. 10.
[7] Robin Cooper and Robert S. Kaplan, "Profit Priorities from Activity-Based Costing," *Harvard Business Review*, May-June 1991, pp. 130-135.
[8] This indictment of accounting as a source of management control information is one of the main themes that is documented and defended in H. Thomas Johnson, *Relevance Regained: From Top-*

Down Control to Bottom-Up Empowerment, The Free Press, New York, N.Y., 1992.
[9] John Holusha, "A Soft Edge for 'Neutron Jack,'" *New York Times*, March 4, 1992, p. C-1.
[10] This is one of the main points I tried to make in H. Thomas Johnson, "Activity-Based Information: A Blueprint for World-Class Management Accounting," MANAGEMENT ACCOUNTING®, June 1988, pp. 23-30. My point there was to urge companies to stop using accounting cost information, even activity-based cost information, to manage and control operations. Now I say: Stop using activity information for any purpose besides costing. To manage and control operations, study and control processes, not activities.

Is this article of interest to you? If so, circle appropriate number on Reader Service Card.	**Yes** 54	**No** 55

IN DEFENSE OF ACTIVITY-BASED COST MANAGEMENT

ABC models can play many different roles to support a company's operational improvement and customer satisfaction programs.

BY ROBERT S. KAPLAN

Recently I spent several hours talking with a colleague. We had last spoken several years ago, and my friend was now quite perplexed by cross-currents that had developed around activity-based cost management. He asked me to explain.

Why is there so much controversy about the merits of activity-based costing? I would have thought people would value an approach that promises more accurate cost understanding?

I have been somewhat surprised myself. Perhaps some people were overselling ABC, claiming that just with an ABC system companies could become world-class competitors. Conversely, proponents of such improvement programs as total quality, business process redesign, theory of constraints, and customer satisfaction were claiming they have the only answer companies need. Consequently, they advocate that other initiatives, such as activity-based costing, are peripheral or even counterproductive to the particular program for which they are proselytizing.

In my opinion, neither view is accurate. ABC systems provide valuable economic information to companies, especially companies active in process improvement and customer satisfaction programs. But ABC information is certainly not the only data managers need to survive and prosper in today's competitive environment. To be successful, companies are learning how to integrate ABC information with other information on revenues, customer preferences, and process quality and cycle times.

How do you respond to the claim that ABC is merely an accounting or general ledger system?

Activity-based cost management is not an accounting exercise. An activity-based cost model is a system designed to inform management about the economics of its past, current, and future operations.[1] The word "cost" appears in the title to remind people that financial and economic considerations are still relevant for management decisions and actions.

The critics who accuse ABC of being an accounting or general ledger system have confused one possible source of data for estimating the model with the underlying structure and purpose of the model. It is true that ABC models can be estimated with financial and operating data generated by the company's historical accounting system. This procedure enables analysts and management to focus their attention initially on actual, not hypothetical, operations. In the initial effort to estimate an ABC model, the analysts must develop a structure for the model and identify available data sources. Rather than attempt to estimate an initial economic model of the organization on hypothetical or forecasted information, analysts usually start by grounding their model in historical experiences. But while the expense data may be collected from financial and accounting systems, other data inputs come from production control systems, sales order systems, and engineering systems as well. You can see why it is illogical to refer to ABC as a "general ledger" system. We could just as easily refer to ABC as a production system, a marketing or sales system, or an engineering system. It is more accurate to view an ABC model as an economic model of the organization that integrates data from many information systems, financial and operational.

I suppose that helps to clear up some semantic confusion, but why do we really care about the cost of an activity, or a product, or a customer last year? Aren't you still being influenced by your accounting background to look backwards rather than forward? ABC, as you've described it, tells me where you have been. Managers want to know how to navigate for the future.

Your question requires two different responses. First, history matters. Recall Santayana's admonition that those who fail to learn from history are doomed to repeat it. This lesson applies to many systems, not simply ABC. For example, TQM concepts stress "management by facts," pareto analysis, root cause analysis of past defects, and a whole array of techniques designed to learn about past operations in order to influence the future. Some people who criticize the relevance of past costs, are, at the same time, strong advocates of Total Quality. These critics, surprisingly, fail to see the internal inconsistency of their beliefs. They advocate studying historical data to learn about the persistent, repeatable causes of defects but criticize the analysis of historical information on product and customer profitability. The analysis of past costs and profits often reveals why certain activities are unexpectedly costly and why specific products and customers are profitable while others are highly unprofitable. Patterns repeat. The same circumstances that led to a costly activity or an unprofitable product, service, or customer last period likely are being repeated today. A clear picture of past operations can stimulate actions in the current period. Management also is more likely to take action when past mistakes—highly costly products, processes, and customers—that are revealed in the ABC analysis are based on actual, not hypothetical, operations. If the past patterns are not repeating, alert managers will certainly be aware of the major changes in current and future operations and are unlikely to be misled by past circumstances that are not persisting.

That may be asking a bit much from busy managers. How do you know they won't be misled?

Before acting, managers can reestimate the model based on current or budgeted information. This is actually the second part of the explanation as to why an ABC model is not a general ledger or "accounting" model. An ABC model is not limited to past financial information. Powerful benefits from an ABC model can be created when budgeted, forecasted, or even targeted expense and quantity data become the data input to the model. The structure of the ABC model enables analysts to estimate activity expense and activity driver information based on forecasted spending information, future activity and process efficiencies, and projected output volume and mix. By estimating a model with current and forecasted information, managers can determine whether the patterns initially revealed from historical data are likely to persist, in the same form and magnitude, in current and future operations.

Nothing in the theory of activity-based cost management implies that it is a system based on historical cost data. Asset values and expenses can be based on replacement cost, budgeted cost, or targeted cost. Several companies already are using forecasts of product volume and mix and process efficiencies to obtain estimated spending for future activities and resources. Used in this way, the ABC model becomes a powerful tool for budgeting future expenses.

Managers in other companies are attempting to eliminate a substantial amount of inefficient nonvalue-added activities from their operations. If managers can estimate the quantity and cost of inefficient operations, these can be excluded from the activity expense data. With this procedure, the company can bid for or price its business based on how it expects to be operating in the future, and operating managers will have an explicit estimate of the amount of expenses they are expected to eliminate during the next 12 to 24 months. By using forecasted activity expenses, based on efficient operations, managers will be using their activity-based model as a target costing mechanism.

Skillful practitioners of activity-based cost management can combine historical information effectively with estimates of future costs and profitability. The ABC model provides the integrating structure by which financial and operating data (past, current, or future) are combined to reveal information managers can act upon.

ESTIMATION NOT ALLOCATION

I see that you don't want to be pinned down to restricting activity-based costing to historical information. But you talk about ABC models revealing economic information on the cost and profitability of products, services, and customers. I'm under the impression that you have to do lots of allocations to get this cost and profitability information. How useful can the information be after you have done all these allocations?

You've found a topic where we certainly may have contributed to some confusion about ABC. When Robin Cooper and I first encountered ABC systems in the mid-1980s, in sites such as Schrader-Bellows, John Deere, and Union Pacific, we described as an allocation the procedure by which operating expenses were assigned, via activities, to products and services. Our use of the term "allocation" alarmed people who have been taught or are currently teaching that allocations are arbitrary and therefore provide no information relevant for management decisions. Once Robin developed and articulated the hierarchical structure of activity-based costing,[2] we understood that ABC was really a contribution margin approach, not an attempt to get "more accurate fully-allocated unit costs."[3] The process we had described initially as an allocation is an estimation. That is, we attempt to estimate the cost of performing a setup or of processing a customer order. In principle, we could install elaborate measuring and monitoring devices to learn exactly the quantity and cost of resources required to perform each setup or to process each customer order. But such instrumentation is rarely justified; we have found that estimates, based on interviews, employee judgments, and available operating data, are usually sufficiently accurate for the managerial use of the information from an ABC model.

I accept your explanation and will try not to say "allocation" in your presence again. Any other confusion from past writings?

The initial sites where we had observed activity-based costing were attempting to obtain more accurate product costs. In our early writings, therefore, we emphasized the product-costing application of ABC to the exclusion of other applications. As we kept observing and working with companies, we learned that just understanding the costs of activities and business processes was itself a major advance over traditional costing systems. Also, we saw that the demand for many organizational activities arose from many different types of outputs, such as services, customers, markets, and projects. The demand for other organizational expenses, particularly corporate support expenses, arose from divisions, facilities, and regions. These observations led us to emphasize ABC's role as a comprehensive economic map of the organization.[4] But some of the ABC critics continue to think of activity-based costing only in relation to the initial studies done in 1985 on product costs.

BENEFITS TO COMPANIES

Many companies are already deeply involved in total quality management and process improvement programs. Some advocates for these improvement programs are skeptical about ABC saying, "Focus on reducing variation and lead-time—the costs will take care of themselves." If companies are already focused on meeting customer needs and "delighting the customer," what benefits will they get from ABC?

This is a vitally important issue to discuss. First, some background. The critics—almost always academics and consultants concerned with manufacturing—have a shop-floor, operations focus. These people have noted the noncompetitive nature of mass-production operations of many leading Western companies and the dramatic improvements that can occur when companies adopt the "lean production paradigm."[5] Lean production includes programs such as employee empowerment, TQM, JIT, DFM, and all the other acronyms associated with organizational learning and improvement activities. Unfortunately, some supporters, in their uncritical enthusiasm for the new manufacturing programs, have developed a mystical faith in the ability of these procedures to solve virtually all managerial and organizational problems. Also, they have observed the frustration of many managers who complain that their company's costing and financial control procedures inhib-

> *The process of obtaining activity and driver costs is an estimation, not an allocation.*

it the organization's attempt to adopt the new production paradigm.

I, too, participated in this criticism of traditional costing systems. But having made this criticism several times in the mid-1980s, I felt it was time to stop complaining and to start contributing to the new financial systems that support the current competitive, operating, and technological environment. Unfortunately, some people find it easier to keep criticizing cost measurement practices, both old and new, than to be creative and devise improved financial measurements and systems.

But how do you respond to the charge that cost systems do not help companies become world-class competitors?

It's not hard to find the counter-examples that reveal the errors in these claims. The idea that costs will take care of themselves if managers focus only on improving quality and reducing lead time makes one wonder how Baldrige Award winners could encounter severe financial difficulties. Documented cases exist where dramatic improvements in quality and lead time were not followed by improvements in financial performance. Even the Japanese, the originators of the lean production paradigm, have now recognized that their model proliferations and rapid new product introductions may have been too expensive. A *New York Times* article[6] described these companies' attempts to reduce the high costs of proliferation:

> The [lean production] system, first developed by Toyota …, involves rapid introduction of models, a flexible manufacturing system that can make many kinds of cars on the same assembly line, low inventories and long-term relationships with suppliers. But now, manufacturers are starting to cut the number of products they offer, slow the pace at which they bring out products, reduce their reliance on low prices as a marketing strategy, keep larger inventories and loosen historic bonds with suppliers.

Don't get me wrong. I'm an enthusiastic supporter of TQM and cycle time reduction. I think it's great that so many organizations are paying attention to these initiatives. I'm just not naive enough to think that all management problems can be solved by blind adherence to these programs. ABC

models help companies understand the linkage between operations improvement programs and increased profitability. There is no conflict between a company's improvement programs and an economic model that accurately identifies the costs of activities and business processes. Managers want to see information on the quality, process time, and cost of their activities. The ABC model provides the cost part of the picture.

ABC AND CONTINUOUS IMPROVEMENT

How do you respond to the claim that activity-based cost systems will "invariably impair companies' long-term performance" if used to direct marketing or operating strategies?

That claim is uninformed nonsense. ABC models can play many different roles to support an organization's operational improvement and customer-satisfaction programs. First, ABC can provide an attention-getting mechanism for companies not yet indoctrinated into the religion of the lean production paradigm. ABC collects data on activities and business processes that cut across traditional organizational functional boundaries. Often managers can see, for the first time, the cost of nonconformance, the cost of design activities, the cost of new product launches, and the cost of administrative activities, such as processing customer orders, procurement, and handling special requests. The high cost of these activities can stimulate companies to adopt the TQM, JIT, and business process improvement programs that will produce a leaner and more responsive enterprise. The ABC model also produces, for individual products, services, and customers, the bill of activities that describes the cost buildup for these outputs. Managers can see how much of any unexpectedly higher cost arises from inefficient or unnecessary activities. The bill of activities information will indicate the opportunities for cost reduction and profit enhancement from improving quality or reducing the cost of batch and product- or customer-sustaining activities. The existing cost for these activities can provide the justification for new technology or for launching major process improvement activities.

OK, so do I understand that ABC systems signal to managers the cost of activities and business processes that can

be the target for future improvement activities?

Yes! As one manager described it, the ABC model indicates the "bucket of opportunities" for these programs. Second, and related to the attention-getting mechanism, the ABC analysis establishes priorities. Without an economic model, the organization may focus on activities that will not have high leverage for improving overall efficiency. For example, the ABC model can focus activity improvement and business process redesign activities on high-cost processes, especially those that contain a high proportion of non-value-added activities.

Let me see if I get this second point. You are saying that organizations need to set priorities for where the improvement programs should be implemented. Otherwise, the efforts could be scattered and unfocused with disproportionate attention devoted to small problems that can be solved easily rather than to where big economic payoffs can be produced from process improvements.

That's a good summary, but not the end of the story. The ABC model actually can be part of the improvement process itself. Despite the rhetoric, not all quality improvements, particularly those that offer enhanced features, service or performance, or cycle-time reductions, come free. When increases in spending are required to achieve the quality or cycle-time improvements, an economic model that compares current with forecasted operations will facilitate a benefit/cost analysis for the proposed spending programs. ABC can shift companies from management by sloganeering towards management by fact.

The ABC model also can be linked to performance measurement. Some companies, after seeing the high costs associated with certain critical activities, have identifed the process drivers for those activities and encouraged employees to work each day to improve those process drivers.

You've lost me. What do you mean by a process driver?

Process drivers are the factors that affect the efficiency of performing the activity. Take an activity such as materials movement. The ABC model will calculate the total cost of performing this activity and then link it to products based on an activity driver such as number of material moves or the distance of the move. Managers have learned, however, that telling operators to reduce the cost of material movements will produce a lot of vacant looks and not much effective action. If, however, managers and operators can identify the drivers of the materials handling process—such as material handling distances, number of inventory stocking points, or number of operations in which material stops between successive operations—then operators can work each day to improve those process drivers.

As another example, the process drivers for setup cost might include the total setup time, the number of setups requiring more than 10 minutes, the number of unique dies required, or the scrap loss after each changeover. By determining the process drivers for *critical* activities, employees and operators are given specific targets for their day-to-day improvement activities which, if successful, should produce large improvements in efficiencies.

Does ABC provide any other information for quality improvement programs?

Any improvements that have been realized from these programs should be observable when the next ABC model is estimated. The ABC model will reveal whether improvements have had bottom line impact. Profits can increase only if companies can either lower their spending or obtain higher prices, margins, and sales volumes. Many organizations have been successful in improving the efficiency and responsiveness of their operations. But these improvements have yet to be transformed into increased profits. An economic or financial model is needed to show whether the operating improvements have been exploited through lower expenses and higher revenues or whether the improvements only created unused capacity and customer services that were not valued in the marketplace.

Are you saying that an ABC model should be used to provide feedback on a company's improvement activities?

The ABC model is not an effective mechanism for providing short-term feedback to employees and operators making process improvements. Several years ago, I wrote an article[7] to explain that short-term feedback on learning and improvement activities is best done by a separate system that collects operating data continuously and reports summary information back to operators on a timely basis. But this short-term feedback informa-

tion is not derived from the ABC system. An ABC system for feedback purposes can assess whether operating improvements have been translated into financial benefits through lower operating expenses or higher throughput or revenues. This information can be estimated quarterly or annually; it is not needed daily or weekly to support shop-floor-level operating activities.

People claim that ABC is deficient for process improvement programs because it does not highlight quality and time dimensions. Is this a valid criticism?

ABC systems do not provide direct measures of quality and process times, but, conversely, systems that measure quality and time do not indicate the quantity and cost of resources used in processes. An organization needs several measurements of its activities and business processes. Cost obviously is important to help managers understand the economics of the process and its outputs, but it is certainly not the only relevant measure. Systems to measure the quality and throughput times of processes will also be vital for management decision making and attention. Measurements on time, quality, and cost of activities and business processes are helpful and informative to managers. The different measurements complement each other; they are not in any way competitive with or contradictory to each other.

ABC AND PRODUCT DESIGN

You have described how an ABC model can support improvements in existing and future operations. Many companies, however, compete by rapid introduction of new products and services that have expanded features and performance. These companies do not attempt to be the low-cost producer of existing or mature products. Does activity-based cost management have a role for these companies?

Absolutely. Several companies have developed an ABC model primarily to provide economic information to product designers and product engineers. The model's output helps designers understand the manufacturing or operating cost consequences from their product-design decisions.

Why do designers and engineers need ABC information to design a product?

Design decisions often involve tradeoffs between cost and performance so an accurate cost model will inform such tradeoffs. Also, designers

often can choose among several options to achieve the specified performance. These options could involve using more specialized but fewer components, common versus unique components, and existing versus new production processes. The greatest leverage to influence future manufacturing costs occurs when these design decisions get made very early in the product's life cycle. An accurate ABC model can guide designers to decisions that will achieve the desired performance while minimizing manufacturing costs.

What about the design process itself? Can activity-based cost management be used to increase the efficiency of the product design stage?

This application has only started to be explored. I know of one company that provided information about the cost of activities performed during the design process itself. Previously the product designers had never seen or been concerned with the cost of their own activities in the total design process. Once they had this activity cost information, they attempted to eliminate or reduce costly and time-consuming activities that did not add sufficient value to the newly designed product. The designers were able to make sensible tradeoffs between effort and value created.

LOW-PRICE VS. LOW-COST SUPPLIERS

Is there anything we haven't covered on the relationship between continuous improvement and ABC?

My responses have dealt mostly with improving internal operations and design. An ABC model can play a maor role in improving supplier relationships as well. These relationships must be a vital part of any quality and cycle-time improvement program.

A key insight is to use ABC to distinguish between low-price and low-cost suppliers. Traditional cost accounting, with its emphasis on purchase price variances, encourages purchasing people to continually scan the population of potential suppliers to obtain low price quotations. Most companies have learned, the hard way, that many of their low-price suppliers are actually extremely high-cost suppliers.

How can a low-price supplier also be a high-cost supplier?

There's no mystery once you include the cost of all activities associated with purchasing items and making them available for productive activities within the organization. Some suppliers offer low prices only when they can deliver large volumes of materials. The purchasing company must then provide adequate storage for these materials. In addition, because of the large delivery volume, the company must check the items in through a receiving dock rather than have them delivered by the supplier directly to the work station where they are needed. Also, low-price suppliers are not always zero-defect suppliers so that the company's receiving or quality assurance department must do considerable inspection before being assured that the items can be released for production. And frequently these inspections reveal defective items that must be replaced, or, worse, they may miss defective items so that the detection and correction activity occurs much later in the production process where the repair cost is several orders of magnitude higher than the actual purchase price. And, beyond large delivery quantities of items with uncertain quality, the actual delivery time of items from low-price suppliers may not be predictable. Uncertain delivery times will lead to additional costs that are due to expediting, rescheduling, unexpected plant downtime, and great increases in confusion.

So the purchase price of delivered items is only one cost element in the total purchase cost?

Exactly! The total cost of having a batch of items available for production must include the cost of ordering and paying for the materials (if the supplier is not linked to us via EDI and electronic funds transfer); the cost of receiving, inspecting, moving, and storing the materials; the cost of scrap, rework, and obsolescence due to defective items; and the cost of scheduling, expediting, and downtime associated with this acquisition. The costs of all these activities can and will be estimated in a comprehensive ABC model, and these costs can be linked to those individual supplier transactions for which the activities are performed.

An excellent supplier makes frequent deliveries of exactly the right mix of parts and materials that do not require any inspection and can be delivered directly to the work station where and just when they are needed. For such a supplier, the purchasing company does not have to commit resources to perform activities such as ordering, receiving, moving, storing,

inspecting, expediting, and rescheduling. Even if this supplier's purchase price is somewhat higher than several other suppliers' quotes, this supplier is likely the low-cost supplier and probably by a considerable margin. The ABC model enables the purchasing company to estimate how much more it is willing to pay such a supplier so that the net gains can be shared between supplier and customer. And the model also helps the company identify the cost and identity of the excess resources that are no longer needed once the bulk of the vendor base has shifted to this new "lean supplier paradigm."

Learning about and developing low-cost suppliers is just another example where managers can benefit from an economic model of their operations. The information helps them make informed tradeoffs among price, quality, and responsiveness. The critics who claim that activity-based cost management has no role in developing a lean production capability seem unaware of the potential for rewarding excellent suppliers with some of the gains from achieving a low-cost relationship.

TOTAL CUSTOMER SATISFACTION

What about customer relationships? Some critics claim that ABC leads companies to charge their customers higher prices for customized products, to shift them from custom to standard products, and to require them to take larger delivery quantities than they would prefer. Don't these actions conflict with "delighting" the customer?

Let me answer this criticism directly and in a perhaps controversial way. I think that an unquestioned belief in meeting all customer needs and making all customers satisfied is demonstrably wrong. A customer-based ABC model can help managers decide when a customer's needs should not be satisfied, at least at the current price. Attempting to meet all customer needs, without regard to the economics of the customer transaction, can lead a company not to the promised land of "world-class" performance but to bankruptcy.

Well it's certainly different to hear someone encouraging companies not to satisfy all their customers. Do you want to expand on this point?

You're right. It is easy for people to misinterpret what I just said. Do I think that the shift during the past decade from product-focused organiza-

tions to customer- and market-focused ones is desirable? Absolutely. Being customer-focused and attempting to learn what customers want and how you can satisfy them, even delight them, is tremendously important. All managers, indeed all employees, should be attempting to satisfy their external and internal customers. But, unfortunately, customer satisfaction can be done badly.

How can satisfying customers be a bad thing to do?

There's a big difference between being customer focused and being customer compelled or sales obsessed. Good marketing companies choose the segments they want to serve and the customers they can serve profitably in those segments. Not all segments or customers' desires can be satisfied economically, even after sensible activity and business process improvement programs have been accomplished. Some customers can make extremely difficult demands and be unwilling to pay for the resources required to satisfy them.

Let me illustrate this point with a real example. A pickup and delivery company (which included overnight express) developed a relatively simple ABC model of its operations. The company discovered that many of its customers packaged their shipments in standard sized cartons and boxes. They were straightforward to handle, and the company had installed excellent processes including bar code reading, remote data entry, and automated sorting technology to move these packages from shipper to destination in a highly efficient pattern. But not all customers packaged their shipments so neatly. One customer used the delivery service to ship mesh bags filled with beach balls. Another one shipped uncrated bicycles, and a third shipped unpackaged mufflers. Servicing these customers caused the companies' pickup and delivery trucks to be filled up quickly, and the items required special handling and sorting in the central facility.

My customer satisfaction zealot friends tell me, "Hey, don't worry about tracing operating costs to outputs [such as beach balls or uncrated bicycles]. If your customer wants this product or service, your job is to improve your operating processes so that you can meet these requirements efficiently. Do a business process redesign so that you can become efficient at picking up, sorting, and delivering mesh bags full of beach balls." I'm not making this up. I have been given this response by academics and consultants deeply committed to but not necessarily experienced in TQM and activity management. I don't doubt that the courier company could devise more efficient processes to handle uncrated bicycles and mesh bags full of beach balls. But at the end of this process redesign, I think it reasonable for the company to know whether the revenues it gets from performing this activity exceed the cost of even the highly efficient and redesigned activities installed to handle this particular line of business. The ABC model helps to identify the segments and customers that can be satisfied profitably. Also, it signals which customers may require significant price increases or changes in demands or terms of trade for the relationship to benefit both parties.

Suppose that a company, after attempting to improve processes, change the terms of trade, and expand volume still has an unprofitable customer. Are you suggesting that the company attempt to get rid of such a customer? I would love to hear you explain to a marketing manager that she has to fire one of her customers because your ABC model has shown it to be unprofitable.

Firing customers is the last possible action to contemplate. Companies may wish to retain unprofitable customers for several reasons. For example, the unprofitable customers may be new, and the sales manager may anticipate "growing the business" with this customer. Other customers may provide some not-easily-quantified benefits. For example, a few customers may provide leading-edge insights about emerging consumer demands or the role for new technologies or production processes. Other customers may be known to be highly critical and demanding so that retaining those customers gives the company valuable credibility for other customers. Experienced marketing and general managers generally are aware of these situations and make good judgments about whether the future or difficult-to-quantify benefits likely exceed the losses reported for these customers.

Other customers, however, are highly demanding, request special features and services not used by most other customers, do not want to pay for the cost of satisfying their demands, provide no learning opportunities, and are unlikely to change in the future. I believe that marketing and sales ef-

The ABC model helps to identify the segments and customers that can be satisfied profitably.

forts can be better spent prospecting for new customers rather than attempting to delight such unprofitable customers.

I keep coming back to the same basic point, but it's fundamental to how ABCM creates value for organizations. All good strategies, whether low-cost or differentiated, and all the good programs, such as TQM, business process improvement, cycle-time reduction, and customer satisfaction, have the potential to create considerable value for organizations. And we should continue to encourage companies to explore all these opportunities. But it seems relevant, even vital, to understand the economics of these programs as well. Blind faith can take you to the promised land. But it also can take you over the cliffs. ABC models provide an economic model of the organization that enables managers to set priorities, make tradeoffs, determine the extent of investment they are willing to undertake for the improvements, and, at the end of the day—or, at least, periodically through these programs—learn whether these programs have increased profits.

Do managers, even with improved information, ever make bad decisions? Absolutely. Can we, in designing information systems, anticipate the bad decisions that managers might make and deliberately distort the information so that they are less likely to make them? Or should we protect managers from making bad decisions by not providing them with any information about the economics of their customer relationships? Such censorship implies that the designers of the information system know more about a manager's business than does the manager. This does not strike me as a good long-term working assumption. I am much more comfortable making the ABC information system as accurate and as representative as can economically be done. Managers generally seem to do sensible things if they are provided with accurate information—not always, but more often than not. I hear many more

horror stories about managers who made decisions based on distorted information, such as from traditional unit cost or direct costing systems, or made decisions that were completely uninformed by the economics of the alternative actions they were contemplating.

ABC is not magic. It is just one of many information systems to help managers make better decisions. Can managers make good decisions without a detailed understanding of their economics? Occasionally, but they also can make mistakes. They might overinvest in certain facilities, technologies, activities, products, customers, and projects that do not provide desired returns, and underinvest in others to which traditional costing systems have overallocated organizational expenses.

It's been an interesting few years of development in activity-based cost management, made slightly more interesting by the criticism of some well-meaning but misinformed commentators. I am sure that, when we talk again, the success stories from activity-based cost management will be even more dramatic and pervasive. ∎

Robert S. Kaplan is the Arthur Lowes Dickinson Professor of accounting at the Harvard Business School.

Author's Note: Helpful comments on the dialogue were supplied by Pierre Loewe of Gemini Consulting and Professors Chris Argyris, Robin Cooper, Marc Epstein, and Robert Simons.

[1] Robin Cooper and Robert S. Kaplan, "Activity-Based Systems: Measuring the Costs of Resource Usage," *Accounting Horizons*, September 1992, pp. 1-13.
[2] Robin Cooper, "Cost Classifications in Unit-Based and Activity-Based Manufacturing Cost Systems," *Journal of Cost Management*, Fall 1990, pp. 4-14.
[3] Robert S. Kaplan "Contribution Margin Analysis: No Longer Relevant/Strategic Cost Management: The New Paradigm," *Journal of Management Accounting Research*, (Fall 1990), pp. 2-15.
[4] This more general framework for applying ABC analysis appeared in Cooper and Kaplan, "Profit Priorities from Activity-Based Costing," *Harvard Business Review*, May-June 1991, pp. 130-135.
[5] James P. Womack, Daniel T. Jones, and Daniel Roos, *The Machine That Changed The World: The Story of Lean Production*, Rawson Associates, 1990.
[6] "A Lower Gear for Japan's Auto Makers," *New York Times*, (August 30, 1992), Section 3, pp. 1, 3.
[7] Robert S. Kaplan, "One Cost System Isn't Enough," *Harvard Business Review*, January-February 1988, pp. 61-66.

Letters *to the Editor*

"It's Time to Stop Overselling Activity-Based Concepts" by H. Thomas Johnson, September 1992, was one of the most controversial articles published in MANAGEMENT ACCOUNTING.® We are publishing some of the first letters received in response to this piece. Ed.

THOSE WHO DISAGREE

ABC IS NOT A PANACEA, BUT IT IS AN ENABLER

As a historian, H. Thomas Johnson presents an enlightening and well-documented description of the evolution of activity-based costing (see "It's Time to Stop Overselling Activity-Based Concepts" in the September MANAGEMENT ACCOUNTING®). Mr. Johnson's assessment of the current status of ABC, in contrast, is noticeably void of documented support. Instead, the article tends to condemn all ABC applications by focusing on the silver-bullet, panacea hype carelessly advocated by a few early ABC zealots.

A quick reading of brochures distributed by the many purveyors of ABC seminars, software, and consulting services indicates that the benefits derived from ABC systems are no longer being oversold. Instead, ABC has found an important niche not only as better product costing methodology but, equally important, as an enabler that supports corporate strategies such as continuous improvement. As an enabler, ABC brings visibility to the true cost of quality, to the prevalence of low value-added work, and ultimately to process reengineering opportunities.

Unfortunately, the article would have readers believe that ABC implementers are naive about the role that ABC plays in pursuit of profitability. This naiveté, if it exists at all, is not pervasive. I recently met with ABC practitioners from 12 large and diverse manufacturing companies to share experiences with the implementation [of] activity-based cost management concepts. Not surprisingly, each company is actively pursuing a variety of initiatives (such as customer satisfaction, cycle-time reduction, employee empowerment, and quality management) *in addition to ABC*. Each company is looking for the appropriate balance of cost,

quality, innovation, and service that will allow it to be competitive in a global economy. ABC is just one of many gears that must work in unison to achieve a world class stature.

By the way, I applaud MANAGEMENT ACCOUNTING® for tempering Mr. Johnson's article by also including the National Semiconductor article "Using ABC to Support Continuous Improvement" in the September issue.

Hal Thilmony
Manager-Financial Systems Implementation
The Clorox Company
Oakland, Calif.

WHAT ABC CAN DO

The September issue is a real winner!

I especially enjoyed Dr. H. Thomas Johnson's review of the history and development of activity-based costing. I was surprised to learn that ABC users expect to make product development (marketing), product design (engineering), or process design (industrial engineering) decisions using cost information describing things as they are at present.

My own involvement arose out of a TQM effort to make cost information responsive to process managers' needs. ABC in that environment was developed by a team including accountants, engineers, production personnel, and material personnel.

We discovered that the principles we developed (which we later learned were ABC principles) allowed us to forecast changes in resources used when process utilization was changed (either through product design or production routing) and to a limited degree when process design was changed. That was all we wanted. The cost history of processes as they are, however accurate that history may be, cannot reliably forecast the costs of new processes. So ABC did not tell us what changes would be responsive to customer needs; that's marketing's job. It didn't tell us how to design more effective or more efficient processes; that's the workers' (under TQM) and engineers' job. It did tell us what resource usage changes to expect when changing process or product designs. Then the most cost-effective solutions could be chosen. Profitability changes could also be estimated if new products or features were added without changing production processes.

Of course, it all depends on whether a company's ABC cost relationships accurately reflect its production and business processes.

Michael E. Woods, CPA

DON'T THROW OUT THE BABY WITH THE BATH WATER

In one sense I wholeheartedly agree with Professor Johnson that it is time to stop overselling Activity-Based Product Costing. But don't throw out the baby with the bath water. I do not agree with Tom Johnson that companies should stop Activity-Based Cost Management.

Activity-Based Costing (ABC) and Activity-Based Cost Management (ABM) are very new technologies. Overly zealous, well-intentioned accountants initially became enamored with ABC without first asking their internal customers a simple, albeit critical, question: "What does our company need, improved product cost or improved product profitability?" A controller said it best right here in the Letters to the Editor column two years ago: "Implementing ABC in my company equates to rearranging the deck chairs on the Titanic!" Most companies' most pressing need is reducing costs (ABM), not reallocating costs (ABC).

Professor Johnson proposes that TQM will automatically result in cost reduction. I disagree. Americans will only play games as long as they can keep score. Seven out of ten quality programs fail! One of the reasons is because companies lack a cost management system that "mirrors" the TQM process. That is, until ABM arrived.

Tom Pryor
President
ICMS Software, Inc.

JUST A TOOL

I agree wholeheartedly with the notion that ABC is not a panacea and cannot solve the ills of any company. Some proponents have taken ABC to such an extent that they lose sight of the fact that ABC is just a tool. How it is used depends on the managers' abilities, not on the abilities of the tool.

Where Mr. Johnson errs is when he assumes that focusing on people not costs is the panacea. TQM and "worker empowerment" theories are hot topics today because they seem to provide worker incentives and company competitiveness which are lacking in the traditional top-down management style. These theories bring about positive change only when measured against what previously existed. ABC is the foremost measurement tool available to managers to judge which changes are best for the company by determining which changes will reduce costs. It is true that some changes should be taken even if they increase costs, but totally ignoring costs would only bring about the demise of the company. By stating that ABC is no longer necessary, Mr. Johnson has done exactly what he accuses others of doing—overstating a position!

Sam Isaac, CMB
President
Automation Consulting
Brighton, Mich.

REALITY IN PRODUCT COSTS

After reading H. Thomas Johnson's article warning us not to waste time with our activity-based costing efforts, I feel he failed to emphasize a crucial point. ABC is a *tool*. It is not an end-all solution to profitability. Armed with this tool, companies can make educated decisions to meet or exceed customer requirements.

His example of the customer's need for small lots of frequent shipments failed to point out that ABC can provide manufacturers with the data necessary to determine the most economical method of producing to meet the customer's demand. ABC can tell us that it may be more economical to produce a one setup, annual supply for a customer, stock the parts, and ship to the customer as needed throughout the year. Yes, customer satisfaction *is* a focus of our corporate mission.

As project leader for our ABC implementation, I have great difficulty swallowing the idea that our ABC efforts are a waste of time A traditional cost system incorrectly allocates material overhead to parts based on purchased cost of components. If we scrap our ABC implementation, are we to continue to pretend there is a relationship between purchased cost and material overhead? Are we also to assume all our overhead can be scooped together and smeared across all parts by direct labor dollars or machine hours? I think not.

Behavior can be influenced by measurements. Marketing managers will pursue the sale of products with the most profit because that is how they are measured. We will continue our ABC implementation to bring some reality to our product costs and product profitability. We will use ABC as it was intended, a tool to help us make educated decisions regarding the products we manufacture.

Alan W. Rupp, CPA
Manager, Cost Accounting
Lord Corporation
Erie, Pa.

THREE VIEWS OF COST

When a colleague such as Tom Johnson speaks, many listen to what is said. Often this is enlightening; however, I believe your September 1992 article and interview with Dr. Johnson (as well as the PR hype for his new book *Relevance Regained*) has created considerable confusion in the minds of many management accountants. Therefore, I am compelled to comment on those issues.

The major concern I have with Dr. Johnson's latest work is that it appears to ignore a key point that he and Bob Kaplan made in *Relevance Lost.* That point being that there are fundamentally three views of costs: operational, strategic, and financial, and no cost system (not even an activity-based one) can effectively and efficiently serve all three simultaneously.

Johnson's point of "It's time to stop overselling activity-based concepts" is extremely valid. However, it is this failure to remember the three views of costs that leads ABC converts into overselling.

Dr. Johnson, Tom Vance, and I attempted to address this problem in a January 1991 *Corporate Controller* article, "The Pitfalls of Using ABC Cost-Driver Information to Manage Operating Costs."[1] Apparently, *Relevance Regained* seeks to make a stronger point but in so doing risks negating the value that ABC does provide when applied to solve a specific problem.

The book and article evaluate the history of ABC, noting it was tried in the 1960s by General Electric but "did not avert declining competitiveness at GE during and after the 1970s."[2] Johnson uses this argument to assert that activity-based costing "as a tool to improve the competitiveness of a business . . . is pure snake oil."[3] While that quote may help Johnson sell books, it does little to promote understanding.

I question Johnson's conclusions first on their premise.

Yes, GE may have used some form of ABC since the 1960s. But is the statement not also true that the basic Deming quality principles (that Johnson correctly says we also need) have been around since the 1940s? Americans first made widespread use of those quality principles during World War II. Though they remained available and to some degree "widely used" in the 1950s through the 1980s, they failed to receive top management attention with many believing that Deming was "selling pure snake oil."

Yet, through Deming's constancy of purpose and the dire needs of a war ravaged Japan, he was able to see implementation take root. The U.S. only began reacting in 1980 when the success of Deming "quality snake oil" resulted in Japan becoming a threatening global competitor. Drucker states that it typically takes 35 years for an innovation to take hold. That was certainly true of the U.S.'s adaptation of Deming's quality principles which is still under way. I believe that is true of ABC as well.

My second challenge to Johnson's statement stems from the hundreds of companies that have improved their operations and competitiveness through activity analysis. The examples are too prolific to ignore.

Johnson states that the goal of business is customer satisfaction. Our clients at Arthur Andersen (including some that Johnson has assisted us with) have found activity-based information extremely valuable. I will readily agree that our focus is on improving operations and not on "accounting."

From Dairy Equipment Company in 1978[4] through the wholesale distribution industry[5] down through the massive restructuring of the telecommunications (PacBell, Southwestern Bell, GTE, and Bell South) and financial services industry (Mutual of New York) of today—literally millions of dollars of improvements are being wrung out of American business by using activity analysis and the costing of those activities as a basis of reengineering the way those operations are performed.

In fact, I have a premise that virtually *all* operational improvement efforts being utilized today *require* some form or use of activity analysis.

Consider how you implement improvement in a company. You first understand the way work is being performed (in other words, you conduct some form of activity analysis). Then you use some criteria (either cost reduction, cycle times to be compressed, quality improvement, etc.) to evaluate that work. Based on that evaluation, you then change the work or activities to achieve better performance on the criteria selected.

Dr. Johnson argues that cost should not be the criterion used when a company evaluates its "operational" performance. He states that quality or customer satisfaction should be. I believe that both of those are important; however, I believe understanding cost should and will remain a key element of evaluating performance.

Quality and customer satisfaction are keys for the 1990s. But as Carl Sewell says in his book *Customers for Life,*" all these rules are not worth a damn if you don't make a profit."[6] It is real hard to satisfy customers in the long run if your company goes broke.

In the final analysis, I believe Dr. Johnson's new work provides an excellent history of activity analysis and activity-based costing. However, his conclusions in *Relevance Regained* may well be as overreaching as the overreaching claims for activity-based costing he rails against. The practitioner should remember that (1) there are three views of cost—financial, strategic, and operational, (2) clearly understand what problem he is trying to solve, and (3) understand how the approach (activity-based or otherwise) will solve that problem.

R. Steven Player
Arthur Andersen & Co.

[1]H. Thomas Johnson, Thomas P. Vance, and R. Steven Player, "Pitfalls of Using ABC Cost-Driver Information to Manage Operating Costs," *Corporate Controller*, January-February 1991, pp. 26-32.
[2]H. Thomas Johnson, *Relevance Regained,* The Free Press, p. 138.
[3]Ibid., p. 132.
[4]Op. cit., Johnson, Vance, Player.
[5]Robert L. Grottke, James W. Norris, *Improving Productivity and Profits in Wholesale Distribution: The Magnifying Glass Technique,* Distribution Research and Education Foundation, 1981.
[6]Carl Sewell, *Customers for Life.*

THOSE WHO AGREE

EMBRACE TOTAL QUALITY MANAGEMENT

Bravo for Tom Johnson! [September 1992 issue] It takes courage to point out that the ABC information set may be empty when professional support for ABC seems overwhelmingly positive.

We cannot do "better" what we always have done and hope to regain respect for accounting. If we know there is a problem such as a cross-product subsidy, ABC can confirm our intuition. However, ABC's focus on independent activities and consumers of those activities diverts attention away from real opportunities for improvement in company processes that are woven tapestries of activities.

Accountants can expand their thinking to encompass the complete operations of a company and develop measures to track critical success factors. We can "dollarize" these measures to standardize the measurement system and weight the severity of any problem. For example, a late order could be "dollarized" by assigning it a penalty equal to the contribution margin that the firm ultimately will realize on the order. This number then can be weighted by multiplying it by the number of days the order is late. The resulting measure has nothing to do with allocating a past cost incurred, but appropriately signals an unfavorable condition and triggers appropriate corrective action.

Our profession must abandon its total absorp-

tion with the allocation of costs and embrace total quality management and theory of constraints concepts. In short, we know techniques galore, but not when and where they should be applied.

Charlene W. Spoede, Ph.D., CPA, CMA
Professor, Baylor University

GOING COMMERCIAL?

It appears that MANAGEMENT ACCOUNTING® is doing its job—by bringing the growing controversy about activity-based costing into the open. While that may be little consolation to the IMA staff that is opening, sorting, reading, and worrying about the avalanche of mail it has received on the heels of publishing Tom Johnson's excellent and thought-provoking article, it is still something to be proud of.

As I understand it, though, much of the early mail you received was quite harsh in its position and language. It appears that some of my colleagues have forgotten their academic foundations, including the fact that debate, and disagreement, is not only healthy, but essential to the growth of knowledge. In addition, unless I have missed something, there is no such thing as the "one best way" to do accounting. Management accounting is based on the notion of different costs for different purposes, and its corollary, different cost systems for different organizations. That means that Tom Johnson's position is as defensible as that of the "ABC'ers." To suggest otherwise is ludicrous.

Which leads me to raise a concern that all management accounting professionals should have: Has ABC been oversold as a panacea for every ill? If so, the very innovation that triggered the much needed reforms in management accounting will also be its death knell. Why? Because ABC is: (1) useful for only a very small subset of the problems practicing managers face; (2) driven by a concern to get every cost in one of four buckets (unit, batch, product-sustaining and facility-sustaining); (3) still myopically focused on manufacturing and the cost of goods sold; (4) ignores long-term, strategic, systemic and process control issues that are critical to developing a sustainable competitive advantage in a global economy; (5) relies heavily on the theory of causality, which focuses everyone's attention on the past, rather than the future; (6) a flawed basis for strategic analysis and ongoing decision support. In other words, ABC is better than traditional standard costing, but only barely.

To suggest that ABC is *"the answer"* is both without merit, in my opinion, and dangerous. As Tom Johnson so clearly points out, doing a better job of getting the costs in the right bucket will not help Western companies regain their competitive edge.

Tools such as target costing, strategic cost analysis, cost control, and related advancements are proving to be helpful here, not ABC.

Dr. C.J. McNair, CMA
Babson College

QUALITY MANAGEMENT

As a manufacturing division controller for a Fortune 100 company, I've been involved with cost accounting for 25 years.

I've used every method from unit-based absorption to ABC. In retrospect, I can say I may have influenced operations through the use of cash flow, NPV, and IRR concepts. The opposite is not true for most of my costing efforts. I know of no significant change I've made in operations from costing work.

I don't believe we need to take *Relevance Regained* as an attack on all cost accounting, ABC, or as a condemnation of our profession. Let's use it as a catalyst to examine whether we truly are satisfying our customers, internal and external. As a whole, I believe we are not. In many cases we simply do a perfect job on products our customers don't need.

If we are to compete in an international economy, we must provide the quality expected. Our customers will eventually get the quality they demand. We need to concentrate on quality management, not run it by the numbers, and give our managers true goals to meet. If customers get the product and quality they pay for, profits will follow.

Accounting results, and some costing, will always be needed, but unless the quality product our customers desire is produced, what will costing do?

Relevance Regained should be another opportunity to examine our profession, provide quality, and get out of micro-managing by numbers.

Richard D. Benedetti
Lake Oswego, Ore.

FOCUS ON PROCESS IMPROVEMENT

Tom Johnson and MANAGEMENT ACCOUNTING® are to be congratulated on moving the profession ahead by publishing such incisive articles as this treatment of ABC. As with *Relevance Lost* and *Relevance Regained* many "professional feathers" are bound to be ruffled. Challenging powerful vested interests with an economic stake in preserving the status quo around ABC is not without risk. The rewards are in moving MANAGEMENT ACCOUNTING® to the forefront of the profession along with Professor Johnson, and focusing the debate around our professional journal.

Weyerhaeuser's experience directly supports Tom Johnson's treatise. Activities are no more than components of a process. Real benefits accrue from process improvement. In *Relevance Regained*, Weyerhaeuser's experience is outlined beginning on page 165. The epilog is that 1992 overhead is below 1989 levels, a reduction of some $12 million. This success has everything to do with process improvement and nothing to do with ABC. A corollary may be the buggy whip business. ABC would have faithfully attributed costs to the irrelevant activities of a dying business. Process improvement would also have costed activities, but in a framework integrated with suppliers and *customers*. The process method would likely have refocused the business on leather interiors for automobiles, while the ABC system for buggy whips simply went out of business.

Dennis A. Loewe
Financial Services Controller
Weyerhaeuser
Former National Vice President, IMA

OVERKILL?

Thomas Johnson's piece helps lift the fog that still envelops performance management. Superior companies train their front-line employees to spot, classify, measure, plot, and attack nonvalue-adding wastes — in natural units. It is overkill for cost analysts to do it, or re-do it, in dollars (ABC-enhanced or not). Though the "dollarization" issue is tending to polarize people, the good news is that those on each side generally profess similar refined beliefs about the strategic importance of quality, response time, flexibility, service, and customer needs — and that management by cost alone is not enough.

Richard J. Schonberger
President
Schonberger & Associates, Inc.

U.S. COMPETITIVENESS

I believe that good cost information is important if you are assessing make vs. buy decisions, target costing or significant cost components of products. Dr. Johnson fears (and I agree with him), that ABC is being marketed and purchased as a competitiveness-enhancement product, when it really is no more or no less than an improvement in cost allocation methodology.

Dr. Johnson correctly points out that no costing system will tell you what your customers really want — either in the short or long term. Also no costing system can tell you what investments must be made now in order to maintain and enhance customer loyalty and satisfaction for the future. Customer knowledge and investment for the future are the true corner-stones to long-term U.S. competitiveness.

Peggy J. Miller
Vice President
Oregon Health Sciences University

KUDOS TO JOHNSON

I commend Tom Johnson on "It's Time to Stop Over-selling Activity-Based Costing." It is extremely grati-fying to see one of the leading gurus of Management Accounting refute positions he espoused in *Relevance Lost,* especially when this book was so well received. I applaud his integrity.

Ernest C. Huge
DELTAPOINT

MUST READ

H. Thomas Johnson's *Relevance Regained* has moved to the head of my "must read now" list.

Although the use of traditional volume based product costing systems can create serious problems, the converse is not true. "Improved" product cost-ing systems, such as those incorporating activity-based allocations, still miss the mark. We must ex-amine the basic thought processes used to analyze and evaluate opportunities and problems. *Relevance Regained* should be read and carefully considered by all management accountants.

John A. Caspari, CMA
Grand Rapids, Mich.

ABC, NO MAGIC

I am concerned about the overemphasis on ABC cost-ing by Dr. Kaplan and thousands of other converts. For the life of me, I cannot see the magic of ABC sys-tem, and I am not stupid! I am amazed at the com-mercialism generated in terms of books, seminars, and articles which claim such magics brought about through ABC costing.

I agree with Dr. Kaplan's proposition on *Relevance Lost,* but I disagree with the proposed cure. The fact of the matter is that we lost relevance in accounting the more we dug into it in spite of all the ARBs, APBs, FASBs, and now ABCs.

We reject replacement costing and current-value accounting, saying that they may be relevant but they are not objective. We reject price-level-adjusted fi-nancial statements, saying that they may be objec-tive but they are not relevant.

We don't capitalize R&D because it is not a con-servative thing to do even though it may be relevant. We don't compute an imputed interest charge on the assets employed because we want to leave it to the world of economics in spite of its relevance.

We reject human asset accounting, saying that it may also be relevant but it can hardly be objectively determined and retain its meaningfulness at the same time. We allow different methods for depreciation and inventory evaluation because that is a democratic thing to do.

This is a nation of compromises. In recent years, no president gets elected unless [he] takes a middle-of-the-road approach. FASB has also taken the demo-cratic approach in dealing with accounting problems and issues whereas many countries seem to be tak-ing a more simplistic or possibly realistic approach to accounting and life in spite of its imperfections.

Relevance predominates in accounting decisions in Netherlands. Conservatism predominates in ac-counting in Germany. Tax code predominates in ac-counting in France. Swedish accounting system has the two elements of conservatism and tax code con-siderations.

British, who are closer to us in their democratic ideals, search for a "true and fair" representation of accounts. It is reported that some Japanese firms dis-allow cost accountants from entering their premises because they believe their thoughts are dangerous and detrimental to the firm's profitability and quality con-trol ideals.

The relevance that Mr. Kaplan is talking about was never there in financial accounting or manage-rial accounting systems, which were extensions of the company's regular accounting systems. Something more than ABC and value-added accounting is needed to save us from the current decline in our for-tune.

ABC is a way of allocating indirect costs to prod-ucts to the extent that a cause-and-effect relationship exists and cost drivers can be identified. It improves product costing through a more accurate allocation of resources. If we don't consider replacement costs and current values, if we ignore imputed costs on assets employed, if we do not charge costs such as R&D to the periods that reap the benefits from such expenditure, if we want to force all costs in a format that each cost arbitrarily or otherwise is related to a cost driver, if we ignore other costing methods be-cause we have supposedly discovered ABC, the ABC discovery will probably do more harm than good in the long run.

Roger K. Doost
Associate Professor
Clemson University

TOM JOHNSON REPLIES

I am pleased to comment on the letters and the article in the November issue of MANAGEMENT ACCOUNTING®

that responded to my September 1992 article, "It's Time to Stop Overselling Activity-Based Concepts."

I believe activity-based cost management impedes companies' efforts to move from the cost-oriented management paradigm that has guided them for the past 40 years to the people-oriented paradigm that I believe they must follow to succeed in the 1990s and beyond. In the old paradigm, the purpose of business is to grow return on investment in order to maximize shareholder wealth; success, old-style, hinges on controlling cost by planning adroitly to capture scale economies, and by managing *consumption* of resource inputs. In the new paradigm (esp. Deming, Senge, et al.) the purpose of business is to profitably create fulfilling jobs in learning organizations that continually enhance people's capacities to realize higher expectations. In that new context, success in business hinges on enhancing the capabilities of resources—above all, people.

I believe the main barrier to change, from the status quo to the new learning organization, is top management's entrenched belief that success hinges on controlling cost, particularly by slashing resource inputs. I believe a company cannot succeed in the long run if its top managers believe they improve performance by cutting costs or by selling higher margin products. Long-term improvement results only from investing in people's abilities to improve customer-focused processes.

I am not saying companies should not know their costs, nor am I saying that profit doesn't matter. Information for planning and estimating the financial consequences of actions is always vital to the success of a business. What is lethal, in my opinion, is to believe it is possible to improve performance in the long run by having everyone in the business manipulate operations to achieve planned financial targets. As a consequence, top managers view people and resources as costs, not as a source of competitive strength.

Cost-focused thinking impairs performance in today's companies by undermining a sense that everyone connected with an organization is part of a larger whole, a system. It encourages people to think of their work as disconnected, decoupled activity. What goes unseen is the larger system from which cost results flow. With cost seen as *the* variable to manage, not seen simply as a *result* of management efforts, people believe that efforts at cost management address fundamental causes when in fact they simply chase symptoms. Interventions to manage cost can, of course, produce short-term "improvement." But by leaving root problems unattended, they exacerbate long-term performance. Cutting training budgets will, for example, reduce certain costs and may even raise bottom-line results—for a while. But that

cutting is almost certain to deepen the company's malaise in the long term.

Cost management thinking also impedes success by causing managers to focus marketing (and sourcing) decisions on cost and margins rather than on the organization's competencies and the customers' opportunities. I would argue there is no necessary connection between customer satisfaction and product margins (estimated with ABC or not). Hence, there is no necessary connection between long-term profitability and efforts to sell more higher margin products. It is far better to profitably make what customers most want, and be ready to adapt flexibly as customers' opportunities change. That is the essence of "new paradigm" thinking.

- I do not unequivocally denounce ABC. I distinguish between information to plan or estimate the financial consequences of decisions and information to direct and control people's work. Activity-based costing techniques may give better information to assess financial consequences—to cost new products, to estimate the costs of processes, to estimate the costs of quality or nonquality, and so forth. But managers must not act, or encourage others to act, solely to improve financial outcomes. (I do not mean steps taken to conserve or marshall cash when a company is on the brink of a financial crisis; that is a different matter, and obviously has to be done on some occasions.) I have no objection to tracking the financial results in well-run processes—timely scorecards on the wall are important and useful. Just don't let anyone slip into the habit of driving processes to achieve financial results. That *always* is a self-defeating strategy in the long term. To improve normal operations, continuously improve the capability of people and processes to exceed customer expectations profitably.

- Some readers say I refer to activity-based costing as an accounting exercise. In fact, that's exactly what it was, in its original forms at GE and at the companies that pioneered ABC product costing in the late '70s and early '80s. Moreover, virtually every ABC presentation, case or implementation that I have seen since I first encountered this concept in 1984 has focused on making a better "rack and stack" of indirect costs from an accounting source. However, nothing says that activity-based concepts, especially those articulated in the GE cross-functional activity analysis framework, cannot lend themselves to economic modelling and cannot accommodate market-based or forecast price information. I would applaud the idea of using such models and that information for planning and estimating. But I would be concerned if such models and cost information were used to make choices and to drive operations to achieve what the economic model says is most profitable or least costly. If an activity-based economic model suggests that you can't profitably satisfy customers with your present processes, then work on improving people's abilities to remove constraints and make processes capable of profitably satisfying customers — don't waste time trying to figure out ways to force something on the customer because your model says it is profitable.

- Many readers associate my message with "TQM." Actually, I try never to use the acronym TQM. I envision a business as a system of interrelated processes in which people are continually learning and inventing more fulfilling ways to profitably exceed the expectations of customers (internal and external). Call that vision "quality," if you must call it anything. To achieve it, I say that companies, and top managers in particular, must adopt a radically new mindset about business. I don't advocate mastering a program of steps to achieve quality. Today's businesses are sold too much of that in the name of "TQM." TQM often is nothing more than a palliative, like activity-based cost management, that top managers adopt who don't want to abandon the old paradigm. Everyone in the company gets "involved" and "committed" to a "TQM initiative" while top management retains all the trappings of top-down manage-by-the-numbers (perhaps dressed up a bit with activity-based cost management). This may generate good press copy, for a while at least, but in the long run it can't generate solid improvements in performance. That's why we read so many stories about "TQM" programs that fail. Of course they fail! They are more of the old wine in new bottles — they have nothing to do with quality.

- In response to Bob Kaplan's November article, I do not care if activity-based costs draw on historical, market, or future data. That issue misses the point. The point is that managers should use lots of different financial, cost, accounting, and economic information to plan, estimate and forecast; but they should *never* roll such information down to drive operating performance and process improvement. Activity-based information (ABC, ABM, whatever) can provide useful input to the planning process; it can never drive operational improvement and customer satisfaction.

- Several letters and Bob Kaplan's article suggest that many problems in American business can be remedied by creating new and improved financial measurements and systems (à la ABC and

ABM). I disagree completely. The problem in American business is not poor management accounting. The problem is managers believing it is proper to control people's work with remote, top-down accounting information at all. I develop that theme at length in *Relevance Regained: From Top-Down Control to Bottom-Up Empowerment.* Now I go even farther than I did in that book and say that the problem isn't just accounting information *per se* — the problem is *any* information that triggers "end justifies the means" behavior. It is more important to focus attention on the behavior, not on the particular type of information that prompts it.

- It would take pages and pages and still I could not address all the fallacies in the claim several readers make that managers must have *cost* information to prioritize improvement programs, to select optimal product mixes, and to know, in general, what course of action to take. That cost-focused view epitomizes the traditional management paradigm that I say companies must root out and destroy if they are to succeed in the long term. Long-term success is achieved by enhancing the competencies of people to fulfill customer opportunities profitably, not by taking steps to cut costs or raise margins. This view was put very well in a recent *Fortune* article exploring the causes of fading productivity in American industry. There the writer said, "U.S. business raises productivity well by cutting inputs, but only investing more in people and innovation to increase outputs will raise living standards." (10/19/92, pg. 55) I contend that we will not begin to develop people and to innovate until we stop driving everyone to see business through the lens of cost. People must be trained and enabled to spot and remove constraints that cause delay, excess, and variation — key impediments to profitable customer satisfaction. Success at removing such constraints will not automatically reduce costs or increase revenues. But it will create resource redundancies and revenue opportunities. Smart companies react, then, by redeploying redundant resources to search for and capture more revenue.

- Many of the letters and the article printed in November defend ABC by telling how its use led a company to discover things that I would expect well-rounded 10-year-olds to have known in the first place. Here are two types: (1) ABC cost information helped Company X ferret out "unreasonable" customers whose special demands triggered extra shipments, extra storage, extra handling, and extra time not required to serve "reasonable" customers. Does it take a massive investment in costing technology to alert us that time, space, people, and transactions cost money? If it does, we have problems much graver than any costing technology is designed to handle. Otherwise, insist on charging more when more is given. And if a customer behaves like a spoiled brat, act accordingly. (2) After an ABC implementation caused Company Y to raise prices, they discovered that for some time they had unwittingly charged far less than customers were willing to pay. Wow! Sounds like Company Y had been producing gold, didn't know they were and unwittingly charged prices for tin. Do they need ABC to tell them that? Of course not! I believe this story tells much less about the power of ABC than it tells about the failure of Company Y to take customer relationship-building seriously. Walk in your customer's shoes, find out just what the stuff you sell them is worth *to them*, and charge what the customer will bear. Basing prices on your costs is a gamble at best, and a fool's game at worst.

■ Some readers suggest that I cannot document the claims I make about activity-based cost management. In fact, I do have *very* extensive evidence from the field showing what I consider to be perverse uses of ABC information in actual companies. This evidence comes from Harvard Business School cases on activity-based cost management, from countless articles about companies' ABC experiences, and from my own observations in scores of companies that I have visited since the mid-1980s and in one Big 6 consulting firm where I was retained in 1989 and 1990 as an ad-

visor on activity-based management. I make references to such field evidence in over two dozen articles that I published since 1987 and in my new book *Relevance Regained*.

Conclusion. The responses to my article are largely from ABC practitioners and consultants. Often people who are closest to an activity are the last ones to know when a paradigm shifts. Customer power and the growing realization that human beings constitute the only source of long-run business success promise to turn the activity-based cost management paradigm into dust. Meanwhile, the cost-focused management paradigm that dominates American business is contributing to a serious human loss—loss of opportunities to create fulfilling jobs and create what Dr. Deming refers to as "joy in the workplace." Activity-based cost management helps reinforce the business community's belief that the old paradigm still works. Unfortunately it may work, in the short run, for top managers' compensation packages and for the revenues of certain consultants and software vendors. But their gain, I am afraid, is offset by society's much greater long-term loss. It pleases me to think that my article may lessen that loss by raising a flag that warns business people to resist the activity-based juggernaut and reject the cost-focused paradigm it reinforces. ■

H. Thomas Johnson
Portland State University
Portland, Ore.

Part **2**

Removing Barriers to ABC Management Systems Implementations

In this section, which leads to ABC business applications, two authors discuss how to remove barriers to ABC management systems implementations. A recently published IMA Bold Step research study sensitized us to the fact that obstacles to ABC implementations may be more common than suspected. In *Implementing Activity-Based Cost Management: Moving from Analysis to Action*, the researchers noted that a number of firms made no significant change in actions or decisions as a result of ABC. They speculate that a number of factors possibly might account for this lack of progress. Among them were inadequate preparation of the organization in thinking and decision making, lack of early identification of the person or group (target) whose decisions were expected to change as a consequence of the information provided by ABC, and lack of a sponsor, a senior person who could authorize the action to be taken by the target person or group.

John M. Brausch and Peter B.B. Turney in their articles suggest different paths to overcoming obstacles. Both would address the organizational barriers. Turney, however, would take a unique course of action — insert and incorporate activity-based management information into the process, turning over the ownership of the information to the process owner or manager.

Brausch, in "Selling ABC," tells us that cost management has to overcome three hurdles just to communicate the need for a new cost management system. (He is not talking about implementation yet.) The hurdles are: (1) the perception that cost accounting as

a discipline is inadequate, (2) proving (especially to manufacturing executives) that a new system will do any better than the old system, and (3) overcoming the high implementation costs. Even if these hurdles are overcome, the new system still won't be successful until it communicates to the customers within the corporate community.

Through a tale of two cost management systems installations, one successful, the other not, Brausch highlights several key organizational preparation steps that he believes necessary for a successful implementation. They are: (1) communicating from the top down that the cost accounting system is of strategic importance, and (2) forming teams or groups to provide direction and project management, to ensure implementation of the new system.

The successful company did just that. It established a cost strategy group consisting of the CEO and VPs of the major functions, a cross-functional corporate project management team to manage the project, and a cost implementation team. These groups encouraged communication and provided the opportunity to turn cost issues into strategic business issues. In contrast, the CEO of the unsuccessful cost implementation was willing to spend half a million dollars on the project but was not willing to take the time to see what the resulting system would do for the company. "He incorrectly assumed that the cost system was not important enough for him to understand."

In "Beyond TQM with Workforce Activity-

Based Management" Turney explains workforce activity-based management (WABM), the process of using information to focus every worker on continuous improvement of profitability, timeliness, and quality. The concept combines three elements: the power of information, group processes involving the entire workforce, and focus, which requires every worker to develop a set of performance measures based on organizational goals. These elements serve to change the organization in important ways. As Turney states, "These include changes in employee empowerment, worker accountability, roles and responsibilities, decision making, and organizational structure."

WABM builds on the ownership of processes throughout the organization. Workers or process owners develop the ABC cost information, and they own the information. Accountants are partners on the workteams. With this information workers can accept responsibility and participate in decision making so that decisions are made at levels below management. When everyone has bottom-line responsibility and knowledge of how to improve profitability, managers are freed to act as coaches and facilitaters in the workforce. The roles and responsibilities of worker and manager are changed forever—the organization is changed. ∎

Selling ABC

New cost systems can flounder if they're not marketed.

BY JOHN M. BRAUSCH

Cost management is suddenly being viewed as one of the keys to helping American firms succeed in a worldwide manufacturing environment. The underlying assumption is that manufacturers don't now know their costs but that they had better in the future. How do they "know their costs"? Increasingly, it is through the use of one of the new and improved cost accounting systems derived from the much touted activity-based costing (ABC) systems.

Are these new systems really necessary? Undoubtedly. The case made over and over is: Manufacturing has changed radically in the past few years; manufacturing accounting has not. But although many academicians and practitioners realize the need for new cost management systems, selling top management on that same idea is an arduous task...especially for individuals more at home with numbers and ledgers than with marketing strategies. Cost accounting management must overcome three hurdles in order to communicate effectively the need for a new cost management system.

Perceived inadequacy of cost accounting as a discipline. "Manufacturing executives have lost faith in their cost accounting systems," is a familiar theme in a spate of articles and seminars during the last seven years. It is important to realize that cost accounting has not been seen as a particularly stringent discipline. "In the last decade, cost accounting has come under increasing scrutiny and criticism. Traditional approaches to cost accounting often fail to meet the needs of managers for purposes of cost analysis and performance measurement."[1] Few CEOs or even top executives have cost

What's the best kind of cost system for a textile mill? Above, warping machines at Culp, Inc. prepare yarn.

accounting backgrounds. Even among fellow accountants, cost accounting has been viewed as a poor stepchild. Auditing, tax, and financial management have been seen as the "glamour" fields within accounting. A recent study indicated that cost accounting ranked dead last in terms of resources consumed by accounting functions. "Many firms of all sizes do no cost accounting or managerial accounting whatsoever. Even in manufacturing, cost and managerial accounting receive meager support."[2]

Fortunately, this state of affairs may be changing. Robert G. Eiler, editor of the *Journal of Cost Management,* reports that "more and more of the brightest students are becoming interested in pursuing a career in strategic cost management."[3]

Also, cost accountants more often than not are on the front lines in manufacturing companies and overwhelmed with an infinite array of detailed-oriented quotidian problems while being somewhat removed from the glitter of corporate accounting and financial staff headquarters. Unfortunately, cost accountants are not respected by manufacturing because many manufacturers see cost accountants as "bean counters" more in tune with pleasing corporate accounting staff and following their own agenda rather than dealing with the intricacies of manufacturing. "The developer of JIT, Taiichi Ohno, has reportedly mentioned that cost accounting is his biggest obstacle to the implementation of JIT at Toyota. Ohno reportedly had to keep the cost accountants out of the plant and 'prevent the knowledge of cost accounting from entering into the minds of his people.'"[4] Cost accounting's unwillingness to keep pace with manufacturing changes has led to a deep distrust of cost accounting by manufacturing personnel.

This perceived weakness makes the task even more difficult: Before management accountants can move to a new system, they must first tell anyone who will listen that the current cost system is not performing its task adequately. Unfortunately, in many organizations this admission is tantamount to suicide because the cost accountants are admitting that the work they oversee is not providing the information needed by their organization.

Proving that a new system will do any better than the old system. Manufacturing executives have indeed lost faith in their cost accounting systems, but convincing them that any new system will provide accurate cost information and has an inherent advantage over existing systems is a very difficult task. Executives don't necessarily see a given system as

WHY IS VARIANCE REPORTING IMPORTANT?

The purpose of plant variance accounting is to provide benchmarks for operational and financial managers to measure the effectiveness of manufacturing site and marketing group performance. Managers participate in establishing budgets for the factors over which they have control based on a combination of factors incorporating planned financial, marketing, and manufacturing goals.

Planned budgets are set based on management's financial expectations for the near future. These expectations are translated by manufacturing and marketing into a workable plan to be carried out by front-line supervisory and sales personnel. Every professional at company B could explain why this step is taken: To communicate goals and to coordinate individual units' conformance to said goals; to provide before-the-fact control to establish and justify resources necessary to meet objectives; to use as a basis for after-the-fact control and performance evaluation; to identify weak areas of the firm; and to motivate managers through involving lower management in the goals, objectives, problems, and policies of the firm.

It is from the budgets developed by marketing, manufacturing, and finance to meet these strategic goals that standard costs are developed by applying those budgets to individual products. Marketing drives the amount of goods to be produced, manufacturing estimates the resources necessary to produce them, and these inputs are used to estimate how much each individual unit should cost to manufacture. This estimate becomes the standard.

Variance reporting simply uses the before-the-fact product cost, production, and sales standards and compares them to after-the-fact results. Did we sell what we thought we would sell? At the price we thought we could realize for it? Did the product cost more or less to produce than we had previously thought? If so, why? Were we as effective in manufacturing the product as we had hoped? These are some of the concerns of variance reporting and the reason we would like to implement it. Variances are simply what we planned to spend (or produce or sell) vs. what we actually spent (or produced or sold).

To report variances correctly, budgets (the planning side) are earned by taking the standard cost of a product and multiplying it by the units produced for the period of time for which we are concerned. This budget is called a flexible or earned budget because it fluctuates based on the actual level of production. If goods are produced and money is spent exactly as was budgeted, then variances would always be zero because earned budgets would exactly equal spending. Each standard cost sheet would then be a precise actual cost sheet, and executive management would know precisely where we were, in which direction we were heading, and at what speed we were getting there.

Unfortunately, we conduct business in less than perfect circumstances, and strategic goals are not always tactically possible. Variance reporting can show that we are missing our targets and can help to answer both why it happened and how it can be corrected. By earning budgets based on "standard" costs, management has a benchmark that shows where we are right now, based on the set of circumstances under which we are operating, as opposed to the "ideal" circumstances upon which forecasts and budgets were made. These details matter because bottom-line profit or loss in and of itself does little to tell the user of the information why it exists.

Variances can help to pinpoint the responsibility for profits or losses which are not always readily apparent. Variances also affect pricing issues. Chronic variances (favorable or unfavorable) will show that the standard cost of products is under or overstated and that pricing decisions based on incorrect standards may be eroding profits or market share. We also will have greater faith that we do in fact have "a handle on our costs" because we see how the standard product costs tie into internal financial reporting. By earning flexible budgets (that is, budgets based on actual production), Company B can judge its progress on what is actually happening as opposed to what was strategically planned. ∎

not being adequate but, rather, view cost accounting in general, and perhaps some cost accountants in particular, as being inadequate. This attitude leaves the cost accountant walking a tightrope of showing that the old system isn't working, that a new system can, and that he or she is the right person for getting the job done.

Tremendous implementation costs. The Institute of Management Accountants' *Cost Management Update* stated that 32% of manufacturing companies responding to an IMA survey spent more than 100K on ABC implementation costs.[5] The cost for implementing an all-encompassing cost system and its inherent production and engineering systems in a company with few or no preexisting systems can very well run to a million dollars, including automated equipment and MIS support, even in a small to medium-sized company. In today's business environment, getting top management to appropriate $1 million for a new cost accounting system, given the disadvantages pointed out above, can be a near impossible task.

These three hurdles are very difficult to overcome. Even if these three hurdles are overcome, it is important to remember that our responsibilities are to communicate the workings of the new systems to the people who are funding their completion. New systems for new systems' sake will not automatically provide better information. New cost management systems will not be much better than old cost management systems if the resulting information is not successfully communicated to their customers within the corporate community.

A TALE OF TWO SYSTEMS

Two medium-sized textile manufacturers recently implemented new cost accounting systems. Overcoming the hurdles listed above was not easy, but making the project a priority in the minds of the entire company was even harder. The systems are nearly identical and incorporate the most fundamentally sound costing strategies. In the long run, however, only one of the two systems will be fully used. It will be used because the goals of the implementation were communicated before, during, and after both the design and implementation stages of the project.

Because the systems per se are nearly identical, project marketing and intracompany communication are identifiable as the difference between the two projects, and hence some generalities can be drawn from these two specific situations. Now, admittedly, some companies are more conducive to change than others, but both of these companies were convinced that their existing systems were inadequate and were convinced that a new system could provide better costing information. One system, however, was built in a vacuum while the other brought a team concept to the project. From these two specific cases can be drawn some general lessons in communication applicable to any cost system implementation.

Company A (a privately held company with $100 million in annual sales and 500 employees) hired an outside engineering consultant with very capable analytical and programming skills to work very closely with the newly hired cost manager. These two individuals were the company's cost implementation group.

The consultant reported to the cost manager who in turn reported to the vice president of administration, another newly created position. The vice president had line responsibility to the CEO and was responsible for implementing an integrated manufacturing system of which cost accounting was but one part. The accounting software package purchased by the firm was inadequate for cost accounting purposes; therefore, the vice president was instructed by the CEO to have a cost accounting system designed specifically to meet the needs of the company in regard to inventory valuation, product costing, and variance analysis. The company already was in litigation with one accounting firm in large part because of its consulting group's failure to implement a satisfactory cost accounting system. In light of the fact that the inadequate software package was recommended by the consulting arm of another accounting firm, the CEO understandably had had enough of accountants in general and cost accounting systems in particular.

The cost manager, hired from a division of a Fortune 50 company, was instructed to design the cost accounting system as he saw fit and to report his work to the vice president. Furthermore, he was requested not to communicate system design or cost strategies to any of the other accountants within the company because no other member of the organization had any cost background and the current accounting staff would be purged and replaced by the time the cost system was implemented. The cost accounting system was to be designed and implemented without any internal costing resources.

The vice president told the cost manager that the other executives, including the CEO, were interested only in seeing that the project was completed and didn't care to be involved in any way in the project's details. This attitude was borne out by an incident during project implementation when the CEO became livid about concern with such "petty system issues." The vice president said that executive level

At Culp, cost management is treated as a strategic imperative. Cost manager John M. Brausch (center) meets with representatives of three manufacturing plants.

communication was his concern and that he would tell the executives what they needed to know about the cost system.

Despite the company's size, it had no industrial engineers and only a one-person MIS staff. Cost accounting systems obviously would have to be built outside the existing system's structure and implemented by the cost personnel who were designing the system. The cost manager worked closely with operations management and designed a production tracking and reporting system as well as engineering product specifications. A cost system was implemented incorporating the most current ABC theory. Despite the normal difficulties associated with large project management and the peculiarities of this particular project, the system was completed by the consultant and the cost manager on time and under budget.

A BLACK BOX

Unfortunately, a very good cost system was built in a black box: The cost manager and the outside consultant knew its workings, but outside of a staff built during implementation no one else did. Result: fiasco. Great systems which no one understood. In fact no one wanted to understand them. The corporate financial and accounting staff was miffed that they had been flanked by outsiders and that new systems were built without their input. They were not purged or replaced and could not understand why they had been bypassed. The manufacturing group was shocked to learn that it was going to be judged on its effectiveness in meeting certain objectives that were heretofore not measured.

When the manufacturing staff representatives realized that theirs was the only group consulted, they denied their involvement in the project. Marketing wasn't thrilled to learn that its price points were not in line with the new company product costing. The CEO, a salesman by trade who had inherited the family business, had no foundation in cost and by the time the bickering began had no desire to get one. The resulting chaos was disheartening and predictable: The systems were largely ignored even though they contained a wealth of strategic information for the company. In time the consultant went on to other projects, taking with him a great deal of knowledge about the company. The cost manager was frustrated and left shortly thereafter with a wealth of information about the company, an implemented self-designed cost management system, and the knowledge of why it wasn't being used and how the same system could be implemented better elsewhere.

You could blame the CEO for this fiasco because he was willing to spend half a million dollars but not willing to take the time to see what the resulting system would do for him. He didn't care to inform his staff of the project and its goals or that he was spending half a million dollars to realize his expectations. He incorrectly assumed that cost accounting was not important enough for him to understand. The vice president failed to communicate to the appropriate parties as was his acknowledged responsibility. He believed that the CEO was going to replace his current accounting staff and that he could introduce his new staff to the cost system at that time. Although he understood the cost system, he felt that no one else needed to be consulted nor understand it.

As for the cost manager, he allowed himself to operate

in a vacuum without following up to see if the communication were carried out. At every stage, there was a breakdown in communication, and the result was that what could have been a great system ended up being not much better than what existed previously.

A SUCCESSFUL IMPLEMENTATION

Company B (a publicly traded company with 1,700 employees and annual sales of about $200 million) is in the process of implementing approximately the same cost management system. The cost manager reports to the V.P.-Controller. Two corporate cost teams have been created: The first is the Cost Management Project team which consists of the V.P.-Finance, V.P.-Controller, Director of Industrial Engineering, Director of MIS, all plant administrative managers and cost accountants, and the cost manager.

The second cost group is the cost strategy group consisting of the CEO, V.P.-Finance, V.P.-Controller, Cost Manager, V.P.-Manufacturing, and V.P.-Marketing. Each group meets periodically and discusses cost management issues in an open forum.

In addition, a cost implementation team that brings together representatives of manufacturing, engineering, cost and general accounting, and MIS has been formed for each of the company's six manufacturing sites. These groups encourage communication and also provide the opportunity to make cost issues strategic business issues. Cost personnel know corporate direction, and executives understand costing issues and concerns. From front-line supervisors to the CEO, those affected by the cost management system are consulted. At company B, cost accounting is of strategic importance and is treated that way from the CEO on down.

The result to date has been successful: good systems that everyone understands and takes pride in. Corporate accounting is thrilled to see better controls on manufacturing financial data. Manufacturing enjoys being measured against more reliable data. Marketing is glad to have more accurate product costs by which to meet price points.

The difference between the two companies? Communication. Each of the three hurdles was overcome by openly communicating to the corporate community about cost management systems in general and their application in particular at Company B. While Company A considered cost accounting a necessary evil, Company B has made costing an integral part of its strategic plans through the two-way communication of costing goals and mechanisms. This is imperative because nothing is of more strategic benefit to a company than knowing what its products cost and why. As noted by a number of observers, accurate cost information can give a company a competitive edge.

COST ACCOUNTANTS: COMMUNICATE

If cost accounting is perceived as inadequate, it is because cost accountants do not explain either the goals or the workings of their jobs. By stressing the accounting fundamentals, management accountants can show the rest of the company why this discipline is essential for the success of the firm.

> *The CEO was willing to spend a half million on the system but not willing to sell it to the staff.*

The sidebar information on variance reporting—"Why Is Variance Reporting Important?"—may seem elementary to most readers, but it represents a wealth of information to those not so well versed in the mechanics of cost accounting. At Company B a more extensive version of what is illustrated in the sidebar was used to explain to executive management the reason why variance reporting is one of the important tools in explaining company performance. Indeed, even though variance analysis is one of the easier concepts intrinsic to cost management, few outside cost accounting understand exactly what makes up the calculation of variances. Given that this is the case, how can we as cost accountants expect the corporate community to understand, much less accept, some of the newer cost theories such as Process Value Analysis and Life Cycle Accounting? By actively communicating rather than waiting to react to problems or complaints, cost accountants will be better able to sell the benefits that cost accounting can bring to an organization. Proving that a new system will do better than the old system and overcoming price barriers are functions of marketing the product.

Yes, new cost system implementation is expensive, but it can be sold as being worth it. Any marketer is an expert at turning perceived weaknesses into strengths. Weak engines, for example, are said to have great gas mileage; gas guzzlers are said to have smooth, powerful engines. If new cost accounting systems are expensive, then a concentrated effort should be made to show that the benefits to be derived outweigh the costs to be expended. Likewise, cost accountants would do well to remember that they must continually sell cost accounting as a discipline as well as sell the concept that better cost systems are an important strategic mechanism for a company. The new theories will have tremendous payback in helping to reduce nonvalue-added manufacturing steps and to assign product costs correctly. But executive management must believe that this is the case. It is imperative that management accountants communicate the importance of cost management to their companies.

Here are some simple steps that will help to open lines of communication between cost management and the rest of the firm:

1. *Make noncost accountants a part of the costing team*. Bring representatives of MIS, engineering, manufacturing, general accounting, marketing, and quality control, among others, together to develop a corporate costing strategy. Each of these areas touches cost either directly or indirectly. Making them a part of the costing team can contribute greatly to goodwill between the groups.
2. *Share cost management articles and theories with interested parties*. Ask questions that help to ensure a response.
3. *Review with executive management the strengths and weaknesses of current costing methodology*. Provide evidence of the strengths and plans to help shore the weaknesses.
4. *Show an interest in becoming involved in the problem-solving process of other departments in the firm*. Because cost management is intertwined with so many other areas, this step can be taken by showing a genuine interest. This demonstrated concern communicates a willingness on the part of cost management to work with others and also ensures that the cost group has a voice in the decision-making process.
5. *Learn the business*. Take the time to study manufacturing processes and product lines. Become familiar with suppliers and customers. Corporate cost staffs need to get out to the manufacturing facilities. Plant cost staffs need to become familiar with other plants in the company, especially those that impact the process at your plant.

By opening intracorporate lines of communication, cost accountants can overcome a perceived inadequacy of cost accounting systems. By developing intracorporate marketing strategies, cost accountants can educate others in how the new costing theories can provide better cost management than current systems and show the cost effectiveness of those systems.

Communicating cost management goals and priorities within your company is no longer optional. The stakes have become higher for companies to be knowledgeable about cost management. By the same token, the responsibility is greater for cost accountants to spread the word. ∎

John M. Brausch is cost accounting manager of Culp, Inc., and may be contacted at P.O. Box 2686, High Point, NC 27261, (919) 889-5161.

[1] Alfred J. Nanni, J. Robb Dixon, and Thomas E. Vollmann, "Strategic Control and Performance Measurement," *Journal of Cost Management*, Summer 1990, p. 33.
[2] Bradley M. Roof and Charles Barill, "How Does Your Accounting Department Measure Up?" MANAGEMENT ACCOUNTING®, Institute of Management Accountants, Montvale, N.J., April 1991, p. 42.
[3] Robert G. Eiler, *Journal of Cost Management*, Fall 1989, p. 4.
[4] John Y. Lee, *Managerial Changes for the 90's*, Addison-Wesley, New York, N.Y., 1987, p. 63.
[5] For an in-depth analysis of selling a cost accounting system, please read Stokes' and Lawrimore's article, "Selling a New Cost Accounting System," *Journal of Cost Management*, fall 1989.

Is this article of interest to you? If so, circle appropriate number on Reader Service Card.	**Yes** 58	**No** 59

BEYOND TQM

With Workforce Activity-Based Management

It builds a sense of ownership at all levels of a company.

BY PETER B.B. TURNEY

That Saturday morning the room was full of people clustered in groups around storyboards. The boards, covered with cards documenting and explaining the work done by the people, were the focal point for intense discussions by each group. These employees of an electronics company were gathered together to launch a new process—workforce activity-based management (WABM). All employees were present—including the president, the janitors, and everyone in between.

What is workforce activity-based management? It is the process of using information to focus everyone on continuously improving profitability, timeliness, and quality. It combines the power of activity-based costing (ABC) information with a group process using storyboards where the development, maintenance, and application of the information involves the entire workforce. Everyone works toward a clear, complete, and measurable set of goals. Workforce activity-based management helps achieve this focus through performance measures of cost, time, and quality that reflect each work team's contribution to the organization's goals. With these measures, everyone understands how his or her contributions affect organizational performance, including the bottom line.

THE GROUP PROCESS

Under workforce activity-based management, employees are divided into work teams—groups of individuals who work together on a regular basis—for the purpose of documenting, measuring, and improving their activities. The primary tools for this process are storyboards, workspaces for attaching cards, dots, yarn, and other items that visually represent information about a team and its work. These communication tools help document and organize a team's ABC information and help employees brainstorm team issues and resolve problems. They do not require extensive training to use, and workers with limited education can create them just as effectively as highly trained engineers or other professionals.

The overall group process is led by a facilitator, who may be a member of the team or possibly a manager or staff person. The facilitator's task is to keep the team in step with

National Semiconductor work team plots activities.

the WABM process and to encourage and focus individual contributions from the team.

The facilitator starts the WABM group process by asking, "What work do we do?" Through brainstorming, team members identify the activities they perform. One member of the team writes these activities on cards, and another pins the cards onto the storyboard. This process continues until all required information is attached.

Once the work has been documented, organized, and measured, the work team moves to the action phase of the process. Here the team contacts the customers and suppliers of the process and asks them to form a joint team.

The joint team develops a storyboard of the overall process, which combines activities and measurements from the separate storyboards of the individual teams. It also includes a determination of key cost drivers for the joint process and their impact on overall performance. This information is used to set priorities for improvement and to develop plans for action.

A POSITIVE IMPACT

The workforce activity-based management group process has a positive impact on an organization and its workforce. This impact results from these characteristics:

■ *The people who do the work have the most knowledge about what they do.* Involving persons who do the work in developing the ABC information improves its quality and usefulness because they understand the work and are best able to improve it.

- *WABM is a bottom-up process.* The work teams develop and maintain the activity-based information, which gives them ownership of the information and increases the likelihood they will use it to improve their performance.
- *The group process is a "shared experience."* All employees share the experience of communicating and solving problems with a common language. This shared experience helps eliminate barriers to communication and cooperation and helps customers and suppliers work together to make changes that have the largest positive impact on their joint performance.
- *Storyboards are easy to learn and use.* Storyboards are not expert tools that intimidate workers. Their simplicity helps make workforce activity-based management an easy process to learn and practice.
- *WABM takes little time from the primary work of the teams.* Workforce activity-based management soon becomes an integral part of a team's daily work. The process is mastered quickly by the work teams and is applied on an ongoing basis without excessive time and effort.
- *WABM integrates information into everyday work.* Activity-based information belongs to the workforce; employees create it, possess it, maintain it, and use it daily. This procedure increases their ability to accept responsibility, bringing empowerment and accountability.
- *WABM allows everyone to function as his or her own accountant.* Each work team and member of the work team participates in the measurement process, which eliminates the need for large numbers of staff to develop and maintain systems and changes the staff's primary role from technician to coach.

ACTIVITY-BASED INFORMATION

This fact-based process uses activity-based information (ABC) to describe work and its results. It applies this information to a wide variety of strategic and tactical issues such as what price to set, what product mix to sell, and which improvements to make.

An ABC model contains two types of information to help answer these questions: cost information and process information. Cost information explains the cost of work and its use. Process information explains why the work is done and how well it is performed, and it describes relationships with customers and suppliers.

Figure 1 shows a graphical representati[on of activity-]based information called the two-dimensional [ABC] cross. Each type of information in the cros[s has a] role in the continuous improvement proces[s.]

Information about activities enhances under[standing of] the team's work and the cost of doing it and is used to iden[tify] costly activities and to reveal nonvalue-added work.

Information about objects of work explains how work and its cost are affected by the volume, lot size, design, or requirements of each product or customer. It helps the work teams plan workload and resource requirements as well as

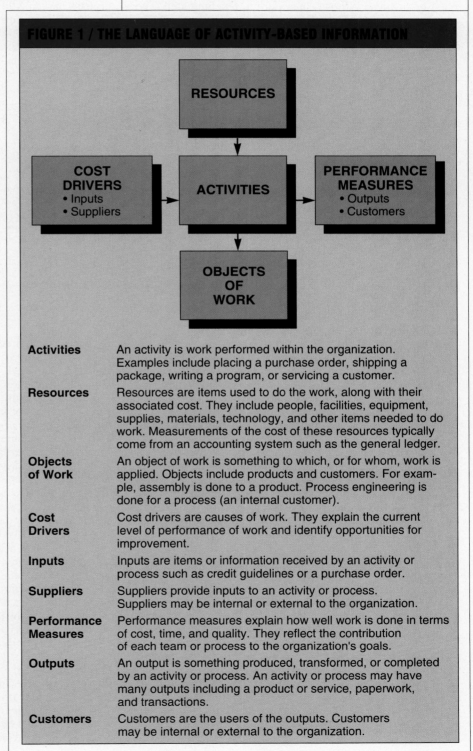

FIGURE 1 / THE LANGUAGE OF ACTIVITY-BASED INFORMATION

Activities	An activity is work performed within the organization. Examples include placing a purchase order, shipping a package, writing a program, or servicing a customer.
Resources	Resources are items used to do the work, along with their associated cost. They include people, facilities, equipment, supplies, materials, technology, and other items needed to do work. Measurements of the cost of these resources typically come from an accounting system such as the general ledger.
Objects of Work	An object of work is something to which, or for whom, work is applied. Objects include products and customers. For example, assembly is done to a product. Process engineering is done for a process (an internal customer).
Cost Drivers	Cost drivers are causes of work. They explain the current level of performance of work and identify opportunities for improvement.
Inputs	Inputs are items or information received by an activity or process such as credit guidelines or a purchase order.
Suppliers	Suppliers provide inputs to an activity or process. Suppliers may be internal or external to the organization.
Performance Measures	Performance measures explain how well work is done in terms of cost, time, and quality. They reflect the contribution of each team or process to the organization's goals.
Outputs	An output is something produced, transformed, or completed by an activity or process. An activity or process may have many outputs including a product or service, paperwork, and transactions.
Customers	Customers are the users of the outputs. Customers may be internal or external to the organization.

entify problem products and customers. At the company level, product cost and customer cost are useful for making strategic decisions.

Cost drivers describe the causes of work. Some causes are positive, such as a customer order that presents an opportunity to serve. Other causes are negative, such as errors in documentation that cause rework. Negative cost drivers explain why work requires excess cost, time, and poor quality, and their removal is the key to permanent improvement.

The identification of inputs and suppliers helps reveal the causes of waste (the cost drivers) as well as the entities that must be involved if those causes are to be eliminated. The root cause of a problem often exists within a supplier's operation, requiring the involvement of the supplier in its resolution. For example, errors in customer specifications (the input) received by engineering may originate in the sales department (the supplier).

Performance measures explain how well the work is done. They cover the cost, time, and quality of the work. They are used to determine the baseline for continuous improvement and can be compared with external benchmarks. They also are used to set targets for improvement.

Customers and the outputs they receive are important because they are affected by changes in work practices. The involvement of customers and suppliers in the WABM process ensures that priorities for improvement are set based on the process-wide impact of the changes.

The availability of activity-based information to the workforce plays an important role in the continuous improvement process:

A typical storyboard.

- *ABC is easy for everyone to understand and use.* ABC can be applied successfully by workers everywhere regardless of industry and culture. This success has been achieved in U.S. companies even where workers have limited formal education and a limited grasp of the English language.
- *ABC removes barriers to communication.* ABC is a common language that transcends conflicting terminology and data. It allows fact-based cross-functional problem resolution and helps customers and suppliers achieve joint performance improvements.
- *ABC is the only source of information about cost, time, and quality, and it allows fact-based decisions about improvement priorities.* No longer just a cost system, ABC contains a full array of activity-based information. Choices can be made based on cost, time, and quality, and priorities for improvement projects are set based on hard facts rather than unquantified preferences.
- *ABC shows all employees how they contribute to the organization's goals.* ABC information reveals how the actions of each work team affect the success of the organization and its customers and allows priorities to be set for maximum improvement in total performance.
- *ABC lets every employee accept financial responsibility for the success of the organization.* Each employee knows how he or she affects financial performance and can take responsibility for actions that will improve the bottom line.

ORGANIZATIONS MUST FOCUS

A focused organization has everyone pointed and moving in the same direction. Its goals are sufficiently clear so everyone understands them, and they represent a complete statement of where the organization wants to be. In addition, the goals are measurable so all employees know when they have been achieved.

Focus is crucial to continuous improvement. Without it, improvement efforts may fail to enhance overall business performance. For example, Company A selects improvement projects based on their impact on quality, but it does not measure their impact on cost. Company A is unfocused because its improvement efforts are prioritized based on the impact on quality alone rather than on quality *and* cost.

Achieving focus requires a vision and a clear, complete, and measurable set of goals based on the vision. The vision and goals must be shared by everyone in the organization. But focus also requires that everyone have a set of performance measures based on the organization's goals. These performance measures allow all employees to see how they contribute to business performance and provide the basis for selecting priorities for improvement.

For example, an automobile manufacturing company has primary goals for the profitability, time, and quality of the vehicles it produces. The company selects vehicles as its primary unit of work. It develops performance measures for profitability, time, and quality per vehicle that match its key goals. The profitability measures are *average sales dollars per vehicle* and *average cost per vehicle*. The timeliness goal is the *average number of days of lead time* from the day an order is placed to the time a vehicle is delivered. The quality goal is *average part per million (PPM) defects*.

Each work team has a similar set of performance measures. Each set of measures is complete (they cover cost, time, and quality) and consistent with overall company goals and performance measures. The work teams collectively are responsible for every component of the company's profit margin, time, and quality. For example, the final assembly work team's responsibility is for the cost, time, and quality of its work. It selected the performance measures *assembly cost per vehicle, assembly lead time per vehicle,* and the *PPM defects in assembly* to reflect these responsibilities.

Clarity is achieved because the measurements are simple, easy to calculate, and few. Each work team has a minimum of three performance measures (one each for cost, time, and quality) and a maximum of seven. Experience has shown the value of a limited number of measures—most people cannot achieve more than seven measures simultaneously.

For instance, the purchasing work team at the automobile company has four performance measures. Its primary unit of work is the *number of purchase orders processed*, so its cost measure is the *cost per purchase order*. The team also tracks the *purchasing cost per vehicle* to show how it fits directly with the company's cost measure. Its other measures are *purchasing lead time* and *purchase order errors*.

WABM provides such focus to everyone. While bottom-up processes fuel employee involvement, they don't always result in improved performance. On the other hand, focused performance measures allow each work team to direct its work for maximum improvement in company performance. Combining focused performance measures with the empowerment effects of activity-based information and the group process yields superior results.

HOW WABM AFFECTS A COMPANY

The three elements of workforce activity-based management—ABC information, a group process, and focus—combine to change an organization in several important ways, which include changes in employee empowerment, worker accountability, roles and responsibilities, decision making, and organization structure.

Empowerment. Empowered workers have "responsibility, a sense of ownership, satisfaction in accomplishments, power over what and how things are done, recognition for their ideas, and the knowledge that they're important to the organization."[1] The group process creates a feeling of job ownership and a belief that the team can change its work practices. ABC information helps workers understand what it is they do. It also shows the workers exactly how they contribute to the goals of the organization and how they can improve organizational performance. The "shared experience" with other team members as well as with customers and suppliers increases their feelings of being connected to the rest of the organization.

Accountability. WABM helps move employees from an attitude of entitlement to one of accountability. An entitled employee is one who says, "I do what I am told to do. Therefore, I am entitled to my pay, raises, promotions, benefits and so on." Entitlement is an inevitable consequence of not understanding how one contributes to the organization. Without information about work and its consequences, and without the responsibility to make business decisions, workers only can be passive in their relationship to the organization. They are mentally disconnected from their work.

WABM involves sharing information with workers. ABC information helps them understand what it is they do and how what they do affects the performance of the organization. This knowledge allows them to make business decisions that improve organizational performance.

ABC information helps workers move from entitlement to accountability. An accountable employee is one who says, "I understand how my actions affect the financial performance of this company. Therefore, I share responsibility for the success of the business."

Accountable employees are mentally connected to their organization. They understand what it is they do, why they do it, and how well they do it. They are fully engaged in the success of the organization.

Roles and Responsibilities. WABM helps change the roles and responsibilities of managers and workers. The traditional role of a manager is to make decisions and give direction. This role is appropriate for managers because, in most organizations, they have the responsibility, knowledge, experience, and information to make these decisions. In contrast, workers do not possess these advantages and only can take direction from managers.

These roles change with WABM because of the availability of information to the workers and because of their involvement in the group process. Workers can accept responsibility, can participate in business decisions, and can develop their skills in addition to doing work. Managers, freed from some of their traditional responsibilities, spend more time as coaches, facilitators, communicators, and resources.

Decision Making. In a traditional organization, decisions are made by managers. With WABM, decisions can be made at levels below management because workers now possess the information they need in order to make knowledgeable decisions.

The extent to which this happens depends not just on the availability of information, but on whether workers have been empowered to take on responsibility for business performance and have been trained to accept this responsibility.

The impact can be significant. The quality of decisions improves because of the accuracy and completeness of ABC information. The speed of decision making increases because those who do the work make the decisions (the chain of command is bypassed). Organizational learning is enhanced as workers grow in experience and knowledge.

Organizational Structure. WABM often reveals organization structure as the root of poor performance. The artificial dividing of work into vertical functions creates communication barriers and results in excess cost and time and in poor quality. Re-engineering the process—such as combining separate work teams into one process-wide work team—is a frequent result. For example, a joint production-sales team may decide, as a result of WABM, to move the production scheduling process into the sales department, putting the work closer to the external customer, eliminating communication problems between the two departments, and cutting overall process cost, time, and errors.

ONCE AGAIN

Let's review. WABM uses information to focus everyone on continuously improving profitability, time, and quality. It integrates ABC into the world of work teams and total quality management (TQM) and goes far beyond what either ABC or TQM can accomplish separately.

WABM uses a group process whereby work teams develop, maintain, and apply ABC information. Teams document and measure their work on workspaces called storyboards and use them for brainstorming and solving team problems. The group process builds commitment to the overall WABM process and fosters ownership of the ABC information.

WABM adds focus to improvement efforts—something that often is missing from TQM. All employees understand how they can change their work to help improve business performance and that they are accountable for their contribution to that performance. Workers accept more decision-making responsibility, and managers become a coach, facilitator, communicator, and resource.

The most important connector is money. With every single employee having bottom-line responsibility, knowledge of ways to improve financial performance, and reasons to do so, a company can't help but become more profitable. ∎

This article is adapted, with permission, from Peter B.B. Turney, Workforce ABM, Cost Technology, Portland, Ore., 1993.

Peter B.B. Turney is president and CEO of Cost Technology and author of the best-selling book, Common Cents. *He spearheaded the development of workforce activity-based management at Cost Technology and has helped implement this new process at companies all over the world. He can be reached at (503) 645-2434.*

[1] William C. Byham, *Zapp! The Lightening of Empowerment,* (Pittsburgh: Development Dimensions International Press, 1989).

Is this article of interest to you? If so, circle appropriate number on Reader Service Card.	Yes 70	No 71

Section 5

ABC Management Systems in Action

A number of practitioners—managers, controllers, treasurers, and others—already have applied the concepts of ABC management systems in their firms. The articles in this section report a wide range of applications, from cost-of-quality reporting to setting the standard for ABC applications for a defense manufacturer. Besides focusing on product costs, many practitioners coupled their work with a quality approach, focusing on the customer and continuous improvement of processes and activities. In most cases the practitioners felt that ABC added value and was an excellent tool for managing activities and providing for continous improvement.

In the first article, "Cost of Quality Reporting: How We See It," Richard K. Youde tells how the firm Sola Optical focused on failures in cost-of-quality (COQ) reporting because their internal failure costs were so high. They used the ABC approach because relating quality costs to activities enhances the usefulness of the report and overcomes a limitation of traditional COQ reporting—the failure to associate costs with activities. Their COQ report compiles the costs of the most important quality-related problems along with their respective cost drivers. In addition to the direct cost of failure (cost of rejected product), ripple costs (complexity costs due to rejected product) are included.

As Youde indicates, "combining cross-functional costs caused by quality failure into a single metric provides management with the information needed to evaluate each type of failure relative to others and focus resources on the most important problem." At Sola, the ABC COQ report is a powerful tool for managing quality improvement activities.

The reader will find the second article, by Thomas E. Steimer, a genuine surprise. The title, "Activity-Based Accounting for Total Quality," does not suggest that the article deals with the assignment of home office costs (corporate G&A) to business units. These costs are assigned using ABC methodology coupled with the TQM approach, which focuses on the customer and continuous improvement of processes and activities. Steimer, manager of government contract accounting practices for Westinghouse, uses his department (part of the corporate controllers staff) to illustrate this application.

He proposes the following guidelines to accomplish the task:

1. Begin by analyzing each function performed by staff members at headquarters to determine if their services are needed. The objective is to perform only those services that are needed and add value. To accomplish this first step you have to identify your customers.

2. Find out whether the customer is satisfied. Then you can rank the activities in terms of importance determined by your customer.

3. Study ways to improve customer service in these activities (continuous improvement) or decide if the activities can be performed more effectively by other headquarters departments or operating units.

4. Allocate resources to activities.

5. Assign the cost of each activity to customers on the basis of appropriate cost drivers (which the author lists for each activity). As Steimer states, services performed effectively at the corporate level will add value to the business units.

Brian Pederson, author of the third article, "Weyerhaeuser: Streamlining Payroll," is manager of payroll services at Weyerhaeuser. As he sees it, costs are driven by or are the direct result of activities, and you have to manage the activities to gain effective cost reduction. For him ABC is a real benefit. He thinks of department activities in terms of measurable processes, in a framework with suppliers as inputs and customers as outputs.

He lists the five steps it takes to get a cost per transaction (divide the cost of the activity by the activity indicator or cost driver) to measure activity improvement. All department employees participate in sessions to support improvements to existing processes, so as to reduce processing time or cost.

Pederson indicates that activity cost profiles and transaction cost trends will be developed annually. His employees have the knowledge to implement process efficiencies that will result in cost reduction.

In the fourth article, "Costing for Warehousing and Distribution," Harold Roth and Linda Sims apply ABC concepts in a service environment, namely warehousing and distribution. Required is the costing by specific activity and customer charging based on the customer's unique usage of warehouse activities.

The authors define seven warehouse activities, identify the resource costs consumed by each activity, and determine the activity charge per unit (activity driver rate) to invoice each customer for the activities used. Roth and Sims indicate that some costs cannot be identified with a specific activity (facility costs) and are assigned to each activity based on an arbitrary allocation. In conclusion, the authors indicate that activity information is helpful in reducing the number of times an activity is performed and facilitates the evaluation and reduction of activity unit rates.

Jack Haedicke and David Feil report in the fifth article, "Hughes Aircraft Sets the Standard for ABC," that their firm's goal was to obtain accurate product cost information to support operations management in making operational and strategic decisions. To do so, costs had to be assigned on "the best causal/beneficial relationships (activity drivers) that can be determined, rather than a single allocation base such as direct labor." As a defense contractor, Hughes Aircraft has to meet not only GAAP reporting requirements but also cost accounting standards required by the Department of Defense and monitored by the Defense Contract Audit Agency. The objective was to create a system that met com-

You have to manage activities to gain effective cost reduction.

petitiveness needs rather than have one forced on them by government regulation and their finance department.

The move to ABC, an evolutionary process, encompassed the following steps:

1. Decentralizing from one to nine product-line segments, each with its own unique burden center.

2. Assigning central service costs to each segment burden center on the direct relationship to the way the burden centers absorb cost. These costs were assigned in consensus with the allocating departments and the operating segments absorbing the costs.

3. Analyzing activities and ascertaining that each was accomplished as cost effectively as possible.

4. Charging resources to activity centers based on effort expended.

5. Determining second-stage driver (activity driver) application rates for assigning to products and/or contracts based on consumption.

Government representatives, who were part of the implementation team, agreed with the Hughes ABC model — its collection of costs into activity centers, the derivation of activity driver rates, and application of these rates to the work orders that consumed these activities.

In the final article, "Activity-Based Costing for Marketing," Ronald Lewis states that several articles from 1968-1973 (including one of his own) isolated the activities in the major marketing functions. Further, that "cost drivers, a modern euphemism for activity bases, were identified for each activity within the marketing function." He then lists the steps to be accomplished, using ABC principles, to provide relevant quantitative data that will assist marketing managers to make informed decisions. For this article, Lewis uses five activities to illustrate profitability by territories and product lines. He suggests other activity bases or cost drivers for the different functions (activities) but indicates only those used by the controller of the Atlanta Company, which presumably had the "main causal effect on cost variability."

The author indicates that direct costs for each activity should be accumulated and separated into variable and fixed categories and that contribution analysis should be applied. However, he does not indicate how the resource costs from the general ledger are assigned to the activities, nor does he illustrate the use of contribution analysis in the exhibits presented. ∎

Cost-of-Quality Reporting:
How We See It

At Sola Optical, we focus on failures in COQ reporting because we want to improve activities that lead to failures.

BY RICHARD K. YOUDE, CMA

Since its founding in 1979, Sola Optical, a manufacturer of ophthalmic spectacle lenses in Petaluna, Calif., has enjoyed rapid and continued growth. While management always had focused on maintaining high levels of product quality and customer service, it had no real understanding of the costs of achieving these goals nor of the opportunities for improvement. Instead, management relied on and gave credibility to traditional financial reporting and cost accounting systems because sales and profits continued to grow.

Three years ago, Sola Optical was given responsibility for the spectacle lens division of a newly acquired business. The integration of additional product lines and three geographically diverse manufacturing plants, along with the doubling of sales volume and the number of employees, added new complexity to the running of the business. Management's attention was focused on the integration process and the bottom line pressures brought with it.

Through this period, management and employees began to think about the application of world-class manufacturing (WCM) concepts such as total quality management (TQM), just-in-time (JIT) manufacturing, quality function deployment, and activity-based costing. While the company had little direct experience with the WCM concepts, many employees had been exposed to them through trade journals and seminars.

The company had no previous exposure to cost of (poor) quality reporting, but through the process of implementing WCM it developed a powerful new approach to cost-of-quality reporting that had a positive impact.

TQM/JIT IMPLEMENTATION

Management's interest in world-class manufacturing concepts led to the hiring of a consultant to help establish an approach for its implementation. The work included development of a TQM/JIT execution plan and the calculation of cost of quality (COQ) for the divisional headquarters site, which included the division's largest factory and all marketing, administrative, and engineering support. Sola Optical's financial results, shown in Figure 1, are typical of U.S. manufacturing companies before implementing TQM, showing 20% of sales dollars being consumed by poor quality.

Management accepted the consultant's proposal for implementing Total Quality Management and Just-in-Time techniques including:

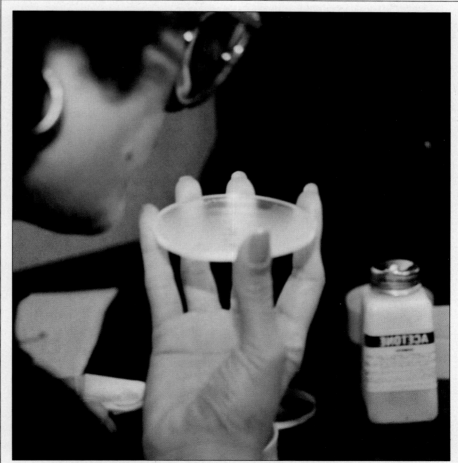

Above: Technician inspects glass moulds for defects. The cost of inspecting products for defects is very important for developing COQ reports.

- Establishment of a TQM steering committee to oversee the implementation,
- Creation of a dedicated cross-functional TQM resource staff as a new organizational entity,
- Formation of four pilot TQM teams, and
- Contracting for the consultant's services to get the project started.

The total quality management effort initially was focused on operational effectiveness. The steering committee included the divisional president, his reporting staff, senior manufacturing managers, and TQM resource staff members who were drawn from manufacturing, marketing, quality control, research and development, and finance. The resource staff was given a charter to facilitate the implementation of TQM/JIT within Sola.

Four pilot projects with the greatest opportunity for savings were selected from the manufacturing area, and each one involved improving process yields and product quality. In a dual-track implementation role, the consulting personnel concurrently facilitated quality improvement teams, beginning with the four pilot teams, and provided training to Sola employees in TQM/JIT techniques. Special emphasis was placed on coaching the TQM resource staff who quickly assumed the responsibility of educating other employees in TQM/JIT techniques and facilitation of quality improvement teams.

To begin the process of cultural change, management decided to provide TQM and JIT overview training to a large number of employees. Overview/introduction classes totalling 20 hours were given to nearly every employee over a period of six months.

The pilot teams and TQM resource staff were successful, and more teams were formed in manufacturing, distribution, and administrative areas. The new teams were assisted by the consultant and TQM resource staff associates. Members often worked in areas of interest to the individual team members, however, and were not focused in the areas known to offer the most opportunity for savings. In retrospect, it was clear that many teams needed better direction, which could have been provided by better cost-of-quality information.

CLASSIC COST OF QUALITY

The initial COQ study prepared by the consultants used the classic approach and identified,

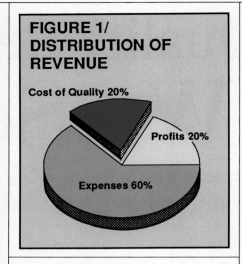

FIGURE 1/ DISTRIBUTION OF REVENUE

Cost of Quality 20%

Profits 20%

Expenses 60%

Through the process of implementing WCM, Sola Optical developed a powerful new approach to cost-of-quality reporting.

through interviews with operating and financial managers and employees, costs of (poor) quality and classified them into four categories: prevention, appraisal, internal failure, and external failure.[1] The purpose of the COQ report was to make management aware of the magnitude of the cost and to provide a baseline against which the impact of future continuous improvement activities could be gauged.

The report demonstrated that relatively few dollars were spent on defect prevention, that appraisal costs were high (because our quality control department used final inspection to assure only good products were transferred to inventory), and that internal failure costs were extremely high. External failure costs were shown to be quite low, attributed to the high level of quality inspections performed and the corresponding high appraisal costs.

TQM teaches that dollars spent in preventive activities such as designing product for manufacturability, training, and development of procedures will be recovered manyfold through reduced appraisal and failure costs. By measuring over time the relative costs of prevention, appraisal, internal and external failure, management can observe whether continuous improvement activities are paying off.

COST-OF-QUALITY STUDY

The COQ study was successful in alerting management to the magnitude of the costs and was a reasonable baseline against which to measure future performance for the site as a whole. It did not suggest specific actions that individual managers and employees could take to make improvements. Therefore, quality improvement teams did not have the information necessary to focus on the most important problems.

The lack of focus by some quality improvement teams contributed to loss of interest in the process by some employees and frustration of both management and quality improvement team members at the slow progress toward achieving real quality improvements.

ACTIVITY-BASED APPROACH

A method had to be devised to ensure that operating managers and quality improvement teams were focusing their activities appropriately in order to assure the success of the TQM/JIT implementation effort. Gaining management's attention and commitment is a basic requirement of world-class manufacturing concepts. Management initially supported the implementation of TQM/JIT and accepted the original cost-of-quality figures. A way was needed, however, to get its buy-in and support of specific quality improvement activities.

One of the limitations of traditional COQ reporting is its failure to associate costs with activities. Activity-based costing has shown that costs cannot be controlled. Rather, one must control activities that in turn cause costs. Relating quality costs to activities greatly enhances the usefulness of the cost-of-quality report.

The solution, in terms of cost-of-quality reporting, lies in applying techniques from world-class manufacturing, such as activity-based costing, JIT and TQM, to the development of quality costs. TQM provides simple statistical tools, such as run sheets and Pareto charts, identifying the most important problems. An activity-based cost-of-quality report works like a Pareto analysis, showing the relative

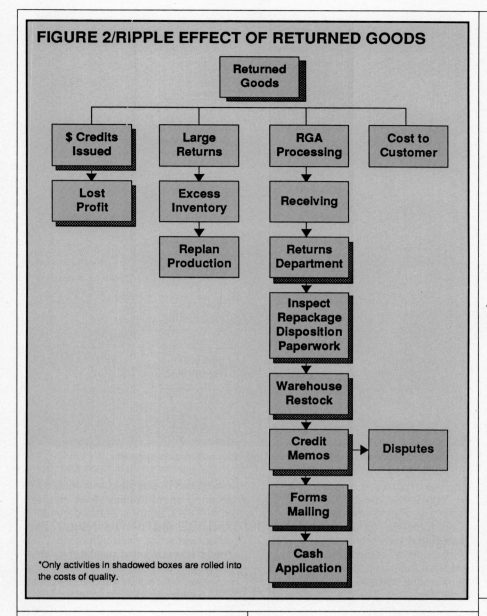

FIGURE 2/RIPPLE EFFECT OF RETURNED GOODS

Returned Goods

- **$ Credits Issued**
  - **Lost Profit**
- **Large Returns**
  - **Excess Inventory**
    - **Replan Production**
- **RGA Processing**
  - **Receiving**
    - **Returns Department**
    - **Inspect Repackage Disposition Paperwork**
    - **Warehouse Restock**
    - **Credit Memos** → **Disputes**
    - **Forms Mailing**
    - **Cash Application**
- **Cost to Customer**

*Only activities in shadowed boxes are rolled into the costs of quality.

ending with the activities associated with issuing a credit memo. When large returns occur, the very complex production and inventory planning cycle is disrupted because of unplanned inventory. Finally, the chart reminds readers that there is a cost to the customer as well.

Inclusion of the ripple effect charts in the COQ report provides readers with a better understanding of their operations. The use of these charts is a powerful tool, drawing attention to opportunities for improvement. Incorporating the ripple costs, along with the direct cost of failures, in the COQ provides the same effect.

DEVELOPING AN ACTIVITY-BASED COQ REPORT

We identified eight steps (see Table 1) in developing an activity-based COQ report.

1. *Identify cost and service problem areas:* The first step in developing an activity-based COQ report is to identify the most important cost- or service-related problems. At Sola Optical, the division president and representatives from marketing, manufacturing, materials, accounting, management information systems, and customer service were asked to identify the five most important problems/opportunities in terms of costs or customer satisfaction. Then a review of the initial COQ report, prepared by the consultants, was conducted to assure no important costs included in it were omitted from the list.

The list was edited to eliminate any

costs of the most important quality-related problems along with the respective cost drivers. JIT is a philosophy promoting the elimination of waste. Quality failures and all the activities surrounding them fall within the definition of waste.

THE RIPPLE EFFECT AND RIPPLE COSTS

At Sola Optical, we focus on "failures" in COQ reporting because we want to improve the activities that lead to failures, the major contributor to cost of quality. Besides the direct cost of failures, such as the cost of rejected product, we wanted to show the complexity the failure itself added to our processes. Thus, we coined the term "ripple effect," defined

as the activities resulting from a real or potential failure. For example, the resources consumed reworking a defective product constitute the ripple effect, as do the activities associated with inspecting a product even when no defect actually exists. We also include in the cost of quality the "ripple cost" (costs of the ripple effect). Results of interviews with managers, supervisors, leads, and workers identified ripple effects of returned goods (see Figure 2).

An analysis of the chart shows that credit memos issued for customer returns result in lost gross profit on the sale. Shown next are the steps in returned goods processing (RGA processing), beginning with the receiving department, followed by the returned goods department and warehouse, and

TABLE 1/STEPS IN DEVELOPING AN ACTIVITY BASED COST OF QUALITY REPORT

- Identify cost and service problem areas.
- Summarize problems to a manageable list.
- Identify ripple effects.
- Calculate ripple costs.
- Condense the list again.
- Summarize information for presentation.
- Review with managers and steering committee.
- Publish and present to employees.

ideas that were not related to COQ. For example, one interviewee had identified the need for employee development. But this was considered inappropriate for this purpose.

2. *Condense problems to manageable list:* The list was summarized and ranked according to the number of responses for each idea. Then a condensed list of ideas was developed based on the number of responses and knowledge of costs and cost of quality. The ideas that remained on the list after this step were those for which data could be collected and for which the cost of quality would be high enough to warrant further consideration.

Some ideas were judged too impractical to include. For example, the cost associated with inaccurate finished goods' inventory records was dropped because of the difficulty in quantifying the costs.

Next, ripple charts were prepared and reviewed with the original interviewees to ensure their accuracy. Changes were incorporated into a final copy of the ripple chart.

3. *Calculate ripple costs:* Several principles guided the development of costs, especially ripple costs. First, it is important to recognize that the intent of COQ reporting is to provide reasonably accurate information for use in allocating resources, not to develop a complex cost accounting system. The purpose of measurement is to tell the organization whether it is heading in the right direction.

Second, the information needs to be absolutely credible. At Sola, we wanted to avoid challenges to the whole process based on disagreements over minor elements of cost. The approach taken was to include only costs that were easily supportable. Not all ripple activities shown on the ripple charts are included in the cost. The reported cost of quality, therefore, is the minimum, and is in fact understated. But employees can recognize that the ripple chart includes other activities that contribute to cost and system complexity.

Finally, we wanted to make monthly reporting very simple. Costs that are readily available, such as the direct cost of rejected product, would be included as calculated. Costs that are not readily available, particularly those combining cross-functional activities, would be estimated on a per occurrence basis. When monthly COQ reports are prepared only the actual number of occurrences need to be collected. Calculations then are based on

Cost-of-quality charts are posted at Sola Optical for supervisors to review.

the per occurrence cost.

The development of yield-loss costs serves as a good example of this process. Yield loss represents the costs associated with product rejected. The direct cost of product rejected was taken from the cost accounting system and broken down by the major production processes. The cost of one major ripple effect, the quality control department (i.e., inspection), also was available from the accounting system.

The remaining ripple costs, which included disposing of product reject, record keeping, and production costs caused by a higher level of starts, were estimated on a per reject basis. The estimated costs of these activities over a six-month period were divided by the number of reject lenses produced for the same period. Ripple costs for the six areas were calculated by the same methodology.

4. *Condense the list again:* It may be necessary to condense the list again if the total costs of any of the potential areas are not significant enough to be included in the report. At Sola Optical, it was our original intent to identify 10 of the most significant COQ areas (more would tend to de-focus management attention). At this point, our list was

condensed to six: yield loss (defective product), mold (tooling) loss, employee turnover, injuries, finished goods stockouts, and customer returns. Two other cost areas, excess finished goods' inventory and machine downtime, looked like strong candidates for inclusion but required more research.

5. *Summarize information for presentation:* The goal of COQ reporting is to present concise, usable information. Presenting too much detail is a sure way to lose the interest of the audience. It is the responsibility of quality improvement teams to develop and present their own detailed information.

The sequence of presentation should be adapted to the business culture. At Sola Optical, we chose to present overall costs first—shown in total, then annualized as a percent of sales and as a cost per employee—followed by the individual COQ areas. Figure 3 shows an example of the total costs chart.

Individual COQ area costs then are shown together on similarly scaled graphs so that relative value of the costs is obvious. Then charts for each of the COQ areas along with their respective ripple charts are presented.

For each area, the total cost per month, annualized cost, percent of the appropriate overall level of activity such as sales or production value, and the activity cost driver are shown.

For each of the COQ areas, costs are broken into direct and ripple costs on the chart.

6. *Review with managers and steering committee:* The first presentation was reviewed with key managers whose acceptance was critical to the success of the whole reporting process. If at this late date any information was to be challenged, it was better to resolve the problem individually than have the validity of the data undercut in a formal presentation.

The next step was to present the COQ report to the TQM steering committee, whose key members already had been exposed to the information. This presentation was designed to generate discussion regarding the use of the information so that management, through quality improvement teams, could address these important problems.

7. *Publish and present to employees:* After the initial report has been reviewed with the steering committee, it is advisable to review it with as many employees as possible so they understand its purpose and contents. Formal presentations to quality improvement teams and to the individual departments within the organization, along with regularly distributed reports, were methods used to improve employee understanding.

8. *Continuously improve the report:* The COQ report is an ever-changing and improving report based on the needs of the company. As quality improvement teams achieve cost reductions, the specific cost areas being measured will change. There is a continuing need to ensure resources are being applied to the most important problems. The entire process described here should be completed each year to ensure the best information is being provided.

A POWERFUL TOOL

At Sola Optical, the activity-based cost-of-quality report is a powerful tool for managing quality improvement activities. Quality improvement teams are focused in the most important areas with the ripple effect concept being key to this method. Combining cross-functional costs caused by a quality failure into a single metric provides management the information needed to evaluate each type of failure relative to others and focus resources on the most important problems. The activity-based cost-of-quality approach can be applied easily in any business environment. ∎

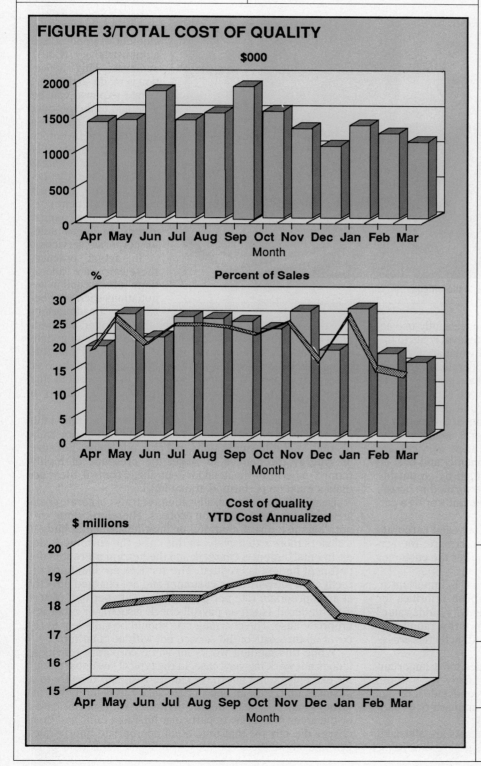

FIGURE 3/TOTAL COST OF QUALITY

$000

Percent of Sales

Cost of Quality
YTD Cost Annualized

Richard K. Youde, CMA, is controller at Attachmate Corp., Bellevue, Wash. He is a member of the Bellevue-Eastside Chapter. This article was submitted through Redwood Empire Chapter.

[1]Wayne Morse, Harold Roth, and Kay Poston, *Measuring, Planning, and Controlling Quality Costs*, Institute of Management Accountants, Montvale, N.J., 1987.

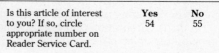

Is this article of interest to you? If so, circle appropriate number on Reader Service Card.	**Yes** 54	**No** 55

Activity-Based Accounting For Total Quality

Analyzing activities means better service to the customer.

BY THOMAS E.
STEIMER

**Certificate of Merit,
1989-90**

Activity-based accounting is ideally suited to total quality management because it encourages management accountants to analyze activities and determine their value to the customer. In the typical multi-segmented corporation concerned with achieving world-class status through the total quality approach, management accountants may successfully use activity-based accounting to assign corporate-level costs to the business units. In following the total quality management approach, the company will provide its operating business units with a great deal of autonomy, reduce layers of management, and optimize the level of corporate staff support.

Author Steimer in his office.

The first step is to analyze each function performed by staff members at headquarters to determine if their services are needed by the customer (the customer is usually the operating business units or divisions). If these services are needed, how can they be performed efficiently and cost effectively? Should the services be performed by an outside contractor or in-house? If services are performed in-house, should they be performed by the operating units or by a corporate entity?

To answer these questions, managers of each corporate activity must determine who their customers are, the services important to the customer, and whether the customer is satisfied with the services.

Furthermore, an understanding of what is important to the customer enables managers to establish priorities for services performed. For example, if the activity "adds value" to the customer, it achieves a higher priority rating. Resources for low-priority or "nonvalue-added" activities are reduced and, if possible, eliminated.

Once managers determine the activities most important to customers, they should continuously study ways to improve customer service in these activities or decide if the activities could be performed by other headquarters departments or operating units more effectively.

In many corporations, corporate staff costs are allocated to operating units on a general base, such as payroll or sales,

where they become an element of general and administrative (G&A) expense. This allocation is made so that corporate expense can be assigned to the product for pricing purposes and for IRS inventory valuation. To comply with Cost Accounting Standards and the negotiation of contract costs, government contractors also must charge business units for corporate services.

In actual practice, these corporate "allocations" often result in negotiations each year between headquarters and the business units. It is either the stronger business units or those units in trouble that may be able to negotiate concessions. Managers may argue, "I can't absorb all this corporate expense without affecting pricing and market share or my profit objective. Besides, I don't need all this service, and probably could do it more efficiently at my own location."

At the corporate level of the total quality organization the objective is to perform only those activities that are truly needed by the business units and that add value. Because of synergy, economies of scale, the presence of highly trained experts, or the need for centralized control, these activities must be performed at that level.

Despite these reasons, allocations of truly corporate costs are subject to the negotiation process. Therefore, some corporations use direct charging or interdepartmental budget transfers more extensively. In this case, the customer's departmental budget is charged, and the headquarters staff department budget is credited. The services are identified directly with the particular customer and are charged directly at an appropriate rate per person-hour, rate per unit of service rendered (such as payroll check issued), or other appropriate base. The charging rate should be sufficient to recover all the costs of the service but with no "markup."

While this method works for some corporate activities, it does not work in every case. In the typical law department, for example, some attorneys can be assigned directly to a business unit, with an appropriate salary transfer. Other attorneys may be able to identify their time with specific cases or the areas of interest to particular business units and then charge directly for that time at an appropriate hourly rate. But what about the corporate tax, antitrust, intellectual property, or labor-law attorney who is involved in issues of corporate policy? Isn't there a better way than either direct charging or allocating on an arbitrary basis? I think there is.

A BETTER WAY

Does your firm have corporate costs that are difficult to charge directly and for which allocations on a general or negotiated base do not provide accurate or acceptable costs to the business units? If so, activity-based accounting can be used effectively.

I recommend an analysis of activities and surveys of customers during the annual financial planning and budgeting process. It is important that managers from headquarters departments and their customers in the operating units discuss the activities that add value and the services performed. Based on these discussions, one or two "cost drivers" should emerge for each activity. Most departments perform several activities. For each, resources must be assigned, the cost determined, and the most significant cost driver selected.

For example, the headquarters treasury department might perform these significant activities: cash management, collections of delinquent accounts, foreign currency management, and debt management. A cost driver must be selected for each one.

FINDING THE COST DRIVER

During the budgeting process, the managers must list their resources and forecast their costs. These resources include employees, computers, and other assets. Costs include salaries, benefits, travel, communications, and office supplies. If a manager uses activity-based accounting, then he or she must identify activities in order of priority, determine the cost of the resources consumed by each activity, and determine the cost driver appropriate for each. After the necessary data are gathered, the cost of each activity can be assigned to the business units.

COMMITMENT TO TOTAL QUALITY

How can an activity-based accounting system be used in conjunction with a commitment to total quality management in assigning corporate home office costs to business units?

Most of the literature on activity-based accounting has focused on the use of an activity-based cost system at a plant or single-location company, particularly those which have introduced advanced manufacturing processes such as computer-aided manufacturing or robotics or "just-in-time" procurement and, therefore, which need a better system for measuring product cost and making pricing decisions than through the use of direct-labor-based overhead rates. Activity-based accounting can be used in the assignment of home office costs, sometimes referred to as "corporate overhead" or "corporate G&A expense," to the business units or segments of a corporation.

First, what is total quality management (TQM)? Although each corporation will develop its own approach to suit its particular culture and management style, certain characteristics are common to most total quality management systems. They are:

- *Focus on the Customer*: Identify the customer, determine his needs and priorities, then do whatever it takes to satisfy him. This process requires a cultural change in many corporations, which may operate on the premise that "I know what my customer wants."
- *Continuous Improvement*: Once the commitment to total quality is made, the job is never done; it is a way of life, and it involves the continuous improvement of every phase of every activity. It is the antithesis of the "If it ain't broke, don't fix it" approach, for there is a better way to perform every task.
- *Active Support and Involvement of Top Management*: The CEO must actively demonstrate his dedication to total quality to employees at every level, to shareholders, and to the community so that everyone is aware of the primary importance of total quality.
- *Active Involvement of All Employees*: Top management must encourage everyone in the corporation, from factory worker to clerical employee to professionals and managers, to become actively involved in the process.
- *Measurable Objectives*: Set measurable objectives, and develop meaningful measurement systems.
- *Provide Recognition to People*: Develop a meaningful award program to recognize achievement of difficult objectives.
- *Training*: Training at all levels is necessary to achieve the culture change required in a customer-focused environment.

At one company, Westinghouse Electric Corporation in Pittsburgh, the CEO, John C. Marous*, is completely dedicated to total quality, which he defines as "performance leadership in meeting customer requirements by doing the right things right the first time." Mr. Marous, in an address at the U.S. Air Force Aeronautical Systems Division's quality symposium in Dayton, Ohio, defined three essential elements of total quality:

- CUSTOMERS. The RIGHT THINGS can only be defined by our customers.
- PROCESS. Process—the active mechanism which makes things happen—must be optimized.
- PEOPLE. Total Quality becomes a reality only when people take ownership and participate.

Mr. Marous has established the annual George Westinghouse Total Quality Awards, in which divisions, business units, and headquarters activities compete in two categories: "Best" and "Most Improved" Total Quality Performance. The Westinghouse Productivity and Quality Center, near Pittsburgh, has formed and trained Evaluation Teams, which do an exhaustive review of each candidate organization's performance to determine a rating. To win, the organization really has to do all the right things right. In 1989, the first year of the competition, the winner in the BEST category was the Thermo-King truck-trailer division, which has achieved a reputation for outstanding customer service. Thermo-King is representing Westinghouse in this year's Malcolm Baldridge Quality Award Competition.

Mr. Marous retired as Chairman and Chief Executive Officer of Westinghouse Electric Corporation on June 30, 1990. He was succeeded by Mr. Paul E. Lego.

Corporate policy should dictate whether it is necessary to assign the actual costs of each activity to the business units on a monthly or quarterly basis or if the budgeted amount can be assigned each month to the business units and the corporation absorbs the variance. If the corporation is a government contractor, "actual" costs must be assigned to each business unit that engages in government business.

In a company committed to total quality management, this is an ongoing process of continuous improvement. This process includes:

- Surveying customers,
- Setting priorities for activities,
- Deciding whether to shift activities from headquarters to the business units or to other headquarters departments,
- Budgeting and allocating resources to activities, and
- Assigning the cost of each activity to customers on the basis of appropriate cost drivers.

Some benefits to companies include a breakdown of departmental barriers, a flatter organization, and fewer layers of management. The process also can encourage the efficient use of cross-functional teams and working groups to bring several viewpoints to bear in discussions on how to provide better customer service. Employees at all levels assume a greater amount of responsibility.

Mr. Steimer and George K. Muhlberg, director of government contract accounting practices, Westinghouse.

ONE MANAGER'S CONTRIBUTION

To illustrate this process, let's look at a typical corporate staff department in a large, diverse corporation that has embraced total quality management. The corporate culture and management style are changing—more autonomy is being given to the business units, and certain corporate services are being decentralized and moved to these units.

The corporate staff functions are examining the activities they perform in order to concentrate resources on those activities which add most value and those which must remain centralized.

The government contract accounting department is part of the corpo-

rate controller's staff. In preparation for the annual financial planning and budgeting cycle, the department manager analyzes the activities his department performs. He lists these seven activities (Table 1). An eighth activity—consulting with the divisions about their particular contracts, auditing, and accounting problems—was discontinued. The divisions must now provide their own expertise.

The department manager performed an initial customer survey, which resulted in this ranking by the divisions of the Table 1 activities: 3, 7, 5, 4, 1, 2, and 6. Armed with this information, he decides to assign more resources to item 3, Negotiation of Corporate Costs; item 7, Training; and item 5, Policy Manual. He will allot fewer resources to item 2, Disclosure Statement, and item 6, Industry Associations. However, in preparing his departmental budget for next year, he sees that his resources are inadequate to provide the improved level of services because one member of his small staff plans to retire. He reviews alternatives and decides to:

- Shift Activity 7—Training—to the Education and Training Department at headquarters. He will consult with them on the specific training programs to offer, and they will include these courses in their catalog at reasonable and competitive prices to the business units. (The person who is retiring handled the training. Perhaps the Education and Training Department can arrange for the retiree to teach the courses or train another instructor.)
- Meet with the manager of the corporate financial policy department, who is responsible for the company's controller's manual. He asks the manager to consider assuming responsibility for the government accounting policy manual. He suggests that the financial policy department hire a freelance writer to supplement its staff because it plans to convert the controller's manual from print to electronic media.
- Cut travel expenses by reducing attendance at industry association meetings next year by 50%.

The manager now has adequate resources to de-

TABLE 1/GOVERNMENT CONTRACT ACCOUNTING DEPARTMENT ACTIVITIES

1. Allocate corporate costs to segments in conformance with the federal government's Cost Accounting Standards (CAS).

2. Prepare the corporate CAS "Disclosure Statement."

3. Submit the "costs claimed" to the government, and negotiate the acceptance of these corporate costs and their allocation to segments, where they are recovered on government contracts.

4. Negotiate "advance agreements" on important elements of cost with the corporate administrative contracting officer (the chief government negotiator).

5. Prepare a "Government Accounting Policies and Practices Manual" to guide operating segments with government contracts.

6. Monitor government regulatory and legislative changes and developments through membership and participation in industry associations.

7. Conduct training programs for government accounting specialists and other accounting and auditing personnel in the business units.

vote to the preparation and negotiation of the Corporate Claim, item 3; the Advance Agreements, item 4; and the Cost Allocations, item 1. These changes will improve the service to his customers and, incidentally, improve relationships with the corporate ACO[1] and his government auditors by devoting more time and resources to their concerns.

Training will be improved because it will be handled by experts. Because the policy and practices manual will be converted to electronic media, only the essential policies will be retained and it will be reduced by 50%. In addition, the business units will be encouraged to establish their own accounting practices within that policy framework.

The next steps are to assign resources to each of the remaining activities; to determine the budgeted cost of each activity; and then to identify cost drivers for activities 1, 2, 3, and 4. Activity 6, Industry Associations, is being cut 50% because it does not add value to the business units. Because it is a necessary corporate activity, it will continue to be allocated as an element of corporate G&A expense on a "residual" or general base. Activities 5, Policies and Practices Manual, and 7, Training, will be transferred to other corporate departments.

The selection of cost drivers may not be easy. Those selected during the initial year should be monitored to see that they accurately reflect a causal or beneficial relationship to the activity being charged. The customers of the government contract accounting (GCA) department are those divisions of the corporation that are in the government contracting business—only those divisions will generate the cost drivers used for assigning the cost of the activities.

Table 2 summarizes the GCA activities; the percentage of departmental resources devoted to each activity, current and future; and the method selected for next year's allocation base.

The use of activity-based accounting to assign corporate costs to customer divisions or business units is particularly valid for government contractors. According to the Cost Accounting Standards Board, the use of a "causal/beneficial" base is preferred to the use of a general or residual base for costs that cannot be charged directly.

CAS 403, "Allocation of Home Office Expenses to Segments," states "The purpose of this…Standard is to establish criteria for allocation of the expenses of a home office to segments…based on the beneficial or causal relationship between such expenses and the receiving segments."

THE FIRST YEAR

The first year of conversion to an activity-based system will be the most difficult because of the culture change and learning process involved. In the typical headquarters staff operation, it may be necessary to have a two-stage assignment of costs. First, the headquarters service departments, such as building maintenance; heat, light and power; typing pools; PC training and service; mail; copy centers; telephone and fax expense, and so on, may have to be assigned to the staff departments—law, treasury, controller, human resources, and others. This may be done through the use of direct charging or cost drivers.

In stage two, the headquarters staff functions, which are the customers of these headquarters service departments, will then follow the allocation process outlined. Each staff function will have a different mix of activities and customers and must choose the appropriate method of charging.

Treasury, for instance, will probably use activity-based accounting to charge most of its services to the operating

TABLE 2/COST DRIVERS

GCA Activity	% of Resources 1990	1991	Basis for Allocation
Allocate Cost	30	35	Dollar value of outstanding government contracts at year-end at each division.
Disclosure Statement	10	10	Man-days of government audit activity at each division annually.
Corporate Claim	30	45	Dollar value of sales to U.S. government customers.
Advance Agreements	5	5	Dollar value of sales to U.S. government customers at each benefitting division.
Policy Manual	5	0	Residual, General Base (for example, Payroll)
Industry Associations	10	5	Residual, General Base (for example, Payroll)
Training	10	0	Direct charge per course.

units. The law department, on the other hand, will probably make use of all methods: direct assignment of staff personnel to the business units; direct charging of the cost of specialists in labor law, environmental law, etc., when working on a specific case; activity-based accounting with appropriate cost drivers when staff attorneys are working on "truly corporate policy" issues; and, perhaps, a general residual base for allocating the cost of the executive vice president who heads the department.

BETTER MANAGEMENT

I believe in the use of an activity-based accounting system for the assignment of corporate headquarters expense to business units in a multi-segmented corporation. The efforts involved in surveying customers, analyzing activities, and determining appropriate cost drivers is certainly preferable to the old authoritarian allocation approach. Managers will feel they are better able to manage their businesses when they know what they are being charged with. Furthermore, when it is clear that services are performed efficiently at the corporate level, it will add value to their businesses. ■

Thomas E. Steimer is manager, Government Contract Costs, Westinghouse Electric Corporation. A certified professional contracts manager, Mr. Steimer is a member of NAA's Pittsburgh Chapter, through which this article was submitted.

[1]The Corporate Administrative Contracting Officer is a U.S. government procurement official appointed by the Department of Defense to negotiate and resolve issues involving costs charged to government contracts.

Is this article of interest to you? If so, circle appropriate number on Reader Service Card.

	Yes	No
	60	61

Weyerhaeuser:
Streamlining Payroll

Activity-based accounting makes it easy to identify cost savings.

BY R. BRIAN PEDERSON

Payroll typically isn't an issue with management accountants. As long as it's running okay, nobody gets too excited about it. Activity-based costing is different. That's something accountants can get enthusiastic about. These two areas aren't mutually exclusive, however, as Weyerhaeuser's Payroll Services Department found out when it began to develop yardsticks for measuring payroll efficiency.

On the surface, the payroll process appears to be fairly simple. The payroll department needs to write a set number of checks on a regular basis and distribute them to employees. To the casual observer, it would seem that the cost to provide this service should be relatively low. A more detailed analysis reveals that the preparation of checks is only one of several services provided by the payroll department. Furthermore, each of these payroll services can be broken down into a series of activities. Because department costs are driven by or are the direct result of activities, any effective cost reduction program requires the management of those activities. Activity-based costing can be a real benefit here.

A department process flowchart is a useful tool for beginning the analysis of costs. Preparation of the flowchart requires management to think of department activities in terms of measurable processes with inputs from suppliers and outputs delivered to customers. Figure 1 displays a payroll process flow. Typical payroll services include:

- Producing regular paychecks,
- Producing special paychecks,
- Updating employee records for other compensation,
- Processing deferred compensation and employee stock options,

A Weyerhaeuser employee team discusses a specific cost reduction idea.

- Processing employee relocation expenses,
- Providing payroll tax reporting,
- Performing payroll department administrative activities, and
- Performing other payroll services.

Activities related to several of these services are as follows:

- Update and maintain employee master file records,
- Process hours worked (time input),
- Process changes to employee deductions,
- Pay deductions,
- Maintain process controls,
- Review system edit reports/audit output,
- Update and modify software programs,
- Calculate checks,
- Prepare labor adjustments,
- Print checks,
- Distribute checks and reports,
- Coordinate bank direct deposit activity,
- Journalize accounting entries,
- Reconcile payroll general ledger accounts,

- Stop pay and reissue checks, and
- Respond to inquiries.

Several activities are specific to particular services:

- Provide payroll tax reporting:
  Prepare federal tax reports,
  Prepare state and local tax reports,
  Deposit/pay taxes withheld,
  Prepare unemployment tax returns,
  Review and interpret new tax law changes, and
  Prepare annual W-2 reporting.

- Payroll department administrative activities:
  Employee performance reviews,
  Staff meetings,
  Budgeting/planning, and
  Sort mail/order supplies.

- Other services:
  Update and revise payroll forms,
  Develop training material for payroll users,
  Provide employment verifications,
  Attend customer meetings,
  Add new payroll groups to the system, and

Attend training sessions/conferences.

Not included in our definition of the payroll process is the maintenance of employee benefit functions, which includes the operation of employee health care plans, retirement plans, and 401K plans, that are performed outside the payroll department at Weyerhaeuser.

DEVELOPING COST PROFILES FOR PAYROLL SERVICES

Once the major services of a payroll department are established and the related activities recorded, their costs can be determined by allocating the employee time spent on each activity. Employees should be asked to estimate the percentage of their time spent on each function over the period of one year. The one-year time frame is recommended so activities that occur only annually, such as W-2s or budgeting, are included in the cost profiles. The majority of activities in a payroll department reoccur on at least a monthly basis, so for most employees this means estimating time spent for a month-long period. If there is general discomfort by employees in estimating their time allocations, a certain period should be agreed upon for tracking the actual time spent.

Figure 2 shows a sample of an employee activity time worksheet that can be used by all employees, including department management, to allocate time spent on department functions. When employee data have been collected, department salaries can be spread to the various activities based on the headcount equivalent assigned to each function. Salaries may be allocated using a single average department salary rate or using multiple salary rates based on different grade levels. It probably is a good idea to avoid spreading salaries based on the actual amounts paid if confidentiality is

FIGURE 1/PAYROLL PROCESS FLOW

Suppliers	Inputs	Activities			Outputs	Customers
		Maintenance	Production	Disbursements		
Personnel Reps.	New hire, termination, rate of pay data	Maintain payroll & tax master files	Process input	Print checks & reports	Bi-weekly paychecks	Employees
		Maintain process controls	Prepare labor adjustments	Distribute checks & reports	Weekly paychecks	Government Agencies
	Bonus, commission pay data	Review system edit reports	Calculate checks		Special paychecks	Business Units
			Stop pay & reissue checks			Human Resource Managers
Compensation Dept.	Deferred comp. & stock option data	Maintain deferred comp. & stock option systems		Pay deductions	Pay stub earnings statements	Personnel Reps.
						Accounting Personnel
Group Insur. & 401K Depts.	Voluntary benefit deductions	Maintain employee benefit structure				Accounts Payble Personnel
Employees	Time cards, employee deductions		Respond to inquiries		Check requests for Accts. Pavable Dept.	Employee Benefits Personnel
Relocation Specialist	Relocation expense reports, moving data	Maintain relocation & other comp. special pays	Process expense/ moving stmts.		W-2 earnings statements	Banks & Credit Unions
Dun & Bradstreet	Tax change data, Software updates	Maintain tax formulas & tables	Prepare tax reports	Pay withholding taxes	Payroll tax reports	
			Modify software programs			
Employees, Government Jurisdictions	W-4s, levies, garnishments				Payroll register reports	
General Accounting Department	General ledger code changes		Prepare journal entries & memos		Journal vouchers & intercompany memos	
Employees, Gov't. Agencies, Personnel Reps., Dept. Managers	Payroll inquiries		Reconcile ledger accounts		Responses	
			Respond to inquiries			

a concern.

The employee activity time work-sheet can be used as a basis for allocating salaries to department activities, but costs other than salaries must be assigned separately to department services. Examples of nonsalary costs are depreciation, computing, and printing charges. These costs can be assigned to related department activities using any reasonable method.

In our example, computing costs allocated from our Information Systems group were assigned to the "calculate checks" activity. Relative job run times were used to break the total computing bill into the service categories of regular paychecks, special paychecks, other compensation, and so on. Printing costs, also allocated from our Information Systems group at three cents a page, were assigned to the various payroll services based on the number of pages printed. Depreciation expense was allocated to activities based on employee use of the depreciated equipment. Thus, depreciation on personal computer equipment used for reconciling accounts was assigned to the "reconcile general ledger accounts" activity, which was, in turn, allocated to the various payroll services based on the percentages of time spent by employees on the reconciliation process.

Any remaining costs not applied as salaries or assigned to specific activities can be allocated to functions based on the time apportionments identified by employees. For example, telephone costs, office rent costs, and office supplies can be grouped and allocated to activities based on the same percentages as the employee time spent on those same functions.

DETERMINATION OF TRANSACTION COSTS

The preparation of cost profiles for payroll services and activities is the first step in developing meaningful statistics that can be used to measure the gains from process improvements. The next step is to establish activity indicators for each cost pool. These indicators can be any quantifiable volume indicator that is a natural outcome of each function. For example, the costs to produce regular paychecks could be measured by the number of regular paychecks produced during a one-year period. Dividing the cost of the service by the related activity indicator provides a cost per transaction figure that becomes a yardstick for measuring progress of cost reduction improvements. Once department personnel discover that each regular payroll check costs $4, for example, any proposed changes in the

FIGURE 2/PAYROLL PRODUCTS & SERVICES (Percent of Time)

NAME _____

Bi-Weekly Paychecks
_____ Process input
_____ Review edit reports/audit output
_____ Prepare labor adjustments
_____ Maintain process controls
_____ Calculate checks
_____ Print checks and reports
_____ Distribute checks and reports
_____ Stop pay and reissue checks
_____ Modify software programs
_____ Maintain files and records
_____ Coordinate direct deposit activity
_____ Pay deductions via check request
_____ Prepare JVs and memos
_____ Reconcile general ledger accounts
_____ Respond to inquiries

Weekly Paychecks
_____ Process input
_____ Review edit reports/audit output
_____ Prepare labor adjustments
_____ Maintain process controls
_____ Calculate checks
_____ Print checks and reports
_____ Distribute checks and reports
_____ Stop pay and reissue checks
_____ Modify software programs
_____ Maintain files and records
_____ Coordinate direct deposit activity
_____ Pay deductions via check request
_____ Prepare JVs and memos
_____ Reconcile general ledger accounts
_____ Respond to inquiries

Special Paychecks
_____ Process input
_____ Review edit reports/audit output
_____ Prepare labor adjustments
_____ Maintain process controls
_____ Calculate checks
_____ Print checks and reports
_____ Distribute checks and reports
_____ Stop pay and reissue checks
_____ Modify software programs
_____ Maintain files and records
_____ Prepare JVs and memos
_____ Reconcile general ledger accounts
_____ Respond to inquiries

Manually Processed Pay Activity
_____ Process manual pays
_____ Process other compensation
_____ Prepare JVs and memos
_____ Respond to inquiries

Relocation Expense Processing
_____ Update & balance relocation system
_____ Reconcile general ledger accounts
_____ Process expense statements
_____ Prepare JVs and memos
_____ Respond to inquiries

Payroll Tax Reporting
_____ Prepare state & local tax reports
_____ Prepare federal tax reports
_____ Pay withholding taxes
_____ Modify software programs
_____ Reconcile general ledger accounts
_____ Prepare JVs and memos
_____ Respond to inquiries
_____ Prepare unemployment tax returns
_____ Consolidate taxes—other P/R systems

Administration
_____ Performance reviews
_____ Staff meetings
_____ Sort mail/order supplies
_____ Budgeting

Other
_____ Customer/problem resolution meetings
_____ Savings bond processing
_____ Document payroll procedures
_____ Update and revise payroll forms
_____ Develop training material for regions
_____ Add new groups to the payroll system

process of producing regular paychecks can be assessed for their favorable impact on the per unit cost.

Other activity indicator examples for payroll services are the number of special paychecks, the number of payroll tax returns prepared, or the number of employment verifications processed. Regardless of the indicator chosen, the volume of activity must be applied to the related cost pool in order to establish the unit cost of each function. As future department activity levels change, total costs may rise or fall, disguising any progress in process efficiency. By comparing unit transaction costs over time, the real change in activity costs can be measured.

USING THE DATA

The development of cost profiles and their related activity indicators produces the necessary data to begin the process improvement phase. Cost data now are available for each major department service and its related activities. This information becomes a tool that can empower employees to implement process improvements and reduce operating costs.

Without a doubt, the most important part of this process is the participation of all department employees. Department staff members have an intimate knowledge of the payroll processes and are in the best position to offer significant cost-saving ideas. Employee participation is needed not only for tracking the time spent on payroll activities but also for suggesting and implementing improvements to payroll processes.

Once the cost profiles are complete, the data need to be shared with all department members. This information sharing should lead to group brainstorming sessions wherein employees suggest improvements to existing processes with emphasis on ideas that either reduce processing time or reduce costs. All ideas should be recorded during these meetings, and employees should be assured that management is interested in everyone's thoughts, with all suggestions given serious consideration. If a large number of ideas are generated during these sessions, the individual suggestions may be grouped by categories for the analysis stage.

The next step is to ask employees to volunteer their time for investigating the ideas to determine which ones offer significant time and cost savings.

The team approach seems to work well in this phase, with several people working on an idea to gather information about the practicality of the proposal and developing an estimate of any potential savings. Ideas that attract no volunteers may be saved for future investigation or may be dropped if the sponsor agrees to rescind the original suggestion.

The group needs to agree on a time frame for completing the analysis of the ideas so that the estimated savings from all proposals can be reviewed at one time and the group can prioritize the proposals based on relative cost or time savings. Once the ideas have been reviewed by the group, employees again are asked to volunteer for participation on teams responsible for planning and scheduling the implementation of the ideas.

THE WEYERHAEUSER EXPERIENCE

Weyerhaeuser's corporate office payroll department provides payroll services for approximately 14,000 salaried and 2,000 hourly employees. Payroll is processed on Dun & Bradstreet HR:M software using an IBM mainframe computer. Monthly cost allocations are received from other corporate groups for their services. Some of these charges are for office rent expense, postage and mail service, mainframe computer usage, telephones, and audit services. The payroll group in turn allocates all its department costs to business and corporate units that use the payroll services. These costs are charged to customers based on the number of employees paid plus additional charges for unique services such as consolidating payroll tax liabilities for multiple manufacturing units within a business. This charge methodology was chosen so that charge recipients could relate their costs to levels of activity clearly.

Weyerhaeuser's payroll department used this activity cost review process during 1990 in an attempt to improve department efficiency and reduce operating costs. All department employees participated in each phase of the program. A total of 111 ideas was identified during the brainstorming sessions, and 31 were selected for further analysis by the teams. Following the analysis, 12 proposals were selected for implementation with projected annual cost savings of $558,500. The payroll department will complete the

implementation of these ideas during 1991 and then revisit the balance of the suggestions generated by the group during the brainstorming sessions. Cost profiles will be developed on an annual basis so that activity and transaction cost trends can be monitored and employees can see the favorable impact of their efforts.

Examples of ideas offered by employees were reducing the number of report pages printed and distributed, standardizing the pay periods for hourly employees, automating the payroll computer job setup routine, outsourcing the data entry function performed internally, and producing special paychecks on a less frequent basis. The implementation of the various ideas resulted in the elimination of two positions in the department. These reductions were accomplished through normal staff attrition as positions left open from employee resignations were not filled.

A similar activity-based costing process was used by other corporate accounting groups to determine the costs of their products and services. Significant cost saving ideas were identified in the General Accounting, Accounts Payable, Accounts Receivable, and Consolidations departments. Our 1991 operating budgets were adjusted to reflect the anticipated savings from implementing the ideas so that department managers could chart their progress during the year.

Activity-based accounting provides an important tool for measuring the efficiency of a payroll department. When provided with departmental cost data, employees have the knowledge to develop and implement process efficiencies that will result in cost reductions. Employee participation is the key to success because programs that do not have work-force participation are never easy to implement. ∎

R. Brian Pederson is manager, payroll services, at Weyerhaeuser in Tacoma, Wash. He holds a B.A. degree in accounting from the University of Washington and is a member of the Mt. Rainier Chapter, through which this article was submitted. Mr. Pederson may be contacted be writing to him at Weyerhaeuser, TB-1100, Tacoma, WA 98477, or by calling (206) 924-7052.

Costing for Warehousing and Distribution

Using ABC in a warehouse can affect the bottom line.

BY HAROLD P. ROTH, CMA, AND
LINDA T. SIMS

In recent years, activity-based costing (ABC) has emerged as a management accounting technique that overcomes some of the limitations of traditional practices. However, most of the literature dealing with ABC focuses on product costing issues and ignores the benefits ABC can provide in a service environment. One service that is particularly well suited for applying ABC concepts is warehousing and distribution.

ABC is based on the principle that activities cause costs. To provide a basis for understanding how costs are driven by activities, Robin Cooper has developed a framework for analyzing activities.[1] His framework consists of four levels of cost-driving activities: (1) unit level, (2) batch level, (3) product level, and (4) facility level.

Unit-level activities are incurred for each unit produced. For example, inserting a bolt or performing a welding operation is a unit-level activity. The key to identifying a unit-level activity is that it is repeated for every unit produced. The cost of these activities can be traced directly to products based on their use of the activity.

Batch-level activities are performed once for each batch or group of units. An example of a batch-level activity is moving a pallet containing 100 units from one process to the next. Batch-level activities are identifiable when the activity is repeated for each group and their cost can be averaged over all units in the batch.

W. Lamar Sims.

Delivery of goods is a significant cost. Here a tanker is being unloaded.

Product-level activities are incurred to support the production of different products. Examples include maintaining bills of materials and expediting production. These costs can be traced to a specific product line but are not identifiable with a specific unit or batch.

Facility-level activities are those that relate to the plant as a whole, such as security, maintenance, and administration. If all costs are to be assigned to products, the costs of facility-level activities need to be allocated to products on some volume-based measure because the activity is not related directly to a unit, batch, or product.

Other writers have suggested that process-level activities should be an additional, separate type.[2] Process-level activities are related to a process within the plant rather than to a unit, batch, product, or the entire facility. These activities include repairing and maintaining equipment and supervising employees. Process-level activities must be conducted if operations are to continue, but they are not incurred in proportion to the number of units, batches, or products. Thus, the cost of process-level activities cannot be assigned directly to a product based on the activity, and some allocation basis such as machine hours will be needed if process-level costs are to be assigned to products.

When ABC is used to cost services and the cost is used as a basis for charging clients, the activities should be classified by levels. Clients then can be charged for unit-level, batch-level, and product-level activities based on their use of the activities. The cost of process and facility (i.e., warehouse) activities, however, will require some allocations based on a volume-related measure if clients are charged directly for these activities. An alternative to direct charging is to add to the other costs a markup sufficient to cover the process and facility costs.

WAREHOUSING ACCOUNTING AND ACTIVITIES

Although warehousing and distribution costs may not be considered a part of most activity-based costing systems, managing warehousing costs is critical to the profitability of many firms. In a study conducted prior to the emergence of ABC, Ernst & Young (then Ernst & Whinney) identified the planning, measuring, allocating, and reporting of warehousing costs as an essential component in effective warehouse management.[3] The firm also noted the role of activities in determining costs as follows:

"There is no substitute for accurate and practical determination and allocation of warehousing costs. The particular method of cost allocation depends on the company and its products, but the proper costing by specific activity and the allocation to products based on their unique storage and handling requirements are critical for effective warehousing management.

Public warehouse operators have progressed beyond most manufacturing and merchandising companies in this area. Many public operators have instituted excellent systems for cost determination, allocation, and reporting."[4]

Although different activities are encountered in different types of warehouses, the study identified six general ones: (1) receiving; (2) put-away; (3) storage; (4) order picking; (5) packing, marking, and staging; and (6) shipping.[5] A brief description of these activities is presented in Table 1.

If these six activities are classified by the levels described earlier, most of them appear to be unit, batch, or product level. For example, receiving, put-away, order picking, packing, and shipping could be either unit-, batch- or product-level activities depending on whether the shipments and orders contained more than one unit and/or product. The storage activity, however, involves costs incurred for the entire warehouse. Thus, if products are charged or clients are billed directly for the space used for storage activities, warehouse-level costs need to be allocated to products or clients to determine the total amount.

The following illustration demonstrates how ABC can be implemented for a warehousing operation. The building serves as a storage and distribution facility for companies that supply yarns, chemicals, and dyes primarily to carpet mills. The services (activities) provided by this warehouse are shown in the first column of Table 2. Although some are the same as the services listed in Table 1, others vary, and an explanation is given in column two.

The cost of the activities listed in Table 2 is used as the basis for billing clients. The billing rate is determined by adding a markup for profits to the cost of performing the activity. The billing process is designed to pick up all charges for every service rendered during the month. Table 3 is an example of how a client is charged for use of activities.[6]

The basis for determining the rates shown in Table 3 depends on the specific activity and the types of costs that are driven by the activity. For most activities, the costs include clerical and administrative costs as well as warehouse labor costs. Because of the record keeping required in a public warehouse, much of the administrative and clerical costs can be traced directly to the cost-causing activity. A brief description of the costs generated by each undertaking and the basis for determining a client's use of an activity follows.

RECEIPT OF MERCHANDISE

Receiving merchandise involves unloading incoming shipments and checking them to verify the items and quantities noted on the bills of lading. For this practice, clients are

---

TABLE 1/GENERAL WAREHOUSING ACTIVITIES

Activity	Description
Receiving	Unload the vehicle. Check products are not damaged.
Put-away	Location for product is identified and inventory records are updated.
Storage	Products are physically stored.
Order Picking	Products are retrieved from storage. Inventory records are updated.
Packing, Marking, and Staging	Products are appropriately packaged, labelled, and placed on loading docks for shipment.
Shipping	Load vehicle. Bill of lading and notification of shipment prepared.

SOURCE: Ernst & Whinney, *Warehouse Accounting and Control: Guidelines for Distribution and Financial Management*, National Council of Physical Distribution Management, Oak Brook, IL, and Institute of Management Accountants (formerly National Association of Accountants), Montvale, NJ, 1985, p. 29.

Forklift operator places tank on scale for weighing as part of the handling process.

W. Lamar Sims.

charged at a rate per 100 pounds received. The rate covers both "in" and "out" labor costs and differs according to the product and the weight per container, with smaller containers bearing a premium rate. The costs prompted by this activity include the expense of warehouse and office labor, the time used by the hyster forklift, and pallets used. The amount of labor and hyster time is determined from time studies of the activity. The cost of the pallets used is based on actual usage.

STORAGE SPACE

The rent charged for the storage activity is based on costs incurred for the warehouse. Thus, the costs are facility-level costs. They include building rent, depreciation on leasehold improvements, repairs and maintenance, and property taxes. They are allocated to the various bays within the warehouse contingent on space (i.e., a volume measure) to determine the monthly charge. Clients are billed on the basis of space used, which is computed by the number of drums, number of pallets, and/or number of cases of inventory.

SHIPMENT OF MERCHANDISE

The shipment of merchandise involves office support for processing orders. Warehouse labor is not included in this activity because it is charged as a part of the receiving rate. The merchandise shipped to a client is determined from the bills of lading. The cost of the office personnel required to process this

document is based on time studies that show the period required to record the order, type the bill of lading, and post

to the inventory records. Office supplies are added to the labor cost of each shipment, and clients are charged at a rate per bill of lading.

INVENTORYING

The inventorying activity involves maintaining perpetual inventory records and verifying the quantities on hand. The charge for this activity is determined by the number of articles inventoried and the amount of detailed information required by the client. Costs incurred in this activity are mainly office labor and supplies. Time studies are used to determine labor, and office supplies are composed of special preprinted forms for each client.

DELIVERIES

The delivery activity involves transporting goods to the client's customers using the ware-

TABLE 2/SPECIFIC WAREHOUSING ACTIVITIES FOR THE EXAMPLE

Activity	Description
Receipt of Merchandise	Chemicals, yarns, and dyes are received via common carrier or boxcar and are unloaded by warehouse personnel.
Storage	Chemicals, yarns, and dyes are physically stored in warehouse bays.
Shipment of Merchandise	Office personnel account for chemicals, yarns, and dyes shipped to clients' customers by company truck, customer's truck, or common carrier.
Inventorying	Inventories are physically counted by warehouse personnel and compared with the perpetual inventory records.
Deliveries	The company truck is used for deliveries to the clients' local customers.
Repackaging	Materials are repacked upon request from the client.
Restenciling	Product labels are changed by removing old labels and replacing with new.

TABLE 3/ILLUSTRATION OF CHARGING FOR WAREHOUSING ACTIVITIES

Activity	Usage During Month	Charge per Activity Unit	Total
Storage-Rent	25,000 sq. ft.	$0.10 sq. ft.	$2,500
Receipt of Merchandise	10,000 lbs.	$1.50 per CWT	150
Shipment of Merchandise	25 bills of lading	$5 per bill of lading	125
Inventorying	1,000 items	$0.25 per item	500
Deliveries	25 bills of lading	$10 per bill of lading	250
	800 lbs. average per bill of lading	$1.60 per CWT	320
Repackaging	2,000 lbs.	$10 per CWT	200
Restenciling	100 drums	$5 per drum	500
Total			$4,545

96

house company's trucks. Delivery activities for each client are determined from the bills of lading. For this activity, an average cost per shipment is calculated by totaling the costs for the month and dividing by the total number of deliveries. Costs include gasoline, repairs, maintenance, depreciation, and labor.

Although an average cost per shipment is calculated, clients are charged for deliveries at a fixed rate of $10 per bill of lading plus a variable charge per 100 pounds. The fixed fee is designed to assure that clients cover the burden of delivering small quantities. COD deliveries are extra because of the responsibility of collecting and mailing the check to the client.

REPACKAGING

Repackaging charges are determined from the inventory change orders, with the rate based on the number of pounds repackaged and the packaging material supplied. The costs of repackaging include labor, warehouse supplies (e.g., paint), and office supplies (e.g., inventory change order forms). A labor time study is used to determine the time required for repackaging, for posting to the inventory records, and for preparing the inventory change order.

RESTENCILING

Restenciling charges are ascertained from the inventory change orders. Time required, the number of packages restenciled, and the amount of supplies (such as paint, stencils, and labels) used make up the rate. The costs used as the basis for the rate include labor, office supplies, and warehouse supplies. The time required for this activity is founded on time studies.

For all of these activities, the labor cost includes wages, payroll taxes, employee benefits, workman's compensation insurance, and employee insurance expenses.

OTHER COSTS

In addition to costs that can be identified with a specific activity, others are assigned to each activity based on an arbitrary allocation, including supervisory and management salaries, commercial insurance, utilities, licenses, advertising, and public relations.

The activity cost data from an ABC system for a warehouse provide managers with valuable information. In a public warehouse, the data can be used as the basis for the rates charged to existing clients and for quoting rates

to potential clients. Thus, to be competitive, warehouse managers need to know the value of providing various services, and activity-based costing provides a method for determining those costs.

Managers of private warehouses of manufacturers and merchandisers also need information about the cost of activities to determine which activities are being performed excessively. This disclosure could show if they are being performed efficiently. Because the activities are the cost drivers, managers should be able to use activity information in two ways to help reduce costs—first, to decrease the number of times an activity is performed and, second, to reduce the cost per unit of activity. Regardless of which method is chosen, managers need information about activities and costs if they are to make the best decisions.

Manufacturers and merchandisers also can use ABC to determine the total cost of a product line. Although warehousing costs generally are treated as an expense rather than as a product cost, they should be traced as accurately as possible to product lines to evaluate the products' profitability. ABC provides the information needed to trace these costs to products. ■

Harold P. Roth, CMA, CPA, Ph.D., is an associate professor of accounting at the University of Tennessee-Knoxville. He is a member of the Knoxville Chapter. Linda T. Sims is secretary/treasurer of Sims Warehouse Inc. in Dalton, Ga. She is past president of the North Georgia Chapter, through which this article was submitted.

[1]Robin Cooper, "Cost Classification in Unit-Based and Activity-Based Manufacturing Cost Systems," *Journal of Cost Management for the Manufacturing Industry*, Summer 1990, pp. 5-6.
[2]George J. Beaujon and Vinod R. Singhal, "Understanding the Activity Costs in an Activity-Based Cost System," *The Journal of Cost Management for the Manufacturing Industry*, Spring 1990, p. 70.
[3]Ernst & Whinney, *Warehouse Accounting and Control: Guidelines for Distribution and Financial Management*, Oak Brook, IL: National Council of Physical Distribution Management, and Montvale, NJ: National Association of Accountants, 1985, p. 11.
[4]Ernst & Whinney, p. 11.
[5]Ernst & Whinney, pp. 27-29.
[6]The rates shown in Table 3 have been modified to maintain relative cost relationships while preserving the confidentiality of the data.

W. Lamar Sims.

Warehouse worker affixes label to stainless steel portable tote tank before it is shipped. Each recyclable tank holds 3,000 lbs. of liquid dyestuffs.

Is this article of interest to you? If so, circle appropriate number on Reader Service Card.

	Yes	No
	66	67

IN A DOD ENVIRONMENT
Hughes Aircraft Sets the Standard for ABC

Once the Activity Centers are carved out, the next challenge is developing relevant cost drivers with the help of operations personnel.

BY JACK HAEDICKE AND DAVID FEIL

The Hughes Aircraft activity-based costing project is helping to usher in a new era of contractor and government cooperation. The aerospace and defense industry companies, while somewhat shielded from foreign competition, now are facing competitive pressures of their own. Recent changes in Department of Defense procurement policies include second sourcing and leader/follower arrangements that have served to increase competition and level the technological playing field. Those contractors who win future procurements will be the ones with the lowest costs and the highest quality, not necessarily the highest technology.

Cost competition between contractors therefore has become intense. Current global politics have furthered these competitive pressures as DoD contractors become casualties of a peacetime economy and face forced consolidations and often painful conversions to commercial product lines.

The good news, perhaps, is that contractors now perceive the need to change. What role can the cost accounting community play in reversing this competitive decline? Do our traditional cost accounting systems provide the strategic information U.S. firms need to address these changes? If inaccuracies exist, what has caused them? What regulations apply in a DoD environment, and do changes need to be made to increase contractor competitiveness? What should be, and is, the government's role in encouraging these changes?

Some answers to these questions will be found in the Hughes Aircraft Company's efforts to implement advanced costing systems. The company's experience highlights a new era of cooperative efforts between contractors and members of the Defense Contract Audit Agency (DCAA) in setting the standard for these advancements.

THE NEED FOR CHANGE

As management teams have turned to traditional financial systems to provide the improved product cost information needed to compete, they have become increasingly frustrated at the lack of relevant and reliable data. Technical support staffs that have moved aggressively to incorporate improved manufacturing techniques such as total quality management, just-in-time, cycle time management, and employee involvement have found themselves faced with a financial system that has not changed in more than 50 years.

Traditional systems typically focus on areas that have little to do with the real causes of production costs. This disparity becomes critical when management is seeking relevant information to control the production process and must use a system designed primarily to bill the customer and to report to shareholders. The situation is exacerbated by an overreliance on direct labor base (DLB) as a system for allocating overhead costs. With continued industry specialization, outside procurement will increase. This factor, along with increasing factory automation, will make direct labor decrease even more, and current methodologies for the allocation of cost will become even less relevant.

As an example, the introduction of new or complex products typically requires significant support in the early stages of development. If these products are produced in the same burden center as more mature products, the increased support costs will be subsidized by the more mature product lines. Making a strategic decision to subsidize an introductory or complex product to gain market share in a commercial arena may be a perfectly sound strategic decision, but it is a decision that should be made with full knowledge of the cost relationships. Otherwise, management may draw false conclusions about the profitability of a product line and even terminate products that in reality are profitable. Alternatively, if the subsidy is significant, it can offer a competitor entry into the mature product niche.

EVOLUTION, NOT REVOLUTION

The reason we at Hughes have been successful in implementing advanced costing concepts is that we have evolved these systems carefully over a period of five years, thereby allowing members of local audit to grow and learn with us as equal partners. The evolutionary process we have experienced progresses from the DLB allocation methodologies developed primarily in the era of Sloan and DuPont at General Motors to today's advanced concepts of activity-based costing. In essence, this transition recog-

nizes that in today's environment, activities rather than products are the absorbers of cost. These activity costs should then be assigned to the product on the basis of the best causal/beneficial relationships (drivers) that can be determined rather than on a single allocation base such as direct labor. Our goal is to obtain accurate product cost information. Without it we will be unable to support the operations management in making operational and strategic decisions.

It is an evolution rather than a revolution for many reasons. Perhaps the most important reason is the completion of the educational process for the government and our own staff and the smoothing of any cost shifts that may occur between contracts and business units. After all, we are attempting to create a system that meets the needs of all parties rather than one forced on us by the finance department and government regulation. For that reason, the effort must start at the bottom and work its way to the top, gaining the concensus of each level of management as it proceeds. Revolution rarely will gain the type of concensus required to support such a system.

In selected pilot sites we have gone through this evolutionary process, as described below, to reach our present level of experimentation with fully implemented activity-based costing.

STRATEGIC USES OF ABC DATA

The strategic uses of the improved informational capabilities of an ABC-type model have proved significant, as the following brief description shows.

Shop Mix Analysis. At Hughes Aircraft, internal manufacturing capabilities are expected to be cost competitive with off-load vendors for production (i.e., a program manager can seek what he or she feels is the best price for a product whether produced externally or internally). In the past, these make/buy decisions were made on the basis of the distorted pricing information provided by the traditional system. An ABC-type analysis, therefore, may alter significantly the mix of what is manufactured internally and, as a result, lower overall costs.

Investment Opportunities. In addition, if the shop mix analysis indicates that a certain product produced in the facility is not competitive with products from off-load vendors and if the firm wishes to continue making it internally, the need for process improvements or further capitalization of the facility becomes obvious.

Comparison Across Facilities. When a firm has multiple facilities producing the same or similar products, an ABC analysis of these facilities can provide a way of benchmarking one facility against the others. Because the facilities most likely will have been capitalized in different time periods and have different process flows, each facility probably will excel at a different type of work. This analysis will make it easier to pursue a strategy to create "centers of excellence" whereby each manufacturing operation concentrates on production of those items that it is capitalized to perform best.

Estimating. The current method of estimating used in most DoD environments builds up a series of indirect and direct pool costs on top of the direct labor component of a manufactured part. Direct labor is a component of cost that we already have shown to be decreasing in relevance. In addition, because the functions that are pooled typically have no direct tie to the progressive steps of the manufacturing process, it is difficult for both the estimator and the customer to conceptualize the buildup of cost.

On the other hand, an activity-based estimating system simply requires a listing of activity centers following the production process and factoring of the second-stage driver in relationship to the way the part number uniquely absorbs the activity center's cost.

Design to Cost. With the increasing competition in defense contracting, the cost of products has become an issue of increasing importance. Engineering design staffs, while having a global understanding of the manufacturing process, find it difficult to target cost objectives under a DLB buildup of costs.

An activity-based system focuses on the drivers of production costs such as circuit size and complexity of design and allows a design engineer to predict more accurately the impact of design changes. Cost objectives then become increasingly tangible and, therefore, more readily achieved.

World-Class Manufacturing—Empowering the People. Two of the philosophies espoused by R.J. Schoenberger in his text *World-Class Manufacturing* are the work cell and employee involvement in the manufacturing process. In a properly designed activity-based system, there is little or no difference between an activity center and a work cell. Controllers now can add the component of contribution to product cost to the concepts of JIT, cycle time management, and total quality, all aimed at improving the efficiencies of the manufacturing work cell.

Employees within a work cell have been hampered in their efforts to reduce cost because traditional standards of measurement such as direct labor base or realization lead to faulty decision making in a world-class environment. The standard of measurement in an activity-based system becomes the second-stage driver of cost from the activity to the product. A metric has been established, therefore, which includes all costs of an operation and can confirm individual contributions to cost reduction efforts.

Only by adding the component of cost to the measures of quality, cycle time, and inventory management can a manufacturer truly reach its goal of world-class cost management. ■

THE STEPS TO ABC

Step 1. The Move to Multiple Burden Centers. Many firms we have encountered in the United States have multiple product lines existing in a single burden center with up to 15,000 employees. For reasons stated above, the potential for inaccuracies in a system such as this are immense. The first step in improving the accuracy of such a system is to break the burden center into major product–line-oriented segments. This move alone will improve the accuracy of the allocation system dramatically by avoiding subsidies across product lines.

Perhaps more important, the breakup of large burden pools begins the educational process as operations managers and finance personnel perceive the more accurate product–line–oriented reporting capabilities that this system provides. Many European firms have used systems such as this for decades, to the extent of implementing hundreds of burden centers to reflect the activities of a particular plant. In addition, although a change such as this adds some complexity to the audit process, it is fairly easy to negotiate in a DoD environment.

However, breaking cost centers into multiple burden centers is only the first step to a more accurate cost management system. This step occurred in 1986 at the Ground Systems Group of Hughes Aircraft when a 4,500-person manufacturing site was decentralized into nine product–line-oriented segments, each with its own unique burden center. The major failing of multiple burden centers is that an inaccuracy for products within the product line still exists due to the continuing allocation of costs by direct labor alone.

Step 2. Central Service Allocations. Whenever an operation is broken up into product-line-oriented segments, the problem remains of allocating to each of these burden centers the costs of support functions that are common to all but that do not have a large enough critical mass to allow each product line to have its own function. Examples would be certain group or corporate functions (finance, human resources), shipping, receiving, and data processing. These functions typically have been allocated by head count or cost of sales rather than by usage.

A natural step in the progression to a true activity-based system is to assign these costs to the various burden centers using drivers that reflect the complexity, volume, or time taken to perform the services, in direct relationship to the way the burden centers absorb these costs.

Shown in Table 1 are a few of the several dozen central service allocations that either have been implemented or are

TABLE 1/CENTRAL SERVICE ALLOCATIONS

Functions	Drivers	Metrics
Human Resources	Headcount	$/Head
	Hires	$/Hire
	Union Employees	$/Head
	Training Hours	$/Training Hour
Security	Square Footage	$/SquareFoot
Receiving	Number of Receivers	$/Receipt
Data Processing	Lines Printed	$/Line
	CPU Minutes	$/CPU Minute
	Storage	$/Storage Unit

Jan Luttes, our customer representative from the Defense Contract Audit Agency (DCAA), attends weekly ABC task team meetings.

AN ERA OF COOPERATION

Following years of a perceived adversarial relationship between defense contractors and representatives of the DCAA, all parties appear to be moving toward a new era of cooperation in regard to the introduction of advanced costing systems. This may not be as surprising as it first seems.

Both parties in reality are pursuing the same goals, although for different reasons. The goal in the introduction of advanced costing systems is to increase manufacturing efficiencies and thereby reduce costs. The government's interest in this process is obvious. The contractor realizes that cost reduction is vital to his own survival in a shrinking and increasingly competitive global marketplace.

Although government representatives are just beginning to take a lead in these efforts, the contractor's responsibilities to local audit when implementing such systems can be summarized in three words—INFORM, EDUCATE, INVOLVE.

1. *Inform*. No matter how far we have progressed in recent history, lingering suspicions still exist as to the intent of both parties when implementing such systems. The most advisable approach is to gain local audit's concensus and cooperation by informing them as soon as a pilot site for experimentation is initiated.
2. *Educate*. While the overall concepts of implementing advanced cost systems may be rather intuitive, the practical realities of implementation in a DoD environment are complex. As much time should be spent educating your local audit staff as is spent with your own implementation team. It is foolhardy to believe that this education process can be completed within the 60-day notification period required for accounting changes.
3. *Involve*. In our own case at Hughes Aircraft Ground Systems Group, our local audit manager participates in each of our weekly task team meetings aimed at the implementation of advanced costing systems. We have gone to great lengths to ensure that all levels of government audit are involved in the implementation process, including our regional audit manager and DCAA's Department of Policies and Plans in Washington. The government's role in these weekly meetings is not so much to suggest new ideas for innovation as to act as a sounding board for the practicalities of audit and the regulatory process. The real benefit of this involvement has been an enhancement of the educational process for both parties and a much more streamlined approach to the full implementation of our ABC pilot project.

There is evidence that the process we have experienced at Hughes Aircraft is spreading quickly to other parts of the industry. The Institute for Defense Analysis hosted a meeting in July 1990 to bring contractors and government representatives together for an in-depth discussion of how advanced cost systems best could be initiated in a DoD regulatory environment.

Participating in this conference on behalf of DoD contractors were Hughes Aircraft, United Technologies, General Dynamics, GE Aerospace, Harris Semiconductor, and Rockwell International. During this meeting each contractor, with a member of the local audit staff, was asked to describe current efforts in implementing advanced costing systems and what they saw as the regulatory impediments to such implementation.

Perhaps the most significant recommendation was that a mechanism be established for a continuing discussion between defense contractors and the government. Specifically, this mechanism would be a steering committee composed of Council of Defense and Space Industries Associated (CODSIA) representing industry, and DCAA, representing the government, with CAM-I (Computer Aided Manufacturing-International) providing the forum for discussion. This step appears to be the most important in several years to resolve what are truly common concerns in maintaining the efficiency, viability, and profitability of the defense contracting industry. ∎

---

under consideration. The allocating department decides on the drivers in consensus with the operating units that eventually absorb the activity costs. Particular attention must be paid to developing drivers that do not simply allocate costs but that create a direct linkage between activity absorption and cost flow.

The allocation of resource costs in direct proportion to the absorption by activities has obvious benefits. However, the side benefits that have occurred from this system may be of even greater significance. For the first time operating units understand, and therefore can control, their level of cost absorption through an evaluation of their own activities. In addition, the metrics derived for each allocation serve as budgeting tools, a method for communication between the providers and absorbers of an activity, and a method for performance measurement in an era of continuous measurable improvement.

Step 3. Activity Accounting. The Hughes Aircraft philosophy is to improve continuously in every aspect of our business. The next logical step in our evolution to advanced costing systems is to decompose our activities and assure ourselves that each activity is accomplished as cost effectively as possible. We define this as activity accounting.

Activity analysis requires an evaluation of each component of cost that contributes to the driver metrics shown in Table 1 (labor, capital, materials, customer requirements). This task can be accomplished in many ways; however, the one that has met with the most success at Hughes is a program called MORE (Measurement of Organizational Effectiveness), developed by the industrial engineering staff of General Motors. This program involves all participants in an activity and catalogs actions that contribute to that activity. The team members and client customers then are brought together to brainstorm and plan appropriate methods for increasing efficiency and reducing costs.

MORE is an accounting project driven by industrial engineers with the intended purpose of developing a team that can create a system of use to all parties.

Step 4. Activity-Based Costing. All of the concepts mentioned above (multiple burden centers, non-DLB drivers, activity accounting) are pulled together in implementing the concept of activity-based costing. At Hughes we are experimenting with two pilot sites for full implementation, which we have defined as taking ABC-derived costs to the general ledger. Figure 1 shows an overview of our design for a fully integrated activity-based costing system.

As shown, all shop resources (labor, materials, square footage charges, depreciation) are charged to the activity centers based on actual usage. Activity centers are defined as logical steps in the production process and generally are identified by geographical location, staffing, or machinery requirements. The number of activity centers depends on the type of process being performed, the diversity of product mix within the operation, and the informational requirements of the department management.

Once the activity costs have been isolated and analyzed, representatives from operations management, finance, industrial engineering, and data processing working as a team determine the most relevant second-stage drivers for each activity center. Once determined, the second-stage driver quantities either are loaded into or obtained from the existing shop floor control system. When these second-stage drivers are balanced with projected workload, application rates are derived for forward pricing rates and eventual recording of costs to the general ledger.

The shaded area in Figure 1 represents a step in the evolutionary process developed from modeling. During this step we used the Cooper/Kaplan software, at present being marketed and implemented exclusively by KPMG Peat Marwick, to assure ourselves and the government that ABC was sound conceptually and that the cost shifts were significant enough to continue the implementation process. We discovered that two of the many side benefits of the KPMG ABC system are that it is an excellent vehicle to forecast forward application rates and that it greatly streamlines making the associated cost impact study required by government audit. The treatment of the data is

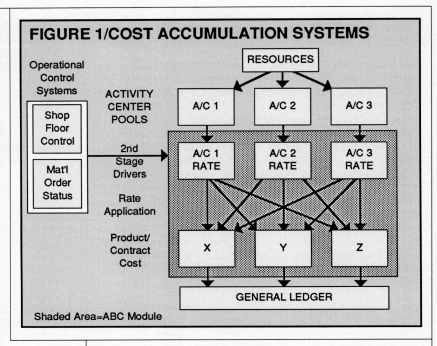

FIGURE 1/COST ACCUMULATION SYSTEMS

Operational Control Systems

ACTIVITY CENTER POOLS

RESOURCES

A/C 1 A/C 2 A/C 3

Shop Floor Control

Mat'l Order Status

2nd Stage Drivers

A/C 1 RATE   A/C 2 RATE   A/C 3 RATE

Rate Application

Product/ Contract Cost

X   Y   Z

GENERAL LEDGER

Shaded Area=ABC Module

clear, concise, and easily auditable (see sidebar, p.30).

The audit points agreed to by the government representatives on our implementation team are: (1) the collection of costs into activity centers, (2) the derivation of second-stage driver application rates, and (3) the application of the second-stage driver to the work order. The use of multiple application rates will greatly complicate the task of audit when compared with a system focusing on hand recording of labor and the application of a single DLB overhead rate. There is an understanding by both parties, however, that the information now being reviewed will be much more relevant to the intended task and may work in concert with the government's own initiatives toward contractor self-governance.

Full implementation of activity-based costing in a Department of Defense contracting environment will require accounting changes. These changes may not be as significant as often publicized. Cost accounting standards that must be taken into consideration when implementing such a system are CAS 418, classification of costs as either indirect or direct; CAS 406, the submission of yearly rates; and CAS 414, cost of money calculations.

We believe that through continued teaming with the government in the CAM-I forum and a practical planned approach to the evolution of our accounting systems, any impediments that may remain can be resolved. A new wind of change indeed is blowing. ■

ABC is helping Hughes make improved strategic decisions in complex manufacturing areas like Printed Circuit Board Fabrication.

John (Jack) Haedicke is division controller of the Product Operations and Quality Systems Division of Hughes Aircraft, chairman of the Hughes Cost Management Systems Committee, and project leader for the ABC program. David Feil is manager of cost management systems and ABC project manager for the Product Operations and Quality Systems Division of Hughes Aircraft. Both authors are members of the Orange County Chapter, through which this article was submitted.

Is this article of interest to you? If so, circle appropriate number on Reader Service Card.

	Yes	No
	80	81

ACTIVITY-BASED COSTING FOR MARKETING

BY RONALD J. LEWIS

Certificate of Merit, 1990-91.

Manufacturing costs and traditional cost accounting systems are not the only cause of America's problems in the world-class competitiveness arena. Marketing functions, particularly physical distribution, are a significant cost factor, yet marketing costs are being ignored in the mainstream discussions today. Also, activity-based costing (ABC) techniques and total cost management (TCM) concepts have been recommended and used by some companies for marketing activities since the late 1960s. How can they be merged with the concepts being promoted today?

THE PROBLEM'S HIDDEN CAUSE

Critics of traditional cost control systems who concentrate on production costs alone are overlooking a significant portion of the total costs of many manufactured products.

Physical distribution is the most effective area for this application.

A major cause of the higher cost of these products is the cost of physical distribution activities and other marketing functions. Marketing costs make up more than 50% of the total costs in many product lines and approximately 20% of the U.S. Gross National Product.

Physical distribution is a major cost factor in the United States. It may not be a major cost factor in geographically small countries, such as Japan or Great Britain, within their own domestic markets. Nevertheless, when foreign companies establish factories in the United States, they face the same logistics problems that U.S. companies encounter.

The theoretical advantages of just-in-time (JIT) methods may not work in all real-life situations, even in Japanese

transplants. In addition, the familiarity that U.S. companies have had with physical distribution problems may be an advantage for them over their foreign competitors. For example, a Japanese-American joint venture established a plant in Michigan to provide parts to a Japanese assembly plant in Ohio. In the Michigan plant, observers found that boxes of parts were stacked to the ceiling in all available floor space of the factory. When asked about JIT and other inventory reduction methods, the plant manager explained that parts were shipped from Japan by freighter to the West Coast, then by rail to Chicago, and finally by truck to Michigan. Therefore, it was more economical to ship in large quantities and store the extra suplies on the factory floor.

The joint-venture supplier in this example is majority owned by the Japanese company, which supplies another Japanese company, an automobile manufacturer, with these particular parts. Competition is not a factor because the two Japanese companies have prearranged agreements, so these physical distribution costs are considered unavoidable under the circumstances.

Although this example illustrates the fallacy of assuming that the Japanese have some magic formula for manufacturing efficiency, it also indicates that marketing costs, particularly the costs of physical distribution, are a major factor in worldwide competition and should not be ignored in discussions of performance measurements and integrated cost systems.

ABC TECHNIQUES FOR MARKETING

The objective of marketing cost analysis is to provide relevant quantitative data that will assist marketing managers in making informed decisions regarding such important areas as profitability, pricing, and adding or dropping the product lines or territories. In achieving this objective it is necessary to be able to trace costs directly to product lines or to territories where possible and to establish a rational system of allocating nontraceable costs to the cost objective. The accounting profession has not pursued this challenge!

ABC principles can be applied in attempting to trace marketing costs to product lines and territories in order to measure profitability. I'll show you how. All you have to do is follow the procedure outlined next.

1. Establish activities performed as advertising, selling, order filling, shipping, and warehousing.
2. Accumulate direct costs for each activity, and separate into variable and fixed categories.
3. Determine cost drivers for each activity. For *selling*, the cost driver is gross sales, or orders received, or number of sales calls. For the activity of *order filling, shipping,* and *warehousing*, the cost driver would be number, weight, or size of units shipped. For the activities of *credit and collection* and *general office*, the cost driver is number of customer orders or number of invoice lines.
4. Calculate unit costs for each activity. The unit cost of each activity is determined by dividing the total activity cost by the cost driver selected. Where conditions justify the practice, the unit cost can be used as the basis for budgeting and for the establishment of standards in a standard cost system.
5. Apply contribution cost analysis. The accumulation of direct costs

and the allocation of indirect costs to marketing activities enables management to assign total cost responsibility to each marketing activity although the identification of total costs does not always provide relevant information for specific decisions. Only by applying contribution analysis will the company be able to determine profit contribution by product line or by territory.

Tables 1–5 were prepared by the controller of Atlanta Company to provide information about marketing prof-

itability. Table 1 shows selling prices, unit manufacturing costs, units sold, and other bases of variability. Table 2 shows total variable and fixed costs for each activity and develops unit rates for variable and fixed costs of each major marketing activity: selling, warehousing, packing and shipping, and general office.

Selling. The selling function is represented by the dollar value of sales. There may be justification for basing variability of selling cost on other factors, such as the number of sales calls or orders obtained, and the controller

TABLE1/ATLANTA COMPANY PRODUCT LINE DATA YEAR 19X1

Product Line Information	Product Line		
	A	B	C
Selling price	$10.00	$ 8.00	$ 12.00
Unit manufacturing cost	$ 8.00	$ 5.00	$ 11.00
Quantity of units sold and shipped	50,000	30,000	20,000
Average weight of units sold	2.0 lbs.	3.0 lbs.	4.0 lbs.
Number of customers' orders	100	200	200
Variable portion of manufacturing cost	60 %	60 %	60 %

TABLE 2/ATLANTA COMPANY CALCULATION FOR PER UNIT COST RATES

TOTAL COSTS

Marketing Activity	Cost Driver	Total Volume	Cost of Marketing Activity	
			Total	Unit Rate
Selling	Dollar value of sales	$ 980,000	$49,000	5.0 %
Advertising	Quantity of units sold	100,000	$40,000	$ .40
Warehousing	Weight of shipped	270,000 lb.	$27,000	$ .10
Packing and shipping	Quantity of shipped	100,000	$20,000	$ .20
General office	Number of customers' orders	500	$10,000	$ 20.00

VARIABLE AND FIXED COST RATES

Marketing Activity	Variable Cost	Unit Rate	Fixed Cost	Unit Rate
Selling	$ 29,400	3.0 %	$19,600	2.0 %
Advertising	$ 10,000	$ .10	$30,000	$ .30
Warehousing	$ 13,500	$ .05	$13,500	$ .05
Packing and shipping	$ 12,000	$ .12	$ 8,000	$ .08
General office	$ 2,000	$ 4.00	$ 8,000	$ 16.00

must select the basis that has the main causal effect on cost variability. Atlanta Company uses the basis of dollar value of sales.

Advertising. Advertising is a promotional activity, similar to selling, which logically could be attributed to the same factors. Atlanta selected units of product sold. Note that advertising may or may not have variable cost characteristics. Some companies increase their advertising when sales are down, so the cost may bear an inverse relationship with sales. Atlanta found that a portion of advertising varies with sales and that a larger portion is fixed.

Warehousing. Warehousing is the physical distribution function of storage and terminaling. The factor of variability selected by Atlanta is weight of product sold.

Packing and Shipping. Another physical distribution function, packaging and shipping, usually has a greater proportion of variable expenses and is related to the quantity of units of product shipped. Atlanta assumes units shipped are equal to units sold.

General Office. Atlanta needs clerical, accounting, credit and collection, and other activities to service the overall marketing function. Each service has its own variability, but Atlanta assumes that number of orders affects all.

Table 3 provides additional product and territory transactions data. For example, the quantity of product C sold in the West territory during the period is 14,000 units. Customers' orders for product A in the South total 50. These data form the basis for the determina-

TABLE 3/ATLANTA COMPANY SALES AND ORDERS BY TERRITORY (IN UNITS) YEAR 19X1

Transaction by Territory	Total	Products A	B	C
Products sold:				
West	60,000	26,000	20,000	14,000
South	40,000	24,000	10.000	6,000
Total	100,000	50,000	30,000	20,000
Customers' Orders:				
West	280	50	80	150
South	220	50	120	50
Total	500	100	200	200

TABLE 4/ATLANTA COMPANY PROFITABLITY STATEMENT BY TERRITORY (ALL PRODUCTS) YEAR 19X1

	Total Company	Territory West	South	Allocation Basis
Sales revenue	$980,000	$588,000	$392,000	
Less: cost of sales	770,000	462,000	308,000	
Gross margin	$210,000	$126,000	$84,000	
Less: Expenses				
Selling	$49,000	$29,400	$19,600	5% of sales
Advertising	40,000	24,000	16,000	$.40/unit sold
Warehousing	27,000	16,800	10,200	$.10/lb. shipped
Packing and shipping	20,000	12,000	8,000	$.20/unit sold
General office	10,000	5,600	4,400	$20/order
Total expense	$146,000	$87,800	$58,200	
Operating income (Loss)	$64,000	$38,200	$25,800	

Uniphoto/Jim Olive.

Production costs have been the center of attention in management accounting recently, yet marketing costs can be 50% of a total product line.

tion of the cost calculations in subsequent tables.

The profitability analysis by territory (shown in Table 4) reveals that both territories show a profit from operations. Table 5 shows the total company profitability by product line. The profitability statement by product line provides additional information for marketing managers. Product lines A and B are profitable, whereas product line C shows an operating loss of $16,000. This statement has revealed that although the overall company shows a profit and that both territories are profitable, one product line requires further analysis. Additional tables could be presented with data by product line for each territory separately to further isolate the operating loss of product C.

As you can see, "Charging costs directly to products eliminates the need

TABLE 5/ATLANTA COMPANY PROFITABLITY STATEMENT BY PRODUCT LINE
(ALL TERRITORIES) YEAR 19X1

	Total Company	A	Product Line B	C	Allocation Basis
Sales revenue	$ 980,000	$ 500,000	$ 240,000	$ 240,000	
Cost of sales	770,000	400,000	150,000	220,000	
Gross margin	$ 210,000	$ 100,000	$ 90,000	$ 20,000	
Less: Expenses					
Selling	$ 49,000	$ 25,000	$ 12,000	$ 12,000	5% of sales
Advertising	40,000	20,000	12,000	8,000	$.40/unit sold
Warehousing	27,000	10,000	9,000	8,000	$.10/lb. shipped
Packing and shipping	20,000	10,000	6,000	4,000	$.20/unit sold
General office	10,000	2,000	4,000	4,000	$20/order
Total expense	$ 146,000	$ 67,000	$ 43,000	$ 36,000	
Operating income (Loss)	$ 64,000	$ 33,000	$ 47,000	$ (16,000)	

to allocate or assign costs. Costs that cannot be charged directly should be assigned to the product through activity-based costing."[1]

This modern advice dovetails with my illustration, which demonstrates that the techniques recommended for marketing cost analysis at least 20 years ago are conceptually equal to those now being recommended for production costs by Robert Kaplan, William Ferrara, Michael Ostrenga, and others contributing to the deluge of activity-based costing literature[2]. The only differences are that only marketing costs were involved, the state of technology was less developed, and the accounting profession did not recognize the importance of marketing costs and the methods being recommended.

WE MUST EMPHASIZE MARKETING COSTS

The main theme of management accounting journal articles in recent years has been world-class competition, emphasizing the gradual slipping of U.S. manufacturers, particularly in comparison with Japanese manufacturers. Production costs have been the center of attention, while marketing costs have been ignored. We must focus on marketing costs as an important component of the total cost of a product.

The use of activity-based costing techniques for marketing functions arose during the years 1968 through 1973 when marketing executives urged members of the accounting profession to develop a better system of

Marketing costs, particularly physical distribution costs, must be taken into account when pricing products and making other management decisions.

identifying, classifying, and allocating physical distribution costs. At that time, several articles (including one of mine[3]) isolated the activities in the major marketing functions. Cost drivers, a modern euphemism for activity bases, were identified for each activity within the marketing functions.

Techniques that resemble the recently discovered activity-based costing system and the total cost concept, which is the forerunner of total cost management, were discussed thoroughly and recommended for physical distribution costs at the request of the marketing managers of several hundred U.S. corporations. The accounting profession largely ignored the recommendations of the practitioners and

overlooked the fact that physical distribution activities have cost characteristics similar to those of production activities. Now, 20 years later, accountants are attaching new names to these same techniques. Activity-based costing techniques have been and should continue to be applied to marketing costs to assist companies in management decision making. ∎

Ronald J. Lewis is professor of accounting at Central Michigan University in Mt. Pleasant, Mich., and a member of the Saginaw Valley Chapter of the IMA, through which this article was submitted. He holds A.B. and A.M. degrees from Wayne State University and a Ph.D. degree from Michigan State University. Formerly he was the vice-president of academic affairs at Tri-State University, Angola, Ind. He may be reached at (517) 774-3796.

[1]Michael R. Ostrenga, "Activities: The Focal Point of Total Cost Management," MANAGEMENT ACCOUNTING®, February 1990, pp. 42-49.
[2]Robert S. Kaplan, "The Four-Step Model of Cost Systems Design," MANAGEMENT ACCOUNTING®, February 1990, pp. 22-26. Also, William L. Ferrara, "The New Cost/Management Accounting: More Questions than Answers," MANAGEMENT ACCOUNTING®, October 1990, pp. 48-52.
[3]Ronald J. Lewis, "Strengthening Control of Physical Distribution Costs," *Management Services* (AICPA), January-February 1968. Also, J.L. Heskett, R.M. Ivie, and N.A. Glaskowsky, Jr., *Business Logistics Management of Physical Supply and Distribution*, The Ronald Press Company, New York, N.Y., 1964.

Part **3**

Section 6

Incorporating Traditional Cost Concepts to Improve Managerial Decision Making

In many respects this is a most unusual section. Here we find academics and practitioners uncovering deficiencies in the ABC model and at the same time proposing enhancements that will improve managerial decision making. They suggest these improvements be made by incorporating traditional cost concepts, such as fixed-variable, different volume measures for capacity, and overhead absorption rates.

The key is in maintaining cost behavior distinction in activity cost pools. In addition, we are asked not to violate the ABC assumptions of homogeneity and proportionality.

In the first article, "Are You Distorting Costs by Violating ABC Assumptions?" Harold Roth and A. Faye Borthick issue a warning to ABC practitioners—if you do not satisfy the cost assumptions implied for ABC systems, the costs ABC provides may be no better than those provided under traditional volume-based systems.

What are these assumptions? They are homogeneity and proportionality, applied to each cost pool. When seeking homogeneity, you must ascertain that the costs in a pool are driven by a single or many highly related activities. The focus is on the identification of activities. It means that a change in the level of one activity is accompanied by a proportional change in the other activities. You violate this concept if the costs in a cost pool are driven by two or more not highly related activities, and you use one of the activities as the activity driver (cost driver) to assign costs to products, based on consumption of this driver. When seeking proportionality, the focus is on the relationship of activity levels to costs—that is, all

costs in the cost pool should vary proportionately with changes in the activity level. You violate this assumption when both fixed and variable costs are in the same pool, and they are assigned to product costs as if they were strictly variable costs. Another term used in the past to identify proportionality is cost behavior. The authors provide examples of cost distortions in product costs that occur when these two underlying assumptions are violated.

How do you ascertain conformance to these assumptions? The answer is—through regression analysis. The authors used the reference function of Lotus 1-2-3, version 2.01. Scattergraphs (charting) and the least squares method are among the techniques used in the past.

The authors counsel that it is a good idea to carry out this evaluation before using ABC costs or product costs. For another view on this same subject, readers should refer to "ABC Puts Accountants on the Design Team at HP," in Section 7, for a practice application.

Attributable costs, as defined by Douglas Sharp and Linda F. Christensen in the second article, "A New View of Activity-Based Costing," are any costs that would be eliminated if a particular activity were discontinued. This concept would include overhead costs directly associated with an activity (fixed and variable) plus "the activity's share of allocated costs which could, in time, be eliminated if the activity were discontinued and capacity reduced accordingly." Their thesis: attributable costs are needed for managerial decision making, and ABC needs to incorporate this concept.

Using a product profitability analysis, the authors illustrate the outcomes under attributable costing and full costing concepts (ABC) to support their hypothesis. They indicate that the fundamental nature of costs does not change under ABC—they are just a better measure of resource consumption.

What do the authors suggest for ABC? They suggest the use of "direct" ABC costs for decision making and "full absorption" ABC costs for reports requiring total resource consumption.

In the third article, "Completing the Picture: Economic Choices with ABC," Michael Woods indicates that ABC has a weak point. Even though it may correct deficiencies in comparing resources consumed to ultimate products, ABC mixes fixed and variable costs. It thus makes economic choices difficult and requires special analysis to gain this information.

He suggests a refinement to ABC—keeping fixed and variable costs separate throughout a firm's cost accounting structure—thus maintaining the advantages of ABC and allowing for rational decision making. To do otherwise, says Woods, would deny managers vital information, a situation that could lead to irrational decisions.

If the refinements to ABC costs can be accomplished as suggested by Christensen and Sharp in the fourth article in this section, "How ABC Can Add Value to Decision Making," ABC not only will maintain its value for strategic decision-making purposes but will become relevant for managerial short-term and intermediate decision making.

Why do Christensen and Sharp want to refine ABC costs? Because, they say, ABC costs: (1) include committed fixed costs that will not cease in the long run (facility-sustaining, entity-sustaining), (2) include short-term fixed costs that do not change in proportion to an individual product in the product line, (3) assume that costs will be reduced proportionately—even when warnings are provided that cost reductions will occur "in time," (4) assume that there are more profitable alternative uses for the capacity released with the decision.

They recommend the following steps to overcome ABC deficiencies.

1. Separate activity costs into short-term variable, short-term fixed, and committed fixed cost pools (cost categories not aggregated).

2. Determine allocation rates for both categories

of fixed costs and applying costs on the basis of capacity provided.

They also offer a framework to support their thesis that cost variability should be made explicit in both the management accounting system and in management reports. This framework would incorporate the following cost definitions and observations.

1. Short-term variable costs change in direct proportion to the cost driver used. They are volume driven, by appropriate cost driver, unit level, or batch level.

2. Short-term fixed costs are not subject to directly proportional results and incorporate a time element—they usually can be affected by management within a year. They could be subject to batch-level and product-sustaining drivers (semivariable/semifixed costs).

3. Committed fixed costs can be affected by decisions only in the long term. Examples are product-sustaining and facility-sustaining costs.

4. Capacity utilization potentially affects both short-term and long-term fixed costs, making idle costs a possibility in both categories.

Using this framework to support their recommendations, the authors illustrate and apply these concepts to support product profitability, pricing decisions, make-or-buy decisions, and cost reduction efforts. Production costs computed under "revised ABC," using allocation rates for both categories of fixed costs, are significantly different from those computed under "traditional ABC."

Gilbert Yang and Roger Wu, the authors of the fifth article, "Strategic Costing and ABC," are aware of the underlying assumptions and full costing philosophy of ABC. They seek to modify ABC by incorporating a future price index for variable costs and capacity utilization measures for fixed costs, where overcapacity exists. They indicate that products are underpriced when unit variable cost is underestimated and overpriced when unit fixed cost is overestimated.

Using a service company illustration, a phone center servicing a bank mortgage department, they develop several volume-related costs per call answered. The cost per call variation is explained by the amount of fixed cost absorption, which is a function of the capacity denominator used. Different ca-

> *The fundamental nature of costs does not change under ABC — they are just a better measure of resource consumption.*

pacity concepts are defined. They are: (1) simple capacity, which is the number of activity minutes (number of telephone calls times the average number of minutes per call) in a 12-month period; (2) capacity ABC, which represents the total capacity in minutes of a fully staffed center; and (3) strategic ABC, which is the percent of total capacity in minutes that the company wants the operation to achieve over its useful life. The lowest cost per minute would be achieved by dividing total period cost by the capacity ABC denominator.

They recommend using the strategic ABC capacity concept. This concept, however, has to be modified to incorporate normalized depreciation (changing from accelerated to straight line methods) and increasing variable cost annually, to reflect the inflation factor. As the authors indicate, strategic ABC is a close approximation of true long-term costs that can be used for strategic advantage.

The final article, "Customize Your Costing System," by Jacci Rodgers, S. Mark Comstock, and Karl Pritz, covers a forms manufacturer that changed its product costing system. The new system combines the concepts of ABC, direct costing, and absorption costing.

Common overhead is assigned to the directly identifiable costs in the press department (machine operators, support personnel, and supplies). A capacity measure, press units, is used for allocating common overhead to both the press and collator departments. A total unit cost per machine (per press and per collator) is developed, which then is converted into a cost per machine hour, per year. This is the cost driver used for estimating press and collator costs. Material costs are added to the press and collator costs, plus a markup, giving a total used for costing bids.

Cost drivers — the items that differentiate and determine the cost of the jobs — include type and amount of paper consumed, size of form, number of parts, type of paper, number of colors, composition, construction, special services, and the machine time to complete. ∎

ARE YOU DISTORTING COSTS BY VIOLATING ABC ASSUMPTIONS?

Homogeneity and proportionality are key factors in cost data decisions.

BY HAROLD P. ROTH, CMA, AND A. FAYE BORTHICK, CMA

Recent articles[1] on activity-based costing (ABC) make the process seem easy: identify cost drivers, establish driver-cost relationships, implement the drivers, and bask in the glory of better decision making based on knowledge of *real* product costs. But are you sure you picked the right drivers? Are you sure the relationships are meaningful? Can the required data be collected on a regular basis to monitor driver-cost relationships?

If you answered yes to these questions, keep basking in the glory of bet-

ter decision making. If you answered no to any question, or even if you are just uneasy about a response, then you may have encountered a pitfall of activity-based costing—failing to satisfy its underlying assumptions.

Although ABC systems often provide better product cost data than volume-based systems, they are based on a number of assumptions that should be evaluated before ABC costs are considered superior. If the data do not satisfy the assumptions,[2] ABC costs may not be any more reliable than the costs provided by simpler volume-based systems.

Two assumptions underlying activity-based costing are:

1. The costs in each cost pool are driven by homogeneous activities.
2. The costs in each cost pool are strictly proportional to the activity.

The first assumption, homogeneity, means that the costs in each pool are driven by a single activity or by highly correlated activities. *Highly correlated* means that changes in the level of one activity are accompanied by proportional changes in the other activities. The ideal situation is to have perfect correlation (correlation value of one), which means that proportional changes in related activities are identical.

The homogeneity assumption will be violated if the costs in a cost pool

Uniphoto/Jim Olive.

In textile mills such as the one above, will an activity-based costing system give you more reliable cost data than a volume-based system?

are driven by two or more not highly correlated activities but only one of the activities is used to assign all costs in the cost pool to products. Under these conditions, some costs are assigned to products on an arbitrary basis. The arbitrarily assigned costs are those caused by an activity or activities not used as the cost driver.

The second assumption, proportionality, means that all costs in the cost pool should vary proportionally with changes in the activity level. This assumption will be violated by several conditions, including the presence of nonlinear costs. For example, costs that are subject to the learning curve phenomenon will violate the proportionality assumption. The assumption also will be violated if both fixed and variable costs are included in the same cost pool and they are assigned to products as if they were strictly variable. Finally, joint costs will violate this assumption when they are not strictly proportional to the activity.

When any of these conditions exists, ABC may not produce better cost data than traditional volume-based costing. The following illustration shows how violating these assumptions can result in distorted product costs.

THE DANGER OF NOT SATISFYING ABC ASSUMPTIONS

To illustrate how an ABC system may provide unreliable cost data, assume that a company produces two products, A and B. During the month, the company produces 10,000 units of each product. Costs incurred for production during the month are shown in Table 1, Part A, and the activity data are shown in Part B.

The product costs in Table 1 include raw materials, direct labor, and overhead that can be traced directly to each product. In addition, two overhead costs, i.e., setup and power department costs, have not been assigned to the products. These two costs will be used to show how product costs will be distorted if the two assumptions discussed earlier are violated. The setup costs illustrate the danger of using a cost pool containing nonhomogeneous drivers. The power department costs illustrate the danger of using a single activity to assign costs when the cost pool contains some costs that are not strictly proportional to the activity.

Distortion from nonhomogeneous cost drivers. To illustrate the distortion from nonhomogeneous cost drivers, let us assume setup costs are assigned to the products using a single activity when actually they are driven by two activities. If the activity used for assigning costs is setup time, the minutes for that activity as shown in Part B of Table 1 will be used to assign the costs. When the total setup costs of $30,000 are divided by the total setup minutes of 3,000, a rate of $10 per minute results. Multiplying this rate by the

TABLE 1/COST AND ACTIVITY DATA

A. Cost Data

Source	Product A	Product B	Total
Raw materials	$20,000	$20,000	$40,000
Direct labor	5,000	5,000	10,000
Traced overhead	15,000	15,000	30,000
Indirect overhead:			
Setup			30,000
Power			54,000

B. Activity Data

Source	Product A	Product B	Total
Number of units produced	10,000	10,000	20,000
Setup activities:			
Minutes to perform setups	1,200	1,800	3,000
Units of supplies used	100	50	150
Power department activities:			
Kwhrs used in production	200,000	400,000	600,000
Kwhrs used at capacity	600,000	600,000	1,200,000

TABLE 2/ASSIGNMENT OF SETUP COSTS TO PRODUCTS: TIME AND SUPPLIES

A. Calculation of Rates

Rate for time-related costs	$15,000/3,000 minutes	= $5 per minute
Rate for supplies costs	$15,000/150 units	= $100 per unit

B. Assignment of Costs to Products

Source	Product A	Product B
Time	1,200 X $5 = $6,000	1,800 X $5 = $9,000
Supplies	100 X $100 = 10,000	50 X $100 = 5,000
Total	$16,000	$14,000

TABLE 3/ASSIGNMENT OF POWER DEPARTMENT COSTS

A. Calculation of Rates

Usage rate	$24,000/600,000 kwhr	= $0.04 per kwhr
Capacity rate	$30,000/1,200,000 kwhr	= $0.025 per kwhr

B. Assignment of Costs to Products

Source	Product A	Product B
Variable costs	200,000 X $0.04 = $8,000	400,000 X $0.04 = $16,000
Fixed (capacity) costs	600,000 X $0.025 = 15,000	600,000 X $0.025 = 15,000
Total	$23,000	$31,000

minutes for each product assigns $12,000 ($10 x 1,200) to Product A and $18,000 ($10 x 1,800) to Product B.

The flaw with this assignment is that the setup costs really are driven by two factors, time and supplies. Assume an analysis of the setup costs shows that $15,000 is related to time and $15,000 is related to supplies. Table 2, Part A, shows the calculation of the rate per unit of activity, and Part B shows the costs assigned to each product when they are assigned using the appropriate bases. With these bases, the setup costs assigned to Product A are $16,000 and to Product B, $14,000. Thus the setup costs assigned to Product A should be higher than those assigned to Product B. However, the use of a single rate based on time causes more of the setup overhead to be assigned to Product B, resulting in distorted product costs.

Distortion from nonproportional costs. The power department costs illustrate how the assignment of a cost that is not strictly proportional to the activity can distort costs. In this illustration, the total cost of the power department is $54,000, as shown in Table 1. A single rate for each kilowatt hour (kwhr) used in the production process would be $.09 ($54,000/600,000). This rate assigns $18,000 ($.09 x 200,000) to Product A and $36,000 ($.09 x 400,000) to Product B.

The flaw with using a single rate for assigning the power department costs is that some of the costs are not strictly proportional to the kwhrs used. They are the costs incurred to provide the capacity to manufacture some maximum quantities of Products A and B. Assume an analysis of the power department costs shows that $30,000 of the total are fixed costs incurred to provide capacity and $24,000 are variable costs incurred in generating the electricity. If the maximum capacity for each product requires the kwhrs shown in Table 1, better product cost data will be provided by assigning the variable costs on the basis of kwhrs used and the fixed costs on the basis of capacity. Table 3 shows the assignment of costs using this procedure. The results are $23,000 of power department costs assigned to Product A and $31,000 to Product B.

When you compare the costs assigned to each product in Table 3 with the costs using a single rate, you see that Product A's costs are understated using a single rate and Product B's cost are overstated. Thus, the costs are distorted when the assumption of

costs proportional to activities is not satisfied.

Table 4 summarizes the distortion in this illustration. If the costs are assigned using a single rate for each pool, Product A has a cost of $7 per unit and Product B, $9.40. However, using cost drivers that do not violate the assumptions results in a unit cost for Product A of $7.90 and for Product

B, $8.50.

EVALUATING WHETHER THE ASSUMPTIONS HOLD

Because ABC may produce distorted product costs, accountants and managers need to be able to evaluate each cost pool to determine if the assumptions are met.

TABLE 4/COST SUMMARY

A. Nonhomogeneous Setup and Nonproportional Power Costs

Source	Product A	Product B
Raw materials	$20,000	$20,000
Direct labor	5,000	5,000
Traced overhead	15,000	15,000
Assigned overhead:		
Setup	12,000	18,000
Power	18,000	36,000
Total	$70,000	$94,000
Cost per unit	$7.00	$9.40

B. Homogeneous Setup and Proportional Power Costs

Source	Product A	Product B
Raw materials	$20,000	$20,000
Direct labor	5,000	5,000
Traced overhead	15,000	15,000
Assigned overhead:		
Setup (from Table 2)	16,000	14,000
Power (from Table 3)	23,000	31,000
Total	$79,000	$85,000
Cost per unit	$7.90	$8.50

TABLE 5/REGRESSION RESULTS FOR SETUP COSTS AND ACTIVITIES

A. Minutes as the independent variable

Constant	553.2312
Standard error of the estimate	130.4427
R-squared	0.009238

X Coefficient	0.779479
Standard error of coef.	1.165131

B. Minutes and supplies as independent variables

Constant	0
Standard error of the estimate	0
R-squared	1

	Minutes	Supplies
X Coefficients	5	100
Standard error of coef.	0	0

The regression equation

   Total setup costs = 0 + ($5 x setup minutes) + ($100 x supplies used)
   The incremental costs of $5 and $100 per unit of activity are the
   X coefficients from the regression results.

The two assumptions considered here may be evaluated with regression analysis, performed with statistical software or spreadsheet programs. The data for this illustration were analyzed using the regression function of Lotus 1-2-3™, version 2.01.

Evaluating homogeneity of cost pools. To evaluate whether all costs in a cost pool are driven by a single activity, you can conduct a regression analysis using the activity as the independent variable and the cost as the dependent variable. This analysis will provide a statistic that can be used to evaluate whether the costs are associated with a single activity. R^2, known as the coefficient of determination, will have a value between zero and one. An R^2 of one means that costs vary exactly with changes in the activity. An R^2 of zero means that none of the changes in costs is associated with changes in the activity. An R^2 between zero and one means that some, but not all, of the changes in the costs are associated with changes in the activity.

In analyzing setup data for the example using minutes as the independent variable, the R^2 is .009 as shown in Table 5, Part A.[3] Thus, using time as the sole cost driver does not account for very much of the change in the setup costs, and some other activity must be driving some of the costs in that cost pool. In this case, the other activity is supplies used. When both supplies and minutes are included as activities (i.e., independent variables) in the analysis,[4] the R^2 is approximately 1.00, and all of the changes in the costs are accounted for by the regression equation. The results of the regression analysis are shown in Table 5, Part B, followed by the regression equation. The high R^2 occurs because the costs are a function of just these two activities. In practice, the R^2 probably would be somewhat less than one, and the accountant's professional judgment would be needed to determine whether the assumption was satisfied.

Evaluating proportionality of costs. The second assumption, that costs are strictly proportional to the activity, also can be evaluated with regression analysis. If kwhrs and costs for the power department are available for several months, a regression analysis can be conducted to determine if there is a significant constant term. If there is, all the costs are not strictly proportional to the cost driver activity.

To determine whether there is a significant constant term, assume the data in Table 6, Part A, represent pow-

er department costs and kwhrs used for the year.[5] The regression results in Table 6, Part B, show a significant constant term of 30,000.[6] If this constant term represents capacity costs, assigning them to products using a measure of capacity will provide better costing results than assigning all costs using a measure of actual activity.

As we have shown, although activity-based cost systems generally provide better cost data than volume-based systems in complex, multiproduct production environments, they also can distort product costs if the assumptions underlying ABC are violated. Two of these assumptions can be evaluated using regression analysis, which can be performed readily on a personal computer with statistical software or a spreadsheet program. It's a good idea to carry out this evaluation before using ABC costs as relevant product costs. ∎

Harold P. Roth, CMA, CPA, is an associate professor of accounting at The University of Tennessee-Knoxville. He holds a Ph.D. degree from Virginia Polytechnic Institute and State University.

A. Faye Borthick, CMA, CPA, is also an associate professor of accounting at The University of Tennessee-Knoxville. She has a DBA degree from The University of Tennessee. Both authors are members of the Knoxville Chapter, through which this article was submitted.

TABLE 6/REGRESSION ANALYSIS OF POWER DEPARTMENT COSTS AND KWHRS USED

A. Data

Month	Kwhrs Used	Cost
1	500,000	$50,000
2	450,000	48,000
3	525,000	51,000
4	620,000	54,800
5	630,000	55,200
6	740,000	59,600
7	490,000	49,600
8	620,000	54,800
9	640,000	55,600
10	550,000	52,000
11	570,000	52,800
12	590,000	53,600

B. Regression results: kilowatt hours as the independent variable

Constant	30,000
Standard error of the estimate	0
R-squared	1
X Coefficient: 0.04	
Standard Error of Coef. 0	

[1] H. Thomas Johnson, "Activity-Based Information: A Blueprint for World-Class Management Accounting," MANAGEMENT ACCOUNTING®, June 1988, pp. 23-30; Robin Cooper and Robert S. Kaplan, "Measure Costs Right: Make the Right Decisions," *Harvard Business Review*, September-October 1988, pp. 96-103; Harold P. Roth and A. Faye Borthick, "Getting Closer to *Real* Product Costs," MANAGEMENT ACCOUNTING®, May 1989, pp. 28-33; Robin Cooper, "Cost Classification in Unit-Based and Activity-Based Manufacturing Cost Systems," *Journal of Cost Management*, Fall 1990, pp. 4-14.

[2] George J. Staubus explored several assumptions of activity costing in *Activity Costing and Input-Output Accounting*, Richard D. Irwin, Inc., Homewood, Ill., 1971, and Eric Noreen discussed the necessary and sufficient conditions for the relevance of activity-based costs in "Conditions Under Which Activity-Based Cost Systems Provide Relevant Costs," *Journal of Management Accounting Research*, Fall 1991, pp. 159-168.

[3] The Lotus command to perform the analysis is: /D(ata)R(egression), where the X-range is set to the column containing the minutes (the independent variable), the Y-range is set to the column containing the setup costs (the dependent variable), the I(ntercept) is set to compute, the Output-range is set to the upper lefthand corner of a range of cells to receive the regression output, and G(o) generates the regression.

[4] The Lotus command is like the earlier one except that the X-range is set to include the two columns, which must be adjacent, containing minutes and supplies (the independent variables).

[5] The X-range is set to the column containing kwhrs used and the Y-range, to the column containing costs; otherwise, the Lotus command is like the previous ones.

[6] Lotus does not provide the level of significance, but the constant term must be significant if the R^2 is one. If necessary, the significance can be evaluated with a test of the standard error of the constant, or the regression can be performed with statistical software that gives the significance level.

A New View of Activity-Based Costing

What costs would be eliminated if a product weren't made?

BY DOUGLAS SHARP
AND LINDA F.
CHRISTENSEN

Certificate of Merit, 1990-91.

Cost information that helps management assess the profitability, effectiveness, and efficiency of subsegments of the business—products, processes, departments—is critical in planning, directing, and controlling operations. Important decisions impacting the strategic position and direction of the company emanate from these analyses. Accordingly, great care must be exercised to ensure that the cost information provided does not give incorrect signals.

Most management accounting text and reference books recommend against the use of *full absorption costs* whenever an analysis of a subsegment is attempted. Although such costs may approximate the *resources consumed* by a particular segment, depending on the accuracy of the allocations involved, they may not represent the resources that would *cease to exist* were the segment not to exist. Accordingly, the argument is advanced that any such analysis should focus on those costs (and revenues where appropriate) that are *avoidable* in the absence of the particular segment.

Proponents of activity-based costing (ABC) have challenged the idea that full absorption costs are inappropriate for managerial decision making. Contending that all costs are variable in the long run—and thus subject to management action—ABC proponents argue that our problem has not been the concept of full cost but the methods used to allocate costs to a particular cost object. Better measurements of resources consumed are achieved if we identify correctly the factors that cause a particular cost to change and use these cost drivers as our allocation base. This approach, if valid, should be applicable to any segment analysis.

Activity-based costing is the most appropriate basis for allocating costs to products and segments and results in a more accurate measurement of resources consumed by a particular product, service, or business segment. When ac-

Superstock/Charles Orrico

ABC is an accurate measure of resources consumed by a product such as these jet engine parts.

tivity-based costs are advocated for many managerial decision-making situations, such as product profitability, pricing, and the like, do they represent those costs that could be avoided if the product, service, or segment were eliminated? If not, what refinements are necessary to make them better decision-making costs?

Answers to these questions are extremely important. For example, when management is assessing product profitability, relevant costs are those costs that could be eliminated if the product is not produced and sold. If activity-based costs do not provide a reasonable approximation of relevant costs, management accountants will not enhance their credibility through the provision of such data.

Activity-based costs are an attempt to determine the *full cost* of a cost object. As such, they suffer a deficiency common to all full cost approximations: Not all *resources consumed* by a cost object are *avoidable* in the absence of the particular object. If the distortions are significant, use of such data in decision making can lead to incorrect decisions.

The thesis advanced here is that, for managerial decision making, activity-based costs need to incorporate the concept of *attributable cost*. Cost measurements representing *resources consumed* are needed, but the management accounting system also must be capable of alternative cost measurements if it is to be of maximum benefit to management.

THE CONCEPT OF ATTRIBUTABLE COST

Almost invariably a measurement of "resources consumed" (i.e., full cost) of a business segment will not be the same as the resources that would not exist if the segment were eliminated. For example: The plant manager's salary is part of the resources consumed in manufacturing a product; it is doubtful that this cost would be eliminated if the product were not produced and sold (assuming a multiple-product manufacturing operation).

The example is illustrative of a well-developed, valid cost phenomenon in many business organizations: There are true "common" or "joint" costs incurred, and the further you subdivide the business, the more significant these costs become. These costs are considered "resources consumed," but they are not "attributable" to a particular segment.

An attributable cost, as used here, refers to any cost that could be eliminated if a particular activity were discontinued. Attributable costs would include all costs, whether fixed or variable, associated directly with the particular activity and the activity's share of allocated costs which could, in time, be eliminated if the activity were discontinued and capacity reduced accordingly.[1] Some authors have called these costs *avoidable*; we prefer the concept of *attributable* cost.

Management accountants often use full cost (either traditionally determined or activity-based) as a surrogate for attributable cost. Does full cost represent attributable cost accurately? If not, is the difference sufficiently immaterial to permit use of full cost as a surrogate? By means of three examples, we shall attempt to demonstrate that the answers to these questions appear to be "no."

Example One: Service Department Cost Allocation. The Wichita Plant of the Kansas Company has seven production departments and four service departments. Product X is processed in Department 1 and finished in Department 2. Product X is one of many products these two production departments work on every month. This example evaluates the cost of Product X under different allocation methods for Service Department S. Relevant information concerning departments S, 1, and 2 are presented in Tables 1 and 2.

Full Absorption Costing—The costing rate for Department S services would be $9.50 per service hour ($13,300/1,400). Assuming "normal" conditions, $2,850 (300 hours @ $9.50) of Department S costs would be allocated to Department 1 and $1,900 (200 service hours @ $9.50) to Department 2. Allocation to individual products in both departments would be:

Department 1:
$2,850/25,000 pounds = $.114 per pound.

Department 2:
$1,900/10,000 hours = $.19 per direct labor hour (DLH).

Thus a unit of Product X would be allocated the following Department S costs: Department 1 (10 pounds @ $.114 = $1.14) and Department 2 (five hours @ $.19 = $.95). The unit cost impact on Product X under full absorption costing would be $2.09.

Attributable Costing—Given that this is a multiple-product plant, it is doubtful that either supervision or depreciation costs would be affected significantly by the elimination of Product X. Accordingly, these costs would not be allocated under attributable costing. The unit cost for Product X under attributable costing would be:

Department S Costing Rate:
$10,140/1,400 = $7.25 per hour of service.

Department 1 Allocation Rate:
(300 x $7.25)/25,000 = $.087 per pound.

Department 2 Allocation Rate:
(200 x $7.25)/10,000 = $.145 per direct labor hour.

Unit Cost Impact on Product X:
(10 x $.087) + (5 x $.145) = $1.595.

Example Two: Alternative Service Sourcing. Department 3

TABLE 1/MONTHLY BUDGET, DEPARTMENT S

Service labor	$ 9,800	*
Supervision	1,400	**
Supplies	280	*
Depreciation	1,750	***
Other costs	70	*
Total	$ 13,300	
Normal volume in service hours	1,400	

   * Proportionately variable with volume.
  ** Salary of department head.
*** Straight-line amortization of equipment; would remain for other products produced if "X" were eliminated.

TABLE 2/NORMAL MONTHLY OPERATING STATISTICS

	Department 1	Department 2
Normal monthly operating volume/ basis for allocating overhead	25,000 lbs. of output	10,000 direct labor hours
Normal monthly consumption of Department S services	300 service hours	200 service hours

Consumption of Department S services varies in direct proportion to changes in operating volume.

One unit of Product X weighs 10 pounds and requires five direct labor hours in Department 2.

TABLE 3/COST AND OPERATING DATA, UTILITY, INC.

	Advanced	Basic
Product Data:		
Selling price	$ 5.00	$ 2.00
Manufacturing cost:		
Direct material	$ .50	$ .30
Direct labor	1.00	.50
Overhead	1.50	.75
Total	$ 3.00	$ 1.55
Overhead Rate Each Product:		
Variable	$ .75	$ .30
Traceable fixed	.60	.30
Allocated fixed	.15 *	.15 *
Total	$ 1.50	$ .75
Sales discounts and allowances (percent of gross sales)	5%	1%
Sales commission per unit	$ .25	$ .05
Advertising and other direct selling costs (per month)	$20,000	$40,000
Sales promotion, general company administration, etc.	$78,000**	

 * $4,000 of nontraceable fixed costs would be eliminated if either product is dropped.
** These costs could be reduced by $10,000 per month if either product line is dropped. Now they are allocated on the basis of gross sales dollars.

is another production department in the Wichita factory, and it uses a good deal of Department S service (100 service hours each month for routine work plus one service hour for each 100 direct labor hours in Department 3). Normal value in Department 3 is 10,000 DLHs per month, on which a departmental overhead rate is computed.

Department 3 uses an outside company, Missouri, Inc., to do some work the Wichita plant's own service departments are not equipped to do. Missouri has offered to expand its service by doing the work now done by Department S but for a flat fee of $1,400 a month. The decision is to be made by the manager of the Wichita plant. Department S will continue to service the factory's other departments in any case.

Full Absorption Costing—Under normal conditions, Department 3 would be allocated $1,900 of Department S cost (200 hours @ $9.50). This cost compares most unfavorably with the $1,400 bid price from Missouri, Inc., and would indicate that acceptance of the contract would be profitable.

Attributable Costing—Assuming the same definition of "attributable cost" as previously, the cost allocated to Department 3 would be $1,450 (200 hours @ $7.25). Now the case for acceptance of the contract is not so clear.

Example Three: Product Profitability. Utility, Inc., has two products, known by the trade names *Basic* and *Advanced*. *Basic* was introduced several years ago to compete on a price basis in a mass market. *Advanced* serves customers interested in a product of high quality and who are willing to pay for it.

The original forecasts called for *Basic's* sales to reach 300,000 units a month this year. This year's budget established a more modest objective of 250,000 units a month. Volume was only 200,000 units last month, while sales of *Advanced* were at their budgeted level of 50,000 units. At this volume, revenues don't even cover costs.

Management questions the desirability of keeping *Basic*. If *Basic* is dropped, Utility, Inc., will become a one-product company again. Cost and operating data for the analysis are presented in Table 3. In order to emphasize the concept being presented, we will assume that, except for volume, no other cost variances occurred. Similarly, we assume that the Table 3 data are typical of what can be expected for the foreseeable future.

Full Absorption Costing—A profitability analysis of the two products, in which all costs are allocated to the products, is presented in Table 4. Indicating a monthly loss of $34,500, it would suggest that *Basic* should be dropped.

Attributable Costing—A profitability analysis using attributable costing is presented in Table 5. This analysis suggests that a decision to drop the *Basic* product would increase the firm's loss by $37,000. Clearly, a decision to eliminate a particular segment should be made only if its revenues do not exceed the costs "attributable" to that segment.

DOES ABC CHANGE THIS ANALYSIS?

A reasonably convincing argument can be advanced that the answer is no. The costs being incurred by a company do not change with activity-based costing. ABC only changes how we allocate these costs, not the fundamental nature of costs. Costs which are or are not "attributable" do not change their colors magically by adopting activity-based costing. Therefore it appears reasonable to expect that distortions similar to those illustrated would continue to exist.

A convincing case can be advanced that ABC should be modified to allocate only those costs that can be eliminated over time if that activity were discontinued and capacity were to be reduced accordingly. Perhaps activity-based cost-

TABLE 4/PRODUCT PROFITABILITY ANALYSIS, FULL ABSORPTION COSTING

	Advanced	Basic
Sales (units)	50,000	200,000
Gross sales revenue	$250,000	$400,000
Less: sales returns & discounts	12,500	4,000
Net sales revenue	$237,500	$396,000
Cost of sales (@ normal cost/unit)	$150,000	$310,000
Volume variance (attributed to Basic product)		22,500
Sales commissions	12,500	10,000
Advertising & other direct selling	20,000	40,000
Sales promotion, general administrative, etc.	30,000	48,000
Total costs and expenses	$212,500	$430,500
Net income per product	$ 25,000	($ 34,500)

TABLE 5/PRODUCT PROFITABILITY ANALYSIS, ATTRIBUTABLE COSTING

	Advanced	Basic
Gross sales revenue	$250,000	$400,000
Less: sales returns & discounts	12,500	4,000
Net sales revenue	$237,500	$396,000
Cost of sales (traceable costs only)	$142,500	$280,000
Volume variance (traceable fixed)		15,000
Attributable fixed costs	4,000	4,000
Sales commissions	12,500	10,000
Advertising & other direct costs	20,000	40,000
Attributable general costs	10,000	10,000
Total costs	$189,000	$359,000
Contribution per product	$ 48,500	$ 37,000

ing should be modified to obtain *direct* activity-based costs for the majority of decision-making purposes and *full absorption* activity-based costs for special-purpose reports desirous of identifying total resources consumed. ∎

Douglas Sharp is associate professor of accounting in the School of Accountancy, W. Frank Barton School of Business, Wichita State University. He holds BBA and MBA degrees from the University of Oklahoma and a Ph.D. degree from the University of Missouri-Columbia.

Linda F. Christensen is assistant professor of accounting in the School of Accountancy, W. Frank Barton School of Business, Wichita State University. She holds a BSBA degree from the University of Missouri-Columbia, an MBA degree from Memphis State University, and a Ph.D. degree from the University of South Carolina. Both authors are members of the Wichita Chapter, through which this article was submitted. They may be reached at (316) 689-3215.

[1]Our definition of attributable cost is broader than the one advanced originally. The concept itself was coined by Gordon Shillinglaw. See Gordon Shillinglaw, *Managerial Cost Accounting*, Richard D. Irwin, Inc., 1977. (Examples we used are based on problems included in Chapters 8 and 9.)

	Yes	No
Is this article of interest to you? If so, circle appropriate number on Reader Service Card.	70	71

COMPLETING THE PICTURE:

Economic Choices with ABC

Separate fixed and variable costs and voila! ABC becomes relevant for decisions.

BY MICHAEL D. WOODS, CPA

Certificate of Merit, 1991-92

At the company where I worked previously, line managers ignored the traditional cost accounting system. Instead, factory managers and their staffs depended on the production staffs to prepare the information they really used.

In the company's production facilities, a whole class of workers were accustomed to providing analysis off-line. They used special cost investigations to find causes of deviations that should have been apparent from reports prepared by the system. They viewed cost allocations as uncontrollable tricks "done to us by those bean counters."

These workers treated internal services as free goods. They thought that material cost only what was paid for it and did not consider the cost of providing it at the work site.

Although these circumstances were unfortunate, I discovered they also are common. Manufacturing management literature and the Institute of Management Accountants' study, *Management Accounting in the New Manufacturing Environment*, have revealed that most of American industry is dissatisfied with its cost accounting systems. Production managers just won't use them for their daily decision making.

Aware of these charges, management accountants recognized the need to change cost accounting reports and methods in order to regain their place as valued contributors to their companies' operations. As a result, activity-

Uniphoto.

Both managers and industrial engineers follow the principle that only variable costs are relevant for any managerial or engineering change decision.

based costing (ABC) was developed to assign costs from the point of incurrence through a company's chain of service, support, and production functions to ultimate products.

Activity-based costing has a weak point. It may correct deficiencies in comparing resources consumed to ultimate products, but it mixes fixed and variable costs. Thus, effective economic choices are difficult and require analysis outside a firm's regular cost accounting system.

A refinement can make the ABC system more useful for line managers at various organizational levels. It entails keeping fixed and variable costs

separate throughout a firm's cost accounting structure. Reporting both fixed and variable elements of transferred costs preserves the advantages of activity-based costing and allows management to make rational choices among economic alternatives.

MIXING FIXED AND VARIABLE COSTS

The advantages of ABC are mainly in its rational assignment of costs. The costs allocated to an internal organizational unit or to a final product are those that actually benefit the recipient.

TABLE 1/TYPICAL ABC BASES OF COST ASSIGNMENT (Cost Drivers)

Cost Center	Cost Drivers
Accounting	Reports requested Dollars expended
Personnel	Job change actions Hiring actions Training hours Counseling hours
Data processing	Reports requested Transactions processed Programming hours Program changes requested
Production engineering	Hours spent in each shop Job specification changes requested Product change notices processed
Quality control	Hours spent in each shop Defects discovered Samples analyzed
Plant services	Preventive maintenance cycles Hours spent in each shop Repair maintenance actions
Material services	Dollar value of requisitions Number of transactions processed Number of personnel in direct support
Utilities	Direct usage (metered to shop) Space occupied
Production shops	Fixed per-job charge Setups made Direct labor Machine hours Number of moves Material applied

USE OF THE TERMS "FIXED" AND "VARIABLE" COSTS

In some of his earlier work, Professor Robert Kaplan argues that we are mistaken to treat any costs as fixed because in the long, comprehensive view there are no fixed costs. The term "fixed cost" as I use it in this article refers to the capacity-related, period costs of being in business at this time with this facility. Although this use may seem like a return to "the bad old ways," it agrees with the definition used in microeconomic analysis, where the "firm" is defined by its capital stock and operating unity so that a change of plant requires treating the company as a new and different "firm." Besides, there is surprising agreement among practitioners about classifying the actual costs of any specific real installation. And we are all aware that so-called fixed, capacity-related costs must be managed by different techniques than so-called variable, volume-related costs.

The use of the term "fixed costs" is just a way of connoting the longer-term, process-related methods needed to manage them. We don't really mean "costs that can't be changed no matter what we do." In fact, fixed costs will be treated as variable in making capital investment decisions, and variable costs may be treated as fixed for decisions about direct labor when operations are below capacity but short-time and lay-offs are not wanted. I have not yet talked with anyone who was confused about these applications of economic principles, but most still use the conventional terms in this way. Consequently, I have done so here.

Readers who disagree with this use of terms will find that the principles that are outlined apply equally well if they substitute "uncontrollable/controllable," "capacity/utilization," or even (though care is needed here) "overhead/indirect/direct" for "fixed/variable." The goal is to create better decision support systems with ABC. Ideal decision support systems are probably unachievable in real organizations, each of which is a moving target and is different in products, processes, culture, and present condition. ∎

ABC achieves rational cost assignment by collecting for each production, support, or administrative unit all the costs that can be placed within it reasonably. When the costs of inputs have been collected, the causes of cost within the unit are explored. These causal relationships are called "cost drivers."

ABC seeks to identify and eliminate drivers that are not valuable outputs through process value analysis, a procedure for reviewing activities to find out how much they contribute to customer value. When the cost drivers are valuable outputs, they provide a basis for assigning the unit's costs to users because demand for the outputs generates the costs. (Table 1 gives some examples.)

All costs incurred within an organizational unit, along with costs assigned from other units whose cost drivers it uses, are further assigned to those who use the unit's services or products, with its cost drivers as a base. (Figure 1 illustrates the cost flow.)

If the producing unit is a support or staff section, its costs become part of the using unit's total costs for further assignment. If the producing unit is a production shop, the recipient of its costs will be its physical products. As Figure 1 shows, the chain of cost flows stops at the final product that will be delivered to an ultimate customer. But ABC mixes fixed and variable costs before assigning them to outputs, a circumstance that can lead to suboptimal decisions.

IRRATIONAL DECISIONS

The distinction between fixed and variable cost elements is vital to economic decision making. A basic management principle is derived from a simple economic principle—in managerial decision making, *relevant costs are marginal costs*. Only the costs that will change are relevant for any managerial decision. Those that will not be changed by a particular decision are irrelevant in selecting among alternatives. Industrial engineers study the same ideas under the name "engineering economy."

ABC submerges the old distinction between fixed and variable costs because it assigns all costs of an organizational unit to its cost drivers as an internal transfer price. When it combines fixed and variable costs in valuing an organizational unit's cost drivers, managers are denied vital information. Managers cannot make rational decisions about using the internal cost drivers because they do not know which costs will change for the company.

The marketing department cannot make informed decisions about custom orders. They know only how costs assigned to their units or products will change. But some of the assigned costs are fixed and still will be incurred by the company whether or not transferred to their particular units.

As an example, consider an internal service department such as personnel. Cost drivers for a personnel department may be those shown in Table 1—job actions, hiring actions, training hours, or counseling hours. By making costs that are fixed for the company, such as personnel department overhead, appear variable to shop supervisors (because the shops may decide to use varying amounts of personnel department cost drivers) ABC can lead to irrational decisions about hiring, training, and overtime. Other decisions such as capital investment, make/buy, and production routings require off-line cost studies to separate marginal costs out of the ABC cost centers. Texts and courses on ABC deal with this problem by requiring periodic process value analysis and special studies.

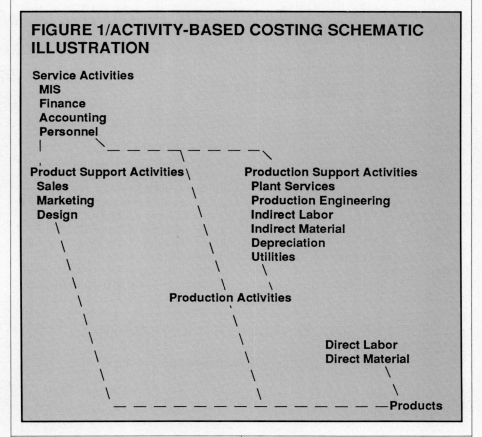

FIGURE 1/ACTIVITY-BASED COSTING SCHEMATIC ILLUSTRATION

Service Activities
  MIS
  Finance
  Accounting
  Personnel

Product Support Activities
  Sales
  Marketing
  Design

Production Support Activities
  Plant Services
  Production Engineering
  Indirect Labor
  Indirect Material
  Depreciation
  Utilities

Production Activities

Direct Labor
Direct Material

Products

Special studies could be reduced if adequate information were available in the ABC cost accounting system. Further, on a day-to-day basis users of cost drivers could make rational decisions about the degree to which they use the services of any department or section. If costs were assigned properly, supervisors would naturally make the best choices for the company. They would not have an incentive to maximize their own cost/value ratio. Thus, the overall company production system would be far more self-regulating.

WE CAN OVERCOME

The information needed for optimal decisions at each organizational level can be furnished by an ABC system. To make the system effective, we must recognize that different decisions require different relevant cost information. Costs that are fixed for one kind of decision will be changed by another. Further, different decisions are made by different organizational units. Therefore, *different organizational units require different relevant cost information.* In order to control their processes, production shop supervisors require direct labor, production indirect labor, and direct material cost information. If other pro-

FIGURE 2/DECISION SUPPORT MODEL

DECISION LEVELS	COSTS	ACTIVITIES
Company Strategic Decisions / Production Capacity Decisions / Administrative Cost Control Decisions / Service Utilization Decisions / Process Design Decisions / Process (Shop) Cost Control Decisions / Process (Shop) Utilization Decisions	FIXED COSTS / VARIABLE COSTS	Product Support Activities
	FIXED COSTS / VARIABLE COSTS	Service Activities
	FIXED COSTS / VARIABLE COSTS	Production Support Activities
	FIXED COSTS / VARIABLE COSTS	Production Activities
	LABOR / MATERIAL	Direct Inputs

duction indirect costs—such as indirect material or utilities—are significant and controllable, the shop supervisor may want to see the cost information. (For example, machining and plating processes typically use electricity as a controllable input, but assembly may not.)

Production planners use the same information as production shop supervisors, but differently. Their job is to choose the most efficient processes for making the final product rather than to control the operation of those processes. They need to select production routings among shops, including outside vendors to whom processes may be contracted.

Facility planners use the same variable costs as the preceding daily decision makers, but they also need some

ABC can be more useful for line managers at various levels if fixed and variable costs are kept separate throughout the cost accounting structure.

fixed cost information (along with non-cost information such as marketing forecasts of required production volume). At a basic level, for example, the initial cost of changing from incandescent to fluorescent lights might be compared along with the actual operating costs of the current lighting and estimated operating costs of the replacements. At the more complex level of selecting among alternative machin-

ing capabilities, maintenance, training, programming, and other production overhead costs also must be considered.

Product design engineers need variable costs for processes that are operating below capacity and total costs for processes that will have to be enlarged. If new processes must be developed, even more cost data will be needed.

Strategic planners use all the costs above. They also use plant overhead, such as costs of production and facility planning staffs and costs of plant accounting and plant management, when deciding whether to construct a new plant. If a projected new plant replaces or enlarges existing capabilities, strategic planners can stop with these costs. But if addition or deletion of product lines is considered, even marketing and sales become variable costs. And at the highest level, that of acquiring or establishing a free-standing subsidiary, virtually all costs vary with the decision at hand.

Managers at each organizational level can make better decisions if both fixed and variable costs are presented. They can select among alternatives for process design, process control, production planning, and production routing, and for deciding whether to continue, enlarge, begin, or eliminate a production process or a product line within an organization.

Current costs are doubly important because the estimated costs of new alternatives also may be based on existing cost data. Figure 2 schematically illustrates the kinds of decisions that require various combinations of fixed and variable cost information. It shows how different organizational units use different combinations of fixed and variable cost information in making the decisions that their responsibilities require.

WHICH TO REPORT— RELEVANT OR FULL COSTS?

Putting the schematic in Figure 2 into concrete form, Table 2 illustrates a cost report that might be

TABLE 2/PRODUCTION SUPERVISOR'S SAMPLE REPORT

Plating Shop Supervisor's Report
February 199X

	Total $	Variable $	Fixed $
Space occupied			
Depreciation (1,574 sq. ft.)	756		756
Heat and light	36		36
Equipment			
Depreciation	1,190		1,190
Maintenance—scheduled PM	344		344
Maintenance—repairs	1,443	1,443	
Internal services			
Quality control (13.1 hours)	419	223	197
Data processing (8 payroll & 5 reports)	539	97	442
Production engineering (6.3 hours)	347	233	113
Personnel department services			
Training (18 hours)	540	432	108
Administration (2 job actions)	76	64	12
Hiring		0	0
Compensation			
Indirect wages and benefits incurred	4,232		4,232
Direct labor and benefits incurred	9,034	9,034	
Direct material and energy			
Electricity (metered)	287	287	
Metal and metal salts	3,896	3,896	
Other chemicals	1,856	1,856	
Material			
Indirect production material	591	591	
Administrative supplies	33		33
Total costs applied	25,619	18,156	7,463
26,275 units plated; cost per unit	.9750	.6910	.2840

Activity-based costing as presently described in the literature would report only the "total" column. As noted in the text, either the full three-column report or only variable components of space, equipment, and internal services may be furnished to line supervisors depending on company preferences.
Note that "fixed" costs are not necessarily invariable, but they are caused by the simple fact that the plant is open and the shop exists. When they change, they do so in response to the supervisor's managerial actions, not directly in response to production volume.

furnished to a production shop supervisor. Whether to report all the information shown or to report only information relevant for each unit's usual decision requirements depends on a company's managerial philosophy. ABC, as described in literature to date, would display only the total cost column. For economically correct decisions, only the variable costs of services used should be reported (shown in bold type). The only fixed cost information managers need is for their own shop.

Providing data on only those elements managers can affect will focus their thinking where they can most help the company. If data are provided on fixed costs managers cannot affect, they may be misled as to their responsibilities. On the other hand, providing such data gives managers a wider perspective and facilitates team loyalty and trust. It might also allow a manager to offer suggestions to the internal service suppliers as to which aspects of their services are worth the total cost, a kind of continuous process value analysis.

In total quality companies, these suggestions probably would occur in quality boards or circles. The choice of whether to supply simpler or more comprehensive information depends on company goals, culture, staff development plans, and the willingness to train supervisors in using the informa-

EARLIER ARTICLES ON ABC DEFICIENCIES

Three IMA Certificate of Merit-winning articles for 1990-91 ("A New View of Activity-Based Costing," September 1991; "Triple Threat Strategy," October 1991; and "Activity-Based Costing for Marketing," November 1991) recognized that activity-based costing is deficient in application to actual managerial problems.

"Triple Threat Strategy" is better on theory and clearly indicates where activity-based costing in its present state is deficient for making rational, effective, economic decisions. It discusses the matter from a direct costing and contribution margin perspective.

"A New View of Activity-Based Costing" shows how separating costs for one type of managerial decision, product profitability, can be done using the ideas of avoidable or attributable costs.

"Activity-Based Costing for Marketing" develops activity-based costing in a new area. In its Table 2 it shows separate calculation of fixed and variable components for application to cost drivers. But in Table 4, the resulting management report, it aggregates them again. In the examples given no false conclusions are likely, but a marginally profitable territory might be shut down mistakenly based on its absorption-cost-based profit when its contribution to fixed costs was significant. Those fixed costs then would be transferred to other territories at the next calculation, and the company would lose profitability at the bottom line.

This article presents a decision support framework that accords with economic theory for as many types of managerial decisions as possible, using activity-based costing while avoiding multiple accounting systems and frequent special studies. ∎

Uniphoto.

> *Only the costs that will change are relevant for any managerial decision.*

tion properly.

ABC was developed to address the concerns of manufacturing managers about the relevance of conventional cost data to the actual manufacturing processes they controlled. ABC meets these concerns effectively by assigning to each product the costs of all activities that are used in its manufacture, but it does not allow for rational economic choices at most organizational levels because it mixes fixed and variable costs.

Separating fixed and variable costs allows managers to apply the proper techniques to reduce waste by managing those aspects of production capacity and process design (fixed) and of production methods and practices (variable) that are within their scope of decision. This refinement of activity-based costing can make it the one cost accounting system a company needs while minimizing off-line investigations and analyses. ∎

Michael D. Woods, CPA, is controller of SMSi in Winston-Salem, N.C. He is a member of the Piedmont Greensboro (N.C.) Chapter, through which this article was submitted. He can be reached at SMSi, (919) 759-7477 or at home, (919) 993-6612.

Is this article of interest to you? If so, circle appropriate number on Reader Service Card.	**Yes** 56	**No** 57

Separating fixed and variable costs allows managers to make informed decisions about those aspects of production that they have the power to change.

HOW ABC CAN ADD VALUE TO DECISION MAKING

Refinements can make an accounting system more accurate and more flexible.

BY LINDA F. CHRISTENSEN AND
DOUGLAS SHARP

If a management accounting system is to be of maximum value to decision makers, it must be flexible and adaptable, providing quality information on demand that addresses the needs of its customers. Activity-based costing provides relevant and accurate information for strategic decisions concerning product pricing, customer and product profitability analysis, and process improvement. Some refinements in cost accumulation and reporting formats for ABC also will, we believe, enhance its value for decision making in both the short and intermediate terms while maintaining its value for strategic decision-making purposes. We further believe that these modifications will provide the necessary database of information from which special studies can be made.

Specifically, we recommend:

■ Categorizing activity costs into short-term variable, short-term fixed, and committed fixed costs rather than accumulating these costs only as aggregated totals.

■ Determining the allocation rates for both categories of fixed costs based on the capacity provided through the incurrence of these costs.

FRAMEWORK FOR COSTS

The fact that all costs are subject to management action and therefore are variable in the long run does not preclude cost categorizations related to the timing of possible management actions. Short-term variable, short-term fixed, and committed fixed costs have different timing implications for management action. In the short and intermediate terms, costs remain that will not be affected by decisions being contemplated. The management accounting system should identify these costs clearly so the decision options available to management can be supported.

Short-term variable costs change in direct proportion to changes in the cost driver used. They are "volume driven," although the volume measure may not be units of product but rather the appropriate cost driver. Thus, decisions related to unit-level cost drivers or batch-level cost drivers (broadly defined as batches, orders, runs, sched-

ules, or setups) potentially have short-term impacts.

The significant difference between short-term variable costs and short-term and committed fixed costs is the time horizon within which management can impact the level of expenditures. The usual length of time for management to affect decisions about *short-term fixed costs* is within a year. Decisions about these costs are not subject to directly proportional results, and short-term fixed costs may result from batch-level cost drivers or product-sustaining activities. Short-term fixed costs subject to batch-level drivers vary with the number of batches (broadly defined) but are independent of the number of units within a batch. Costs of a product-sustaining activity—for example, personnel costs in a purchasing department—would tend to vary in discrete steps.

The impact of decisions related to *committed fixed costs* can occur only in the long term. Decisions about committed fixed costs are not subject to directly proportional results, and, typically, such costs are driven by product-sustaining, facility-sustaining, or entity-sustaining activities.[1] Many costs associated with property, plant and equipment fall into this category, and changing the level of these costs requires substantial long-term adjustments to the capacity provided. The nature of both short-term and committed fixed costs is such that a precise matching of capacity with short-term operational needs usually is not possible.

Finally, the distinction between resource spending (acquiring the capacity to perform activities) and resource usage (actual capacity usage), developed by Robin Cooper and Robert Kaplan,[2] integrates with our cost categorizations. Capacity utilization potentially affects both short-term fixed and long-term committed costs. Thus, idle capacity costs are possible with both cost categories.

These cost categories are being recognized in the field. For example, Michael O'Guin notes that unit cost figures must be recomputed for different product and volume assumptions—explicitly recognizing that not all costs are going to vary by even the cost drivers selected. Kaplan and Cooper support the idea of capacity measures being used. O'Guin concurs but notes the difficulty of establishing a plant capacity for this purpose.[3]

Our argument is that the cost variability distinction should be made explicit in both the management accounting system and in management reports. Most companies encounter difficulties when determining overall plant capacity, but it is much more feasible to establish capacity measures for individual activity areas.

AN ABC ILLUSTRATION

For responsibility accounting purposes, we advocate distinguishing between a manager's controllable (subject to his/her decision) and non-controllable (allocated) short-term and committed fixed costs, even though all costs are controllable in the long term by at least one manager's responsibility level. Therefore, for simplicity, our case example illustrates the entity responsibility level and eliminates the need to identify short-term fixed and long-term committed costs as controllable and noncontrollable. Additionally, the example will deal only with manufacturing costs although the concepts also would apply to marketing and administrative costs.

Traditional ABC.[4] The Wichita Machine Shop produces three types of precisely engineered components for aircraft engines—Model 1000, Model 2000, and Model 3000. Model 1000 is the high-volume basic component. Models 2000 and 3000 are progressively more sophisticated, with higher-quality and a greater number of parts involved in their manufacture. Budgeted production data for these products for 1993 are presented in Table 1.

The company has just implemented an activity-based costing system. Its single manufacturing department has been divided into six activity areas, appropriate cost drivers have been selected, and costing rates for the year have been established (see Table 2). Total and unit costs per product under this ABC system are presented in Table 3.

An analysis of the total costs in each activity area finds that these costs can

Parker Hannifin

An ABC system that measures capacity use can help companies prevent production bottlenecks. The employee above would know the correct number of parts to manufacture.

be subdivided into the three suggested categories of short-term variable, short-term fixed, and committed fixed costs. Using capacity measures for the appropriate cost drivers enables the company to determine cost driver application rates by activity center and cost variable (Table 4). Revised total and per unit product costs are presented in Table 5. Note that costing rates

are based on capacity provided but are charged to production on the basis of actual usage.

DECISION-MAKING IMPLICATIONS

Fully aggregated traditional ABC costs have a number of shortcomings for both long-term and short-term decisions. Specifically, ABC costs:

1. Include costs that will not cease, even in the long run (included would be most of the entity-sustaining expenditures);
2. Include costs that do not change in proportion to an individual product in the product line;
3. Assume that costs will be reduced proportionately—even when warnings are provided that cost reductions will occur "in time"; and
4. Assume that there are more profitable alternative uses of the capacity released with the decision.

TABLE 1/WICHITA MACHINE SHOP BUDGETED PRODUCTION DATA FOR THE YEAR 1993

	Model 1000	Model 2000	Model 3000
Unit production	10,000	5,000	800
Direct materials cost per unit	$80	$50	$110
Number of parts per unit	30	50	120
Direct labor hours per unit	2	5	12
Machine hours per unit	7	7	15
Production orders	300	70	200
Production setups	100	50	50
Orders shipped	1,000	2,000	800

While we do not recommend that the suggested revisions be used blindly and without further analysis, we do believe that the revised data are more useful in at least the following respects:

1. Costs that definitely will increase or decrease (short-term variable) are identified clearly.
2. Costs that probably will increase or decrease (short-term fixed), but not necessarily proportionately, are identified clearly.
3. Costs that may decline (committed fixed), assuming there are alternative uses of released capacity or the firm is in a position to liquidate the capacity, are identified clearly.

These refinements increase the management accounting system's flexibility in responding to management's information needs. The cost categorization framework will reduce the lead time in preparing those special cost studies still required.

Next we'll demonstrate this increased flexibility in these decision-making situations: product profitability analyses, both short- and long-term; pricing decisions, both short- and long-term; short-term make-or-buy decisions; and cost reduction efforts.

PRODUCT PROFITABILITY

Assume that the Wichita Machine Shop has been selling its Model 1000 for $300 per unit (price based on cost data used before implementing the ABC system). A product line income statement, using the current volume of 10,000 units per year and the suggested reporting format, would appear as follows:

Revenue		$3,000,000
Short-term variable costs:		
Materials	$ 800,000	
Other variable costs	388,000	
		1,188,000
Excess of revenue over short-term variable costs		$1,812,000
Short-term fixed costs		777,467
Short-term margin		$1,034,533
Committed fixed costs		1,266,327
Income after all manufacturing costs		($ 231,794)

It is apparent that Wichita Machine Shop has been undercosting and un-

derpricing its Model 1000. The previous cost system allocated overhead on the basis of direct labor hours. Model 1000 used relatively fewer hours than the other models so was allocated less cost. It also is apparent from the product-line income statement, however, that eliminating Model 1000 will, in the short and intermediate term, increase the company's profitability only if alternative profitable uses exist for the company's current capacity or if the company is in a position to liquidate that portion of costs identified as committed. Until it has analyzed the situation and devised its planned course of action, Wichita Machine Shop should maintain its production of Model 1000. As our suggested reporting format indicates, Model 1000 does not show a loss until after committed fixed costs have been allocated.

PRICING DECISIONS

First, we suggest that allocating fixed costs on the basis of capacity measurements improves the accuracy of the cost data. For example, given the capacity assumptions of the re-

vised ABC system, a comparison of unit cost figures in Tables 3 and 5 suggests that cost differentials can be significant—9.4%, 8.8%, and 7.4% for the three products, respectively. Cost-based pricing systems still exist in business, especially when market-based systems are less feasible. In a highly competitive global environment, differentials of 7% to 9% can make a big difference in the competitive pricing of a product. Resources representing excess capacity are important and should be highlighted for management's attention, but they should not be reported as a cost of producing the company's products.

Additionally, capacity-adjusted figures guard against year-to-year price changes based solely on temporary swings in demand and actual production. ABC costs that fail to incorporate this capacity dimension tend to encourage price changes based on temporary volume changes instead of costs.

Not all pricing decisions, however, are long-term strategic situations. We could cite, for example,

1. Special-order price negotiations;

TABLE 2/BUDGETED ACTIVITY-BASED CONVERSION COSTS

Activity Area	Cost Driver	Costs	Cost Driver Total	Costing Rate
Material handling	# of parts	$258,400	646,000	$ .40
Production scheduling	prod. orders	114,000	570	200.00
Setup labor	prod. setups	616,300	200	3,081.50
Automated machinery	mach. hours	3,053,700	117,000	26.10
Finishing	direct labor hours	1,092,000	54,600	20.00
Packaging and shipping	orders	190,000	3,800	50.00

TABLE 3/TOTAL AND PER UNIT COSTS TRADITIONAL ACTIVITY-BASED COSTING

	Model 1000	Model 2000	Model 3000
Direct materials	$ 800,000	$ 250,000	$ 88,000
Conversion costs:			
Material handling	120,000	100,000	38,400
Production scheduling	60,000	14,000	40,000
Setups	308,150	154,075	154,075
Machinery	1,827,000	913,500	313,200
Finishing	400,000	500,000	192,000
Packaging/shipping	50,000	100,000	40,000
Total costs	$3,565,150	$2,031,575	$ 865,675
Cost per unit	$ 356.52	$ 406.32	$1,082.09

2. Pricing decisions for a new, untapped market when the product has lost its value in its original markets; and
3. Pricing decisions during the declining product life cycle phase.

The cost categorization framework provides management with the ability to test prices for both short- and long-term profitability.

MAKE-OR-BUY DECISIONS

Assume, for example, that Wichita Machine Shop is notified by one of its key suppliers that, due to labor problems, it will be unable to meet Wichita's requirements fully for a particular component during the second quarter of the year. Wichita has the capability of producing the component internally or of securing the component from another supplier.

What is the relevant internal cost figure Wichita should use to try to make the most appropriate decision? Given this short-term situation, we suggest comparing the outside bid with only the incremental costs associated with the possibility of doing the work internally. The suggested cost categorization and reporting format clearly identifies relevant costs and provides a more useful basis to determine exactly which incremental costs apply.

Materials costs and identified short-term variable costs are involved. Short-term fixed costs probably are not relevant because existing capacity is available in most activity centers (see Table 4). It also is apparent that capacity exists in terms of committed fixed costs. In fact, available capacity would be a prerequisite for even considering the alternative of producing internally.

COST REDUCTION EFFORTS

Successful cost reduction efforts depend on the ability of the company to become more efficient in terms of the activities that cause costs to be incurred—one of the most important benefits of activity-based costing. The ability of the company to reduce its costs, however, is affected by a time horizon also, as well as a knowledge of how costs will behave with respect to cost drivers selected. Without this detail, the management accounting system provides only rough indications of the extent to which costs can be reduced over time and in some fashion.

Already it is being recognized that it is important to subclassify costs in terms of such categories as unit-driven, batch-driven, product-driven, and the like. We concur with this refinement because the data clearly indicate to management the nature of the effort that must be undertaken in order to affect the level of costs incurred. Additionally, the nature of the decision to affect committed fixed costs is significantly different from a decision to impact either short-term variable costs or short-term fixed costs. The latter can be impacted either immediately or within a budget cycle, whereas the former requires more drastic action, including the possibility of capacity liquidation.

An important benefit of the revised system is its ability to provide measures of capacity use. In the planning/budgeting cycle, such measures can indicate the potential for bottlenecks and for excess capacity in the production process. Further analysis of the cost figures would be needed in order to be more precise concerning the extent to which cost levels could be adjusted. The data become more useful when a company explicitly identifies costs in terms of the time horizon management has for decision making.

For performance measurement and

> *An important benefit of the revised system is its ability to provide measures of capacity use.*

TABLE 4/REVISED ACTIVITY-BASED COSTING RATES

Activity Area	Short-Term Variable	Short-Term Fixed	Committed Fixed
Material Handling:			
Total costs	$ 103,360	$ 103,360	$ 51,680
Capacity measures (# of parts)	646,000	650,000	675,000
Costing rates	$ .16	$ .159	$ .0766
Production Scheduling:			
Total costs*	$ -0-	$ 102,600	$ 11,400
Capacity measures (production orders)	570	600	600
Costing rates	-0-	$ 171	$ 19
Setups:			
Total costs	$ 160,000	$ 136,890	$ 319,410
Capacity measures (production setups)	200	200	200
Costing rates	$ 800	$ 684.45	$ 1,597.05
Machinery:			
Total costs*	$ -0-	$ 916,110	$ 2,137,590
Capacity measures (machine hours)	117,000	125,000	150,000
Costing rates	$ -0-	$ 7.32888	$ 14.2506
Finishing:			
Total costs	$ 655,200	$ 218,400	$ 218,400
Capacity measures (DL hours)	54,600	56,000	60,000
Costing rates	$ 12.00	$ 3.90	$ 3.64
Packaging/Shipping:			
Total costs	$ 76,000	$ 76,000	$ 38,000
Capacity measures (Orders shipped)	3,800	4,000	5,000
Costing rates	$ 20.00	$ 19.00	$ 7.60

*There would, in all probability, be some short-term variable costs in these activities. We have assumed them to be insignificant for purposes of this illustration.

control purposes, particularly in a continuous improvement environment, capacity measures can serve as useful indicators of the extent to which improvements are leading to possible cost reductions. Given increasingly more fixed than variable cost structures, cost improvements will occur from the company's ability to minimize excess capacity or to use existing capacity more effectively to get more production.

Performance reports for evaluating managers of activity centers also would appear to be more useful with capacity-adjusted measures. While managers may not be able to exercise much influence in the short term over the level of fixed costs being incurred, they can, through effective action, impact the extent to which the capacity inherent in these costs is used. Not only will managers be "made aware of these costs"—the traditional argument for making such allocations to responsibility centers—but performance reports (because costs are allocated on the basis of actual use) will reflect the actions of the manager in impacting these costs.

DIFFERENT COSTS FOR DIFFERENT PURPOSES

As we've said, managerial decision making in today's environment is both complex and variable. The current emphasis of activity-based costing is on strategic decisions, but short- and intermediate-term planning and control decisions also are required. A company's accounting information system must be flexible and adaptable and designed to provide cost data focused on the particular decision that must be made. There is not a single cost concept that can fulfill this function. The phrase "different costs for different purposes" should be on every management accountant's desk.

Refining ABC to incorporate time-horizon cost categories and applying costs on the basis of capacity provided will increase both the accuracy and the flexibility of a management accounting system. Even direct costing, used in the appropriate decision-making context, may be relevant once again.

Most, if not all, traditional cost concepts—product/period, direct/indirect, controllable/noncontrollable, variable/fixed—are still cost-type information the management accounting system should be able to deliver in the particular decision-making context.

TABLE 5/TOTAL AND PER UNIT COSTS REVISED ACTIVITY-BASED COSTING SYSTEM			
	Model 1000	Model 2000	Model 3000
Direct materials	$ 800,000	$ 250,000	$ 88,000
Conversion costs:			
Unit short-term variable:			
Material handling	48,000	40,000	15,360
Finishing	240,000	300,000	115,200
Batch short-term variable:			
Setups	80,000	40,000	40,000
Packaging/shipping	20,000	40,000	16,000
Unit short-term fixed:			
Material handling	47,700	39,750	15,264
Machinery	513,022	256,511	87,947
Finishing	78,000	97,500	37,440
Batch short-term fixed:			
Production scheduling	51,300	11,970	34,200
Setups	68,445	34,223	34,223
Packaging/shipping	19,000	38,000	15,200
Commited fixed:			
Material handling	22,980	19,150	7,354
Production scheduling	5,700	1,330	3,800
Setups	159,705	79,853	79,853
Machinery	997,542	498,771	171,007
Finishing	72,800	91,000	34,944
Packaging/shipping	7,600	15,200	6,080
Total costs	$ 3,231,794	$1,853,258	$ 801,872
Cost per unit	$ 323.18	$ 370.65	$1,002.34

The phrase 'different costs for different purposes' should be on every management accountant's desk.

The problem never has been that the concepts are bad but that companies have applied or used these concepts inappropriately in the decision-making context. Avoiding misconstrued applications is the real challenge for management accountants in the new environment we face. ■

Linda Christensen is assistant professor of accounting in the school of accountancy, W. Frank Barton School of Business, Wichita State University. She holds a Ph.D. degree from the University of South Carolina.

Douglas Sharp is associate professor of accounting in the school of accountancy, W. Frank Barton School of Business, Wichita State University. He holds a Ph.D. degree from the University of Missouri-Columbia.

Both authors are members of the Wichita Chapter, through which this article was submitted. They may be reached at (316) 689-3215.

[1] The term "entity-sustaining activities" refers to activities, such as the president's salary, that support the business entity rather than the production facility.
[2] Robin Cooper and Robert S. Kaplan, "Profit Priorities from Activity-Based Costing," *Harvard Business Review*, May/June 1991, pp. 130-135.
[3] Michael O'Guin, *The Complete Guide to Activity-Basecd Costing*, Prentice Hall, Englewood Cliffs, N.J., 1991; Alfred M. King, "The Current Status of Activity-Based Costing: An Interview with Robin Cooper and Robert S. Kaplan," MANAGEMENT ACCOUNTING®, September 1991, pp. 22-26.
[4] This case illustration is adapted from material contained in *Cost Accounting: A Managerial Emphasis* by Charles T. Horngren and George Foster, Prentice-Hall, Englewood Cliffs, N.J., 1991, pp. 168-169.

Is this article of interest to you? If so, circle appropriate number on Reader Service Card.	Yes 58	No 59

MANAGEMENT ACCOUNTING/MAY 1993

Strategic Costing & ABC

Create high-quality products and services at the lowest possible price.

BY GILBERT Y. YANG, CMA AND
ROGER C. WU, CPA

Recently a regional bank wanted to determine how much of the cost of its mortgage department's customer telephone service center should be allocated and how these costs could impact future product pricing, staffing, and resource allocation. Like many companies, the bank had devoted significant resources in developing an effective activity-based costing (ABC) system and used the resulting cost information to aid in its decision making.

Unfortunately, some executives and managers consider ABC the solution to all cost accounting problems and ignore the extra steps necessary to understanding the underlying assumptions and costing philosophy. For example, product unit cost, developed under ABC using historical cost data, is often used to make pricing decisions without considering either the future price index (for variable cost) or capacity utilization (for fixed costs) in case overcapacity exists. Thus, products are underpriced when unit variable cost is underestimated or overpriced when unit fixed cost is overestimated.

Recognizing this problem, the bank incorporated capacity utilization into ABC costing and applied different measures of unit cost. As a result, its phone center stayed profitable and efficient.

CUSTOMER SERVICES

The bank's mortgage department offers two products—fixed rate mortgages and adjustable rate mortgages (ARM). The activity and expense reports for the phone center are shown in Table 1.

The telephone center receives calls regarding:

- Current offering rates and terms.
- Mortgage application status.
- Loan portfolios serviced by the bank (payment processing, tax escrows, and rate adjustment for ARM loans).
- Nonproduct related calls. These include inquiries about branch locations and office hours. They are categorized under "other calls" in the activity report.

The phone center has 10 phone/terminal sets linked to the bank's mortgage database. This equipment is in its first year of operation, and it is used under the double-declining balance method of depreciation.

When a prospective customer contacts the bank, an operator reads the current offering rate/term information from the terminal monitor. To answer questions concerning existing loans and applications, the operator retrieves customer information from the bank's database. Complicated questions go to the mortgage department.

The phone center employs three full-time operators and a number of part-time operators to work during peak hours. If incoming calls are clustered and cannot be answered immediately, they are queued and put on hold.

FOUR COSTING METHODS

Traditionally, unit cost for a phone center operation is developed by dividing the cost center's total historical expense by the number of calls answered. This is a volume-based or output-based approach.

The amount allocated to different products and overhead is determined by multiplying the unit cost per call by the number of calls for each product/overhead. For the bank, the unit cost per call is $3.75 per call answered. The amount allocated to each product/overhead is calculated as shown in

Uniphoto/Frank Siteman

Strategic ABC revealed the strengths, weaknesses, and opportunities in this bank's customer phone service center.

TABLE 1/PHONE CENTER ACTIVITY REPORT

Activity	Total Calls Answered	Average # of Minutes Per Call	Total Activity (Minutes)
Inquire Rates and Terms:			
1. Fixed Rate Mortgages	75,000	3.00 min.	225,000 min.
2. Adjustable Rate Mortgages (ARM)	60,000	5.00	300,000
Inquire Mortgage Application Status:			
3. Fixed Rate	4,000	10.00	40,000
4. ARM	2,500	10.00	25,000
Problem Solving – Servicing			
5. Fixed Rate	1,500	7.00	10,500
6. ARM	11,000	15.00	165,000
7. Other Calls Answered	6,000	3.00	18,000
8. Total Calls Answered	160,000 calls		783,500 min.
Subtotals:			
9. Fixed Rates	80,500		275,500
10. ARM	73,500		490,000
11. Other Calls	6,000		18,000
12. Total	160,000 calls		783,500 min.

Expense Report from General Ledger	Past 12 Months
Variable Expenses:	
13. Salary & Benefits	$128,000
14. Other Variable Expenses	72,000
15. Total Variable	200,000
Fixed Expenses:	
16. Depreciation – Equipment	200,000
17. Office Rent	200,000
18. Total Fixed	400,000
19. Total Expense	$600,000

Table 2. The underlying assumption of the volume-based approach is that each call, regardless of its purpose, takes roughly the same amount of expense to service.

Simple ABC acknowledges that products, by definition, are not homogeneous and the activities and level of effort required to service and produce them are different. According to ABC, activities consume the resources, and products consume activities. Therefore, activities have to be identified for proper costing.

In the bank's phone center, the primary resource is the amount of time available to answer calls. The hours worked, number of operators, physical facilities, and machines serve as the constraints. The total capacity of the fully staffed phone center (a combination of full and part-time operators) is 1.44 million minutes. (300 workdays, 8 hours per day, 60 minutes per hour x

10 phone/terminal sets.)

At a high level, the phone center performs one activity—answering phone calls. This activity consumes all the resources of that department, including the operator's time.

The bank's activity report (Table 1) provides an average number of minutes per call and the number of calls answered for each individual activity (i.e., different types of phone calls). This information can be gathered through historical tracking over a period of time or through an operations/activities study.

Using these two statistics, the total number of minutes in operation of each activity and the total number of minutes in operation for the phone center during the past 12 months are calculated. As shown in Table 1, the total number of minutes in operation is 783,500, which represents 54% of the capacity 1.44 million minutes. The total cost per minute in operation is equal to

$600,000/783,500 minutes, or $0.766.

When a company has a significant fixed-cost component, capacity is a key issue in incremental decision making. With a higher capacity utilization rate, the fixed cost is spread throughout a larger volume and thus drags down the overall per unit cost. Many companies practice using capacity unit cost for aggressive pricing purposes.

Capacity ABC costing calculates unit cost of resources *assuming a full 100% capacity utilization*. Consequently, in the bank's case, the denominator of fixed cost per minute is the 1.44 million capacity minutes instead of the 783,500 minutes in operation (actual capacity utilized) used in Simple ABC. The resulting fixed cost per capacity minute and total cost per capacity minute are $0.278 and $0.533 respectively (Table 2).

The variable cost per unit under Capacity ABC remains the same as the cost per unit under Simple ABC at $0.255 no matter how the fixed cost of the denominator changes.

The Capacity ABC approach is intended for incremental decision making such as pricing. However, this approach also is optimistic and often results in an underestimated price, primarily because:

- No operation operates at 100% all the time.
- During the first few periods of an operation, the capacity utilization rate is usually low.
- A company usually begins further expansion of facilities when the existing capacity utilization exceeds a certain "high" rate, i.e., 90%.
- Fixed and variable expense rates usually increase as an operation approaches full capacity due to overtime, maintenance, or fatigue.

To accommodate the above factors, a capacity utilization rate of lower than 100% should be assumed to be the operation's long-term (lifetime) average utilization rate. The bank's first-year actual utilization rate is 54%. Assume for the next four years the utilization rates are estimated to be 62%, 70%, 78%, and 86%. This results in a five-year, estimated lifetime average utilization rate of 70%. Note that when the average utilization rate is too high, a customer may have to wait on hold for a long time during peak time even though all 10 machines are being used. Customer complaints and lost business opportunities would increase, which is a qualitative factor for the incremental decision making.

The Strategic ABC unit cost is a variation of the Capacity ABC unit cost. The only difference is that instead of assuming a 100% capacity utilization (1.44 million minutes in the sample case), it selects a capacity utilization rate that the company wants the operation to achieve over its useful life or planning horizon.

Assume the bank's five-year estimated average capacity utilization rate of 70% is selected. To calculate the cost per "strategic" capacity minute, the denominator of the $400,000 fixed cost is calculated by multiplying 70% by 1.44 million minutes, which is 1,008,000 minutes. The resulting total unit cost of $0.652 per strategic capacity minute is presented in Table 2.

Table 3 illustrates the unit cost of information for each activity under different ABC methods. This is done simply by multiplying the average number of minutes of each activity by the total cost per minute under the different ABC methods calculated previously.

While the unit variable cost for all three ABC methods is the same at $0.255 per minute, the three fixed costs per minute are drastically different, representing three different capacity utilization levels.

The 54% (actual) capacity utilization of simple ABC provides a direct link to the general ledger's expense. The Capacity ABC method's 100% capacity utilization represents the lowest possible cost that can be achieved for cost estimation purposes in incremental decisions. The 70% strategic capacity utilization rate is most appropriate for cost estimation for the planning horizon. Strategic ABC leads to more aggressive pricing using Simple ABC and less aggressive pricing than the Capacity ABC method.

The actual historical cost of the phone center allocated to the two products (fixed rate and ARM) as well as overhead is calculated in Table 3. The total minutes in operation for each product are multiplied by the total cost per minute.

Table 3 provides a mathematical proof that cost allocation using Simple ABC costing reconciles with general ledger expense ($600,000). The total cost allocated under the Capacity ABC method ($417,639) and the Strategic ABC method ($510,913) do not. They are calculated based on the planning horizon and do not have to tie into any period's general ledger.

A general ledger account (strategic idle capacity) can be established to capture the difference between $600,000 under Simple ABC and $510,913 under Strategic ABC. Another account (operational idle capacity) can capture the difference between $510,913 and $417,639.

The "strategic" capacity utilization rate does not have to be the anticipated lifetime capacity utilization rate. It could be the average utilization rate for the next few years or for the remaining life of the operation because all past costs were "sunk." However, when evaluating whether to make a future capital investment for an operation, the Strategic ABC unit cost should be used to calculate the cost base for the products this operation serves because no cost has been incurred.

DEPRECIATION & INFLATION

The capacity utilization rate may vary from period to period, resulting in drastic differences in per unit fixed cost over time. Therefore, in referring to an operation's (or product's) unit cost, it is important to separate average lifetime unit cost from periodic unit cost. By definition, average lifetime unit cost may encompass several periods or years. Therefore, such interperiod cost allocations as depreciation come into play.

Assume the bank's 10 phone/terminals cost $500,000. The double-declining balance (DDB) method of depreciation results in the first full year's $200,000 depreciation expense. The depreciation expense for the next four years under the DDB method are $120,000, $72,000, $54,000, and $54,000, respectively, with no salvage value.

If the Strategic ABC method is used to calculate unit cost per minute, *the decreasing depreciation expense coupled with the increasing capacity utilization rate will greatly distort the unit costs for each period.* The earlier periods' unit

---

TABLE 2/COSTING MEASURES
Volume-Based Unit Cost

Calculate Cost per Call Answered:

$$\frac{\text{Total Cost}}{\text{Total Calls Answered}} = \frac{\$600,000}{160,000 \text{ calls}}$$

$$= \$3.75 \text{ per call}$$

Amount Allocated to:

Fixed Rate Mortgages	=	$3.75 × 80,500 calls	= $301,875
Adjustable Rate Mortgages (ARM)	=	3.75 × 73,500	= 275,625
Other Calls (Overhead)	=	3.75 × 6,000	= 22,500
			$600,000

Simple ABC

$$\frac{\text{Total Cost}}{\text{Minutes in Operation}} = \frac{\$600,000}{783,500 \text{ calls}}$$

$$= \$0.766 \text{ per call}$$

Capacity ABC

Variable Cost	200,000	/	783,500	=	$0.255 per minute
Fixed Cost	400,000	/	1,440,000	=	$0.278 per minute
Total Cost	600,000				$0.533 per minute

Strategic ABC

Variable Cost	200,000	/	783,500	=	$0.255 per minute
Fixed Cost	400,000	/	1,008,000	=	$0.397 per minute
Total Cost	600,000				$0.652 per minute

costs will be significantly overstated, while the later periods' unit costs will be understated.

To normalize depreciation, use straight-line depreciation over the planning horizon in calculating unit cost. The resulting "normalized" Strategic ABC unit cost is a flat $0.553 over the planning horizon (Table 4). In operations with high wear and tear, the units of production method is more appropriate to normalize depreciation expense and other fixed expenses.

Over a period of several years, variable costs change significantly. To estimate a product's future unit cost and competitiveness, all of these factors have to be considered. Assume, in the bank's case, variable cost increased by 5% each year. The Simple ABC, Capacity ABC, and Strategic ABC unit costs per minute are shown in Table 4.

A financial analyst then can take the Strategic ABC information—the current "best estimate" of the future costs—to perform a reasonableness check on the pricing and sales forecast assumption of the budget or strategic plan. For example, in 1993 the $0.566 cost per minute can be used to estimate unit costs for different activities in the phone center. Adding up unit costs for activities, the unit cost of different products can be estimated. Conse-

quently, the reasonableness of a product's pricing, profit margin, and sales volume assumptions can be evaluated using the projected product cost.

HELPFUL MEASURES

Managers often are confused by having an array of unit cost measures from which to choose. However, all these measures are important because they present different perspectives on costs. In addition, many unit cost measures have unique applications associated with them.

The most obvious application is pricing. Cost-plus-profit pricing should use a number of different cost measures. Variable cost per unit should be the "absolute" floor of pricing, while the Strategic ABC unit cost constitutes the "theoretical" floor. Capacity ABC is unrealistically optimistic in pricing application, and Simple ABC is inappropriate because of its focus on a single period.

In performance measurement, Simple ABC clearly has its application because it ties in with general ledger expense. Therefore, it has credibility with product managers.

An efficiency rate approach can be adopted together with Simple ABC in

performance evaluation. For example, assume in 1992 the phone center was staffed to 60% capacity utilization while the actual utilization rate was only 54%. The efficiency rate was then 54% over 60%, or 90%. This 90% efficiency ratio could have been used to measure management effectiveness in work scheduling, to hire peak/part-time operators, and to anticipate the incoming calls. To further enhance Simple ABC's effectiveness, general ledger accounts could be added to represent the "strategic idle capacity" and the "operational idle capacity," as discussed.

Capacity planning is an application of both Capacity ABC and Strategic ABC unit costs. Because capacity utilization and its impact on cost management is brought to senior management's attention at all times, a company can better plan its capacity expansion.

In budgeting and planning, different unit cost measures can be very helpful. By calculating the Strategic ABC unit cost, the budget department can perform a reasonableness check on the pricing, profit margin, and corresponding sales volume assumptions. Of course, Simple ABC and the related product cost allocation calculated for the budgeting period can be tied into the budgeted general ledger.

An organization can benefit from

TABLE 3/UNIT COST INFORMATION

Activity	Average # of Minutes Per Phone Call	Simple ABC $0.766	Capacity ABC $0.533	Strategic ABC $0.652
		Times Cost Per Minute		
Inquire Rates and Terms				
1. Fixed Rate Mortgages	3	2.297	1.599	1.956
2. Adjustable Rate Mortgages (ARM)	5	3.829	2.665	3.26
Inquire Mortgage Application Status				
3. Fixed Rate	10	7.66	5.33	6.52
4. ARM	10	7.66	5.33	6.52
Problem Solving–Servicing				
5. Fixed Rate	7	5.361	3.731	4.565
6. ARM	15	11.487	7.996	9.781
7. Other Calls Answered	3	2.297	1.599	1.956

Product	Volume-Based Costing	Total Actual # of Minutes	Simple ABC $0.766	Capacity ABC $0.533	Strategic ABC $0.652
			Times Cost Per Minute		
1. Fixed Rate Mortgages	$301,875	275,500 min.	$210,976	$146,853	$179,651
2. Adjustable Rate Mortgages (ARM)	275,625	490,000 min.	375,239	261,191	319,524
3. Other Calls Answered	22,500	18,000 min.	13,784	9,595	11,738
4. Total	$600,000	783,500 min.	$600,000	$417,639	$510,913

TABLE 4/IMPACT OF DEPRECIATION AND INFLATION ON UNIT COST

	Actual	Forecast			
	1992	1993	1994	1995	1996
1. Total Capacity (minutes)	1,440,000	1,440,000	1,440,000	1,440,000	1,440,000
2. Estimated Capacity Utilization Rate	54%	62%	70%	78%	86%
3. (Est.) Minute in Operation	783,500	892,800	1,008,000	1,123,200	1,238,400
4. (Est.) Variable Expense per Minute	$0.255	$0.255	$0.255	$0.255	$0.255
5. (Est.) Total Variable Expense ($)	$200,000	$227,900	$257,307	$286,713	$316,120
6. Depreciation ($)	200,000	120,000	72,000	54,000	54,000
7. Office Rent ($)	200,000	200,000	200,000	200,000	200,000
8. Total Fixed Expense	400,000	320,000	272,000	254,000	254,000
9. Total Expense	600,000	547,900	529,307	540,713	570,120
Expense per Minute Calculation:					
10. Simple ABC (Line 9/Line 3)	$0.766	$0.614	$0.525	$0.481	$0.460
11. Capacity ABC (Line 4+Line 8/Line 1)	$0.533	$0.477	$0.444	$0.432	$0.432
12. Strategic ABC (70% Capacity)	$0.652	$0.573	$0.525	$0.507	$0.507
With "Normalized" Depreciation					
13. Straight-Line Depreciation ($)	100,000	100,000	100,000	100,000	100,000
14. Total "Normalized" Fixed Expense ($)	300,000	300,000	300,000	300,000	300,000
15. Total "Normalized: Expense ($)	500,000	527,900	557,307	586,713	616,120
"Normalized" Expense Per Minute:					
16. Simple ABC (Line 15/Line 3)	$0.638	$0.591	$0.553	$0.522	$0.498
17. Capacity ABC (Line 4+Line 14/Line 1)	$0.464	$0.464	$0.464	$0.464	$0.464
18. Strategic ABC (70% Capacity)	$0.553	$0.553	$0.553	$0.553	$0.553
With "Normalized" Depreciation and a 5% annual Increase in Variable Expense per Minute:					
19. (Est.) Variable Expense per Minute	$0.255	$0.268	$0.281	$0.296	$0.310
20. (Est.) Variable Expense	$200,000	$239,295	$283,681	$331,907	$384,246
21. Total "Normalized" Fixed Expense	300,000	300,000	300,000	300,000	300,000
22. Total Expense	500,000	539,295	583,681	631,907	684,246
Total Expense Per Minute:					
23. Simple ABC (Line 22/Line 3)	$0.638	$0.604	$0.579	$0.563	$0.553
24. Capacity ABC (Line 19+Line 21/Line 1)	$0.464	$0.476	$0.490	$0.504	$0.519
25. Strategic ABC (70% Capacity)	$0.553	$0.566	$0.579	$0.593	$0.608

both the process and the end results of deriving and analyzing the cost measures of its operations. As the ABC costing process and subsequent reviews of cost drivers progress, nonproductive activities will be discovered. For example, the bank discovered that a confusing advertisement was causing an increase in "overhead" calls. The ad was corrected and a waste of resources minimized and controls strengthened.

The Strategic ABC method enables the user to calculate a close approximation of true long-term costs and to plot its strategic advantages in the marketplace. As a result, product entry/exit, investment, staffing, and financing decisions can be determined more easily. ∎

Gilbert Y. Yang, CMA, is financial controller for UFO GROUP Co. Ltd. based in Taiwan. Previously he worked for Coopers & Lybrand. He is a member of IMA's Morris-Essex (N.J.) Chapter, through which this article was submitted.

Roger C. Wu, CPA, is corporate controller for Diamond Entertainment, Los Angeles, Calif.

Is this article of interest to you? If so, circle appropriate number on Reader Service Card.
Yes 56   No 57

MANAGEMENT ACCOUNTING/MAY 1993

CUSTOMIZE YOUR COSTING SYSTEM

The best of ABC, absorption, and direct costing leads to profits.

BY JACCI L.RODGERS, S. MARK COMSTOCK, AND KARL PRITZ

Companies without effective costing strategies are in danger of losing market share. This was the case with FMI Forms Manufacturers, a medium-sized printing company that produces business forms. Although the company was operating at full capacity, it was continually "in the red." Management realized that some common denominator was needed to cost its printing services accurately and consistently. The objective was to increase customer confidence, price more effectively, and (most important) make money.

FMI uses authorized independent distributors throughout the country to attract customers, solicit bids from printers, choose the best bid, and finally forward the job to the company's plant in Girard, Kan. The company deals with these distributors exclusively.

During the 1970s and early 1980s, FMI bids were made without any formal cost structure. There were baseline costs, but estimates were not consistent for similar procedures.

Initially, a traditional approach to costing was implemented. The accounting system was designed to compute the direct costs of each job and apply overhead on that basis, but this approach was not accurate. The only real direct cost was the material or paper used in the printing process. Overhead costs could not be allocated accurately to jobs using traditional cost drivers.

FMI is a machine-intensive operation. Nine presses print the forms (nine different jobs can run at once). Six collators are used to combine parts of forms, glue, crimp, punch holes, and/or attach mylar tape as each job requires. Other services are imprinting magnetic numbers (for example, on checks) by an encoding machine, special bindery work, die cutting, and shipping finished jobs to customers.

The cost of any job is determined by the type and amount of paper used, the composition, construction, any special services that are needed, and the time necessary for completion. All jobs, however, are constrained by the time necessary on a press and a collator. An additional constraint is the size of the form. Some of the machines are capable of producing forms of greater width than others.

When it became apparent that allocation based on direct costs was resulting in confusing and inconsistent costing, FMI considered an activity-based costing system. Cost drivers were identified as size of form, number of parts, type of paper, number of colors, composition, construction, and special features. These are the items that differentiate and determine the costs of the jobs.

Different presses have different costs to operate. Wide presses can run narrower jobs, but the reverse is not true. These factors are the correct drivers, but jobs were bid without knowledge of which press actually would run the job. Furthermore, while FMI wanted to remain competitive in its bidding, it also had to acknowledge that fixed costs were not covered. Consequently, the company was not profitable. The FMI controller needed to address these issues properly and produce accurate bids quickly.

FMI's costing system combines activity-based and absorption costing when determining price. It allows estimates to be made quickly (usually within one hour of receiving bid requests) and accurately. The following simplified assumptions are used in the new system.

- Operation at 80% of full capacity is assumed. The plant operates three shifts daily for five days each week, but not all machines are capable of running continually.
- Labor costs are assumed to be constant within each year. The shop is unionized, and contracts are renewed yearly.
- Workers are cross-trained on machines, but not between departments, so each department's pay scale is constant.
- Training is not included in the formula because employee

Former FMI operations manager and coauthor Karl Pritz.

TABLE 1/COMPUTATION OF UNITS

Formula used to allocate indirect department costs:

Press			Collator		
Maximum paper width	12"		Maximum paper width	12"	
Maximum # of colors	x 4		Maximum # of stations	x 2	
Maximum speed of press (per minute)	x 500'		Maximum speed of collator (per minute)	x 800'	
Total units for one press	24,000		Total units for one collator	19,200	

Formula used to allocate all other indirect costs to presses and collators:

Total Press Units (9 presses)
+ Total Collator Units (6 collators)
Grand Total Units

turnover is negligible.

- No setup or changeover time is considered. Thus, every machine is assumed to run at maximum speed continually whenever it is in operation.

The results of the analysis are a much simpler and more accurate activity-based system that involves a two-step process. A formula to compute "units" is derived for each press and collator (Table 1). The units for each press are summed to get "total press units," and this number is used as a denominator for identifiable costs associated with the press department. Identifiable costs for a press include the machine operator, support personnel, and supplies. A similar computation is used for the collators.

Then both the press and collator units are summed to get grand total units. This total is used as the denominator to allocate *all other* costs, in true absorption fashion, including supervision, office salaries, insurance, and any other operating expense item from the previous year's income statement, adjusted for expected increases or decreases during this year. This allocation of costs to presses and collators yields a projected cost *per machine* for the year. The allocation is done at the beginning of each fiscal year, using the previous income statement as a base from which to project current year expenses. Once the yearly cost is allocated to each machine, it is broken down into cost per hour on each machine, assuming each machine continually operates at full speed.

BIDDING PROCESS

When one of the company's independent distributors sends a request for a bid on a particular job, an estimator uses a computerized estimating package to record relevant data. The data are the cost drivers identified above. The only variable cost is determined by the type and quantity of paper.

The estimating program first checks the least expensive machine (allocated costs per machine hour) to see if it can handle the job. This "handling" is determined only by mechanical ability (i.e., a machine with a maximum width of 9-inch forms cannot print an 11-inch form) and not by scheduling constraints. If the least expensive machine is not able to do the job, the algorithm moves to the next least expensive machine and continues until a match is made. The estimated time to complete the job is multiplied by the cost per hour on

the machine to get a press cost for the job. A similar process is used to determine collator cost. Finally, the press, collator, and material costs are summed, a standard markup is added, and the bid is completed.

FMI receives two types of special orders. One requires special features such as desensitizing pressure-sensitive tape or nonstandard perforation and is assigned a higher markup than normal to cover the cost of errors or remakes.

The second type of special order is a rush job, which is usually within two to three weeks. For example, if the company has enough idle capacity to complete the job, the bid price should be no lower than the variable costs of the job. FMI does not use this strategy, which is advocated in cost accounting textbooks and which suggests special orders should be evaluated on the basis of idle capacity. At FMI, actual capacity does not enter into the bid procedure for normal jobs or special orders. Rush jobs are assigned a higher markup than normal because they are considered constraints on capacity—not a way to use idle capacity.

Occasionally FMI has the opportunity to resubmit a bid for a job. The capability to lower an initial bid is determined by using direct costing. First, all variable costs (material) are removed from the bid. The remaining cost is divided by the estimated hours necessary on the press to get a contribution margin per press hour. Past history has determined that the minimum acceptable contribution is $120 per press hour. The bid can be lowered to this rate but not below.

Two methods are used to determine whether or not a job will be profitable—one absorption based, the other direct. First, job costs are compiled for each job using the allocation rates of the machines (press and collator) actually used plus material. This cost is subtracted from the selling price of the job to determine profitability. Second, the contribution margin per press hour is computed as described above. Any jobs with contributions per press hour below $120 are investigated. This process occurs daily for all jobs finished the previous day, and feedback is very timely.

The new costing system really works well. First, allocation rates need to be adjusted only annually. Second, the company is profitable and has increased business in an increasingly competitive market. Finally, FMI's system shows how the "best" (most appropriate) parts of the three prevalent costing methods—direct, absorption, and activity-based—can be combined to create one costing system that will give your company the competitive edge. ∎

Jacci L. Rodgers, Ph.D., CPA, is an assistant professor at Oklahoma City University and can be reached at (405) 521-5824.

S. Mark Comstock, Ph.D., CPA, is an assistant professor at North Carolina State University. They are members of the Raleigh (N.C.) Chapter, through which this article was submitted.

Karl Pritz, who was operations manager at FMI Forms Manufacturers, is currently a consultant.

Part **4**

Section 7

Completing the Picture: Financial Reporting and Continuous Improvement

From about the mid '80s, when early reports on ABC surfaced, management accounting practitioners have been provided with a new way to look at cost accumulation and cost distribution. At its inception ABC focused on improved product costing. It has since reduced this focus as the common denominator and instead shifted its focus to activities and processes and the way work is done every day. Improving process flows by eliminating waste and excess and by empowering workers—the process owners—to achieve continuous improvement is a far better way to manage a business. Accountants, too, are "teamed up" with the other functions of the business, helping to develop and provide information to support these activities and processes. New ABC models are designed to provide information that mirrors the process and production flows.

In the three articles that follow, many of the changes referred to have been incorporated in financial reporting systems and ABC design. ABC continues to unfold and progress along new pathways.

The first article in this section, "ABC Puts Accountants on Design Team at H-P" by C. Mike Merz and Arlene Hardy, may be one of the earliest to report actual experience with using ABC as the primary financial reporting system over an extended period of time. Here is an ABC system that is fully integrated into the company's formal accounting system.

One of the criticisms made against traditional cost systems was that they failed to keep up with changing manufacturing technology. The Boise Surface Mount Center (BSMC) at the Hewlett-Packard Boise site overcomes this criticism by providing a supporting ABC system that mirrors the manufacturing process and evolves continuously. Engineers and production people feel a sense of ownership over the system as a result of the ongoing effort of working together with accounting to identify the appropriate cost pools and their drivers. The accountants at BSMC, using ABC, spend their time helping production manage their costs, in contrast to accountants working with traditional cost systems, who seem to spend more time trying to understand production costs and defending themselves against production managers who don't believe the reports.

Consider some examples of accounting participation at BSMC: (1) Accountants help engineers perform a "what if" analysis to overcome high costs that would seriously derail the introduction of new circuit boards at a predetermined (target) price. (2) They work with engineers and production staff preparing bids to show potential customers how to lower costs by modifying circuit design.

What does the ABC system at BSMC look like? Some specifications:

- Direct and indirect costs associated with an activity are collected in separate cost pools.
- Through 1992, the system used 10 different overhead cost pools (1993 forward, cycle time to be used).
- The cost pools are divided by the volume of the activity driver to obtain the overhead rates for each pool. The cost driver application rate is predeter-

mined for each six-month budget cycle. Significant volume variance can occur if actual volume differs from the planned volume used to determine overhead rates.

■ The standard cost to manufacture their product consists of two elements — direct material and manufacturing overhead. Direct material is small and is combined with manufacturing overhead.
■ BSMC uses a pricing system to charge or credit customers for any volume variance they cause.

A few concluding observations about the BSMC ABC system:

■ About cost pools used by BSMC and the statistical validity of the cost drivers — it was confirmed that cost drivers are correlated with overhead costs in their cost pool.
■ The ABC system has had a dramatic impact on pricing and product design decisions.
■ Effective ABC systems evolve and must have continual "bottom-up" involvement by accounting, engineers, and production people.

In the second article, "ABC: An All-Purpose Solution for Financial Reporting," William Stratton states that the differences in product cost when a company changes from a traditional system to an ABC system have been well documented. He indicates that little has been said, however, regarding the impact of these systems on external reporting. Besides, it long has been accepted that traditional systems are adequate for external reporting.

By way of illustration, Stratton sets out to ascertain the difference, if any, between these systems. He employs a company with two product lines, product line A, characterized by large volume orders and a simple production process, and product line B, characterized by small orders, a more complex produc-

tion process, and frequent engineering changes. The company switches from a traditional labor-based overhead allocation system (direct labor costs) to an ABC system. The author uses two product line scenarios (emphasizing one product line at the expense of the other) to report the differences between systems.

The outcomes reported indicate that higher margins are realized under ABC when emphasizing product line A, the high-volume, low-complexity product line. Traditional costing favors small-order product line B with higher margins. The conclusion: traditional systems distort costs and the reported results of operations.

In the final article, "Using ABC to Support Continuous Improvement," Peter Turney and Alan Stratton show us how to design a two-dimensional ABC system that supports product costing and performance improvement. Using the model built for the wafer sorting process at National Semiconductor Corporation, the authors describe the two main elements of this design, namely, micro and macro activities.

Micro activities are detailed activities that reflect the day-to-day work. The focal point of cost improvement, with cost and noncost information attached, these activities parallel the responsibility structure of the organization and support process improvement in each department. Macro activities are summaries of related micro activities. Each set of macro activities for a process contains the cost of all work performed in a process, including supplier activities consumed. Macro activities facilitate the reporting of product cost.

The authors claim this new design, incorporating micro and macro activities, is an improvement over earlier two-stage models because it focuses on managing activities and processes as the route to continuous improvement. ■

ABC Puts Accountants on Design Team at HP

"Bottom-up" involvement by engineers and production makes cost system effective.

BY C. MIKE MERZ, CMA, AND
ARLENE HARDY

Lybrand Gold Medal Winner, 1992-93.

Engineers in a major circuit board assembly department of Hewlett-Packard (HP) have something to tinker with besides machinery. They can tinker with their "own" activity-based costing (ABC) system, continually thinking of ways to improve it.

In 1989 HP implemented an ABC system at the Boise Surface Mount Center (BSMC) in Idaho. The ABC system was integrated fully into the company's formal accounting system so that cost information in all internal and external reports now contains costs using ABC. Design engineers, customer service engineers, the production team, and the accounting staff routinely use ABC to measure historical costs, value inventory, assess financial results, and forecast future performance.

The ABC system has evolved over the four years since it was implemented—thanks in part to the engineers' tinkering. In addition to the obvious technical changes that ABC brought to the cost accounting system, it also changed the role of the department's accountants dramatically, essentially making them a part of the product design team.[1]

The technical aspects of ABC have been discussed much in the last few years, but actual experience using ABC over an extended period of time seldom has been reported. The unique

Authors Mike Merz and Arlene Hardy (l.) discuss a circuit board with Ken Schrader, service manager, and Ron Ray, production section manager.

aspects of how HP has been using ABC are well worth describing.

CURRENT STATUS

Since January 1993 the ABC system has been fully operational within the BSMC. All cost data pertaining to circuit boards that have been produced, that are being designed for production, or that are being bid on in the process of getting new business come from the ABC cost system. All data are entered into the company's general ledger system so that the ABC system is completely on-line.

It is significant that the ABC system

has been completely operational and on-line for four years because some recent articles imply that ABC analysis should be done "off-line" while the traditional cost system continues to report cost data. The fact that operational people within the department routinely gather and analyze activity data differs markedly from H. Thomas Johnson's recent observation that "activity information is usually compiled and monitored by central staff personnel or outside consultants."[2] The BSMC's use of ABC as a completely operational accounting system to provide all data for cost analysis and reporting represents an advanced application of ABC.

MANUFACTURING ENVIRONMENT

The Boise Surface Mount Center manufactures about 50 different electronic circuit boards for internal customers within HP. With surface mount technology, patches of a semiliquid solder are placed on the surface of a circuit board, and electronic components are placed on the solder patches. Then the board goes through an oven to melt the solder to form a strong mechanical bond and a reliable electronic circuit. The process is highly automated, with computer-controlled "pick-and-place" machines that can select more than 100 different components each minute from the correct reel and place each one on the surface of the board within a tolerance of four-thousandths of an inch. Production volumes for each board vary from a few hundred per month to several thousand. Annual production costs exceed $100 million.

The BSMC operates as a form of cost center that charges out its manufacturing costs to its internal customers, each of which is independent of the BSMC in the organization structure. The BSMC has no "captive" customers! About 700 employees work directly in the BSMC, including production workers and their supervisors, engineers, and material procurement personnel. In the circuit board industry, total volume sometimes is cited as the total number of placements—the number of individual electronic components attached to all boards manufactured. The BSMC makes hundreds of millions of placements annually, so it is a relatively large producer although not as large as several of the industry giants.

Because circuit boards have become a commodity product and because the life cycles of both the product and manufacturing technology are short, the BSMC has to compete in a very dynamic business environment. To get and keep business, the BSMC must compete for orders with other circuit board manufacturers within HP and with outside vendors, based on schedule, quality, and cost. Efforts to get new business require continual interaction with customers to help them design new boards that can be produced efficiently, to prepare cost bids, and to start up production of new boards. Production volumes fluctuate as older boards phase out of production and new boards are introduced. As technology continues to evolve, new equipment is inserted into the production line. The manufacturing environment changes so rapidly that if a few weeks elapse between your visits to the factory, the production line may look completely different next time.

This environment conforms closely to the conditions for which ABC is recommended:

■ Products are very diverse,
■ Overhead costs are relatively high and for some products are higher than the direct costs,
■ Production volumes vary significantly among products, and
■ Operating managers believe that the old system that applied all overhead as a percent of direct material costs did not give meaningful product costs.

EVOLUTION OF ABC SYSTEM

To date, the cost pool and driver system has evolved so it uses 10 different cost pools and drivers, as shown in Table 1. The composition of the cost pools and selection of the most appropriate drivers resulted from an intense analysis of the production process and cost behavior patterns by the accounting, production, and engineering staffs, similar to the process followed by other companies.[3]

Costs are assigned to products in two stages almost exactly as recommended in the ABC literature. First, all of the direct and indirect costs associated with an activity, such as material procurement and handling, are collected into a separate cost pool. Then the volume of activities selected as the driver are accumulated, in this case the total number of unique parts on each board. Dividing the cost pool dollars by the total number of unique parts yields the overhead application rate, say $7.50 per unique part. If a board had 500 total parts but only 100 unique parts, it would be charged $750 for material procurement overhead during the six-month budget cycle. This amount is the total amount charged—if the customer ordered 2,000 of that particular board during the six months, the effective unit cost would be $.375

TABLE 1 / COST POOLS & DRIVERS	
COST POOLS	DRIVERS
1. Panel operations	Percent of a whole panel; if one panel contains four individual boards, then each board is charged 25% of the panel rate.
2. Small component placement	Number of "small" components placed on the board's surface.
3. Medium component placement	Number of "medium" size components placed on the board's surface.
4. Large component placement	Number of "large" components placed on the board's surface.
5. "Through-hole component insertion"	Number of components with wires that are inserted through holes on the board.
6. Hand load component placement	Minutes required to place all components that must be hand loaded rather than automatically placed on the board.
7. Material procurement & handling	Number of unique parts in the board.
8. Scheduling	Number of scheduling hours during a six-month period.
9. Assembly setup	Number of minutes of setup time during a six-month period.
10. Test & rework	Number of "yielded" minutes of test and rework time for each board.

of material procurement and handling. As with most cost systems, each cost driver application rate is predetermined during the budget cycle, and an adjustment for any over- or under-applied overhead in each cost pool is made at the end of the accounting period.

The ABC system is in a state of continuous evolution. As engineers and production people gain experience about how a certain cost driver works or whether overhead costs have been distributed to the appropriate cost pool, they keep coming back to accounting to request changes in the cost system to make it reflect perceived cost behavior patterns. Of the 10 cost drivers currently being used, only three have not been changed in some way during the four years that ABC has been in place. A major benefit of implementing ABC was that engineering and production now feel a sense of ownership over the cost system as a result of the ongoing effort of working together with accounting to identify the appropriate cost pools and their drivers. Another benefit is that the accounting staff must work closely with production and engineering to make sure that costs are assigned to the correct pool and to maintain accurate counts of driver activities.

The BSMC operates as a form of cost center that bills its customers for the standard cost to manufacture their product. Customers receive detailed bills that show how the manufacturing overhead component of their board has been computed using the cost driver system. The manufacturing cost of a board includes only two components—direct material and manufacturing overhead. Because direct labor is such a small percent of total cost, it is included in manufacturing overhead.[4] As mentioned earlier, all manufacturing costs and activity data are collected and recorded using the ABC system. All formal and informal reports, analyses, and forecasts use ABC information.

ACCOUNTANTS INVOLVED IN DECISION PROCESS

Implementing an ABC system dramatically changed the role of the accounting staff in product decisions. Accountants now provide important inputs into product design and development decisions. Under the prior cost system, all overhead was applied as a percent of direct material cost, and it was difficult to understand how changing a board's design would

The circuit board produced by BSMC for HP's Coyote Disc Drive resting upon a completed disc drive.

change manufacturing costs. Also, designers had little motivation to optimize the board for efficient production. With ABC, however, the cost system attempts to mirror the manufacturing process, so that engineers and production managers easily can see how design changes will affect costs.

Two cases in which the accounting staff influenced product design illustrate the important role played by the accountants. In the rush to introduce new products to the market, the circuit boards in the new product sometimes are released for production before the engineers have time to optimize the design for production. If the product is successful, the board design is modified—"rolled over"—later to simplify manufacturing.

During 1991, one particular board produced in high volumes was expensive to manufacture because several components had to be hand loaded rather than placed on the board automatically by a machine. Although the board was scheduled to be rolled over in six months to a design that was easier to produce, the accounting staff worked with engineering and production to prepare an analysis showing the customer how much costs could be reduced by rolling over the board's design sooner. Recognizing that they could save millions of dollars by acting sooner, the customer rapidly changed the board's design.

During the design phase of another new product, the design engineers realized that the cost to manufacture one of the circuit boards in that product was going to be so high that it would preclude introducing the product at

the target price. The BSMC accounting staff was asked for help. Armed with their ABC system loaded into a personal computer, the accountants helped the engineers perform a "what-if" analysis. If four small components were substituted for the one large component, how would cost be affected? If the two components that would have to be hand loaded could be replaced with components that could be placed on the board automatically, how would cost be affected? By trying lots of combinations of different designs, the engineers and accountants were able to lower the board's cost to an acceptable level.

The BSMC's customers seem to like the transparent cost reports from BSMC that show clearly how costs are computed. The general perception in the BSMC is that the ABC system has helped significantly in getting new business.

EFFECT ON PRODUCT COSTS

Prior to adopting ABC, the BSMC applied all overhead as a percent of direct material cost. To measure the effect that ABC had on product costs, and the resulting amounts that customers were billed, the boards that BSMC was producing during late 1991 were "costed" both ways: (1) all overhead applied as a percent of direct material costs, using an ad hoc analysis, and (2) with the ABC system currently used by the BSMC. Such comparisons are not made routinely—ABC has become a way of life within the BSMC.

Table 2 and the bar chart in Figure 1 show the distribution of percentage changes in product costs for all boards that were being manufactured. They also show that the use of ABC increased the total cost of a lot more products than it decreased. The old method for applying overhead was as a percent of material costs. Products with low material costs had low amounts of applied overhead. ABC caused dramatic increases for some of these products.

One board that would have cost about $5 if overhead were applied as a percent of material had a reported total cost of about $25 with ABC—an increase of 400%. Some boards with high material costs received much less applied overhead with ABC even though the percentage change did not appear as dramatic. For example, one board with high material costs would have had $123 of overhead applied as a per-

TABLE 2 / % CHANGE IN TOTAL MANUFACTURING COSTS: EFFECT OF ABC

Percent Change Caused by Activity-Based Costing	Number of Products
> + 100%	1
+ 50% to + 100%	5
+ 20% to + 50%	6
+ 5% to + 20%	23
- 5% to + 5%	13
- 20% to - 5%	9
Total	57

Note: This table shows the percentage change resulting from ABC. For example, if a product would have a total cost of $100 using a single overhead rate based on direct material costs but a total cost of $129 with ABC, then the percentage change would be plus 29%.

cent of material cost but only $45 with ABC. The percent change in total product costs for that board, however, was only about minus 12%. Either cost system would apply, of course, the same amount of total overhead to all the products manufactured.

During a recent six-month forecast and budget cycle, the ABC system resulted in shifting millions of dollars of costs between customers and products and thus had a dramatic impact on pricing and product design decisions.

ABC COSTS NOT 'RELEVANT'

As customers learned to use costs reported by the ABC system to make product design decisions, an unanticipated side effect of the new cost system became apparent. For making decisions, the ABC costs were relevant to the customer but not relevant to the BSMC as the manufacturer. For example, one customer figured out a way to reduce her board's cost by placing two boards on each preprinted panel that goes through the assembly line rather than just one. The effect was that instead of one whole panel operations charge of about $18 for each board, the same charge now was spread over two boards, so the total board cost to the customer was reduced by $9.

From the BSMC's standpoint, however, the actual manufacturing costs did not decline nearly that much because excess capacity existed in panel operations, and no specific cost reduction in labor or other overhead resulted from the design change to that one

board. So even though customers can treat costs determined from the ABC system as relevant to their decisions, the same cost is not necessarily relevant to decisions by the manufacturer, BSMC.

ENGINEERS TINKER WITH COST SYSTEM

Both the production engineering and the production staff participated in defining each cost pool and its appropriate driver for the ABC system. Although the accountants gather data and administer the cost system, the production and engineering people now feel that they own the system. The well-known propensity of engineers to tinker mentioned earlier has had an unanticipated side effect. An almost daily dialogue goes on among production, engineering, and the accountants about how the ABC cost system could be improved to reflect product costs more accurately.

The engineers have instigated a major revision to the cost system that will be implemented this year. After a lot of analysis, discussion, and physical observation of both the production line and cost behavior, management concluded that cycle time is the most appropriate cost driver for most of the production line operations. The first five cost pools shown in Table 1 that now are allocated with a cost driver measured in physical volumes of components placed on a board will be allocated instead with a cost driver measured in minutes or seconds of cycle time required to complete the placements. One of the anticipated benefits of using cycle time as a cost driver is

that the total standard cycle time for all boards that go through a certain operation can be compared with the total actual cycle time to complete that operation during a given time period. This comparison will provide an independent check on the accuracy of the standard cycle times for each operation for each board.

Using cycle time as a driver will require a new set of decision rules. With the current drivers, designers know it costs about $.02 to place a small component on a board or $.15 to place a large component. To help designers make trade-off decisions, new decision rules in terms of dollars of cycle time per placement must be developed.

The HP experience with ABC indicates that a cost system should be in a continual state of involvement for three reasons: (1) As actual experience is gained with the initial ABC model, desirable changes in the way cost pools and cost drivers have been defined become apparent, (2) the cost system must accommodate changes in manufacturing technology, and (3) the cost system must accommodate new products that frequently force changes in the way the production line operates. Thus, having a consultant perform a one-time study and then install an ABC system to be operated by a company's accountants does not seem appropriate in a dynamic environment. Our experience indicates that an effective ABC system must have continual, "bottom-up" involvement by accountants, engineers, and production people. That an ABC system must evolve continually and not be considered static has not been discussed much in previous writing about ABC.

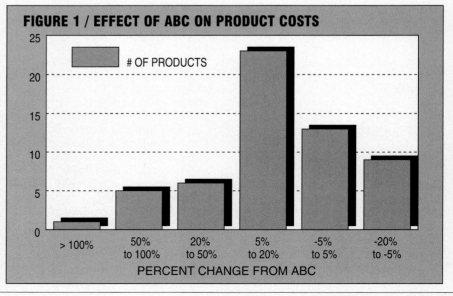

FIGURE 1 / EFFECT OF ABC ON PRODUCT COSTS

OF PRODUCTS

PERCENT CHANGE FROM ABC

STABILITY OF COST POOLS

To test the statistical validity of the cost drivers, we ran a series of simple, linear regressions between the overhead dollars in the cost pools and the cost driver volumes. The linear regression model looks for a fixed cost component (the "Y intercept") and a variable cost component (the "X coefficient"). Applying overhead with a cost driver makes the implicit assumption that the volume of a cost driver is the independent variable X and the overhead dollars in the cost pool are the dependent variable Y. If this assumption is valid, then a good statistical relationship should exist between volume and overhead cost. Five regressions were performed:

1. Material procurement and handling overhead vs. the number of distinct parts purchased, the cost driver.
2. All overhead related to automatic component placement vs. the number of components placed with the automatic machines. Because the definition of automatic placement cost pools had changed several times, several cost pools and drivers had to be combined to have sufficient data points for a regression.
3. Test and rework overhead vs. the number of minutes yielded test time, the cost driver.
4. Through-hole insertion overhead vs. the number of through-hole placements, the cost driver. Through-hole insertion is the older technology in which components have individual wires that are inserted automatically through holes in the circuit board. This technology is being phased out rapidly, and the volume of through-hole insertions during the last budget cycle had declined to almost zero.
5. Total department overhead vs. total component placements. This regression tested the relation between the combined overhead of all 10 cost pools and total component placements.

Actual data were available for fiscal years 1990, 1991, and 1992. Because overhead rates are set for each six-month budget cycle, six data points were available for the regressions—three years with two budget cycles per year. As mentioned previously, many changes in cost pool and driver definitions had occurred during the four-year period since ABC had been implemented, so we did not have

sufficient data to run regressions on all the cost pools.

Regression results are shown in Table 3, "R squares," the squared correlation coefficients for each regression. The R squared measures the proportion of change in the dependent variable explained by changes in the independent variable. Thus, the R squared of .914 for the regression of material handling overhead vs. the number of distinct parts indicates that 91.3% of the change in overhead can be explained by changes in the number of distinct parts. The table also lists the range in cost driver volumes that occurred over the three-year period to give a feeling for whether volumes remained in a relevant range. While no firm definition of the relevant range seems to exist, a rule of thumb is that fixed and variable cost relations remain stable only within a volume range of plus or minus about 20%.

We are reasonably pleased that the regression analyses tended to confirm that the cost drivers selected indeed are correlated with overhead costs in their cost pool. Our experience, though, suggests that such regressions have very limited usefulness in selecting cost drivers for an ABC cost system, for several reasons. After four years of working with ABC, we had barely enough data points to run meaningful regressions.

The main criticism of older cost systems is that they failed to keep up with changing manufacturing technology. An effective ABC system also must change over time, and rarely will a stable time period of historical data occur to permit meaningful regression analyses. While academicians recently have advocated using regression analysis to help select cost drivers,[5] we believe that relying on the judgment of engineers and production people familiar with technical processes is the only practical way to define cost pools and select drivers.

PRICING TO CHARGE FOR VOLUME VARIANCES

The BSMC recently developed a unique method for charging production volume variances to its customers. To avoid having to pass variances along to customers, the BSMC has been defined as a form of cost center called a "performance center," which will charge customers only for standard manufacturing costs. Any variances from standard will be absorbed by the department. The operating goal is to just break even, meaning that the net variance for a budget period will be zero. This system eliminates the argument that when it operated as a pure cost center, the BSMC had no motivation to control costs.

Manufacturing overhead rates are very sensitive to changes in production volume, however, and manufacturing overhead constitutes a very high percent of total product cost. Significant volume variances can occur if actual volumes differ from the planned volumes used to set overhead rates. To charge customers for any volume variance they cause, the BSMC has adopted a volume discount or premium system. Overhead rates are set for each six-month budget cycle based on the volume forecasts for each customer. If a customer's orders exceed the forecast by a certain percent, that customer receives a volume discount approximately equal to the favorable volume

TABLE 3 / REGRESSION RESULTS R SQUARES & VOLUME RANGES		
REGRESSION	R SQUARED	VOLUME RANGE* (+ or -)
1. Material procurement overhead vs. number of distinct parts.	.914	51.2%
2. All automatic placement overhead vs. number of automatic placements.	.923	84.5%
3. Test overhead vs. yield test time in minutes.	.098	19.3%
4. Through-hole overhead vs. number of through-hole placements.	.631	96.7%
5. Total department overhead vs. total number of components placed.	.946	40.4%

*The volume range was computed around the volume mid-point. For example, if the volume varied from 40 to 120 million placements, 80 million would be the mid-point, and the range would be plus or minus 50% [(120 - 80) ÷ 80].

variance resulting from spreading the total overhead over a larger volume base. Conversely, if a customer's actual orders fall below the forecast, they are charged a higher amount. Two volume ranges for price discounts and premiums were established as shown in Figure 2.

Because the price premium for being under forecast is higher than the price discount for being over forecast, customers are motivated to avoid overly optimistic forecasts. Customers have responded favorably to this new system because it permits them to predict exactly what their costs will be. The BSMC has not had enough experience yet to tell how the volume discount or premium system will work in the long run.

NO AUDIT PROBLEMS

The ABC system has been audited four times since it was implemented in 1989—twice by HP's internal auditors and twice by its external auditors. Both auditing groups were familiar with ABC and were able to understand quickly the BSMC's system, which uses ABC costs to value inventory and cost of goods sold. In addition to their usual tests of the accounting records, the auditors verified unique aspects of the cost system. They verified that cost drivers could be measured accurately because accountants typically do not record physical measures such as the number of electronic components placed on circuit boards or the number of setup minutes. The auditors also verified that cost drivers were reevaluated adequately every six months during the budget cycle.

All the audits went smoothly. The ABC system is well documented, and a good audit trail is maintained, so the auditors got satisfactory answers to all their questions. The ABC system passed both internal and external audits with no problems.

HOW MUCH DOES ABC COST?

Managers usually assume that an ABC system with multiple cost drivers will cost more to administer and maintain than a traditional cost system with only one or two cost drivers. We tried to identify the additional accounting costs, if any, required to implement and maintain the BSMC's ABC system. During the study and implementation phase, a cost manager and financial analyst

worked with production, engineering, and materials procurement personnel. After implementation, the BSMC rapidly doubled in capacity as production volumes grew. Even though more accounting support was required, there was no apparent way to determine the specific impact that ABC may have had. Because it has to justify all its costs to customers, the BSMC's cost system must be more complex than if all costs were passed on to a single department or product line, but it is not certain what additional costs, if any, are attributable to ABC. A casual comparison showed that the size of the accounting staff that supports the BSMC was about the same as the size of the accounting staff that supports a similar manufacturing department still using a traditional cost system.

What did become apparent, though, was how ABC changed what the accountants did. Accountants in departments with traditional cost systems seem to spend more time trying to understand why production costs do not make sense and dealing with frustrated production managers who do not believe production cost reports. The accountants who support the departments using ABC spend much more time helping production to manage costs. Another division of HP that uses ABC experienced similar results.[6]

THE OVERALL RESULTS

The Boise Surface Mount Center at Hewlett-Packard's Boise site by now has had more than four years of operating experience with its ABC system. The BSMC took the rather bold step of integrating ABC fully into its computerized financial and cost reporting systems, unlike many companies that do ABC analyses "off-line" while maintaining a traditional cost system for financial reporting.

One aspect of using ABC that has not been described in previous articles is that the system must evolve continually. As the BSMC gained experience with the original model and as manufacturing technology changed, desirable changes in definitions of cost pools and cost drivers became apparent. Most of the cost pools and cost drivers have been modified in some way since 1989 when the ABC system was implemented.

Because the ABC system now mirrors the manufacturing process, the engineers and production staff believe the cost data produced by the accounting system. Engineering and produc-

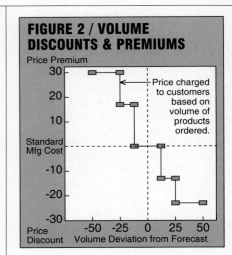

FIGURE 2 / VOLUME DISCOUNTS & PREMIUMS

Price charged to customers based on volume of products ordered.

tion regularly ask accounting to help find the product design combination that will optimize costs.

The accountants now participate in product design decisions. They help engineering and production understand how manufacturing costs behave. They produce cost bids customers understand and that help the department get new business. In addition to producing good cost information, the ABC system makes the professional lives of the accountants more rewarding. ∎

C. Mike Merz, CMA, CPA, is a professor of accounting at Boise State University. He is a member of the Boise (Idaho) Chapter, through which this article was submitted. He can be reached at (208) 385-1268.

Arlene Hardy is a finance supervisor with the Hewlett-Packard Company in Boise. She can be contacted at (208) 396-2797.

[1] In this article, the term accountant is used in the generic sense; actually, Hewlett-Packard distinguishes between various job classifications within the accounting function such as "accountant" and "financial analyst."
[2] H. Thomas Johnson, "It's Time to Stop Overselling Activity-Based Costing," MANAGEMENT ACCOUNTING, September 1992, p. 32.
[3] Robin Cooper, "Implementing an Activity Based Cost System," *Journal of Cost Management*, Winter 1990, pp. 69-77.
[4] R. Hunt, L. Garret, and C.M. Merz, "Direct Labor Cost Not Always Relevant at HP," MANAGEMENT ACCOUNTING, February 1985, pp. 58-62.
[5] Harold P. Roth and A. Faye Borthick, "Are You Distorting Costs by Violating ABC Assumptions?" MANAGEMENT ACCOUNTING, November 1991, pp. 39-42; Adel M. Novin, "How to Find the Right Bases and Rates," MANAGEMENT ACCOUNTING, March 1992, pp. 40-43.
[6] D. Berlant, R. Browning, and G. Foster, "How Hewlett-Packard Gets Numbers It Can Trust," *Harvard Business Review*. January-February 1990, pp. 178-183.

ABC:
An All-Purpose Solution for Financial Reporting

It gives firms an accurate picture of costs and jibes with GAAP.

BY WILLIAM O. STRATTON, CMA

Cost allocation systems are used primarily for economic decision making, motivation of managers, and inventory valuation for external reporting.[1] The dramatic differences realized in product cost when a company changes from a traditional cost system[2] to an activity-based costing (ABC) system have been well documented in theory and practice, but little has been said regarding differences in impact of these two systems on external reporting.[3] In fact, most proponents continue to suggest that maintaining dual systems is appropriate.

Many accountants continue to use aggregate volume bases such as direct labor hours to allocate production overhead for financial reporting, but they use ABC systems internally on an *ad hoc* basis for economic decision making and motivational purposes. A few innovative companies have implemented fully inte-

Products arriving at the distribution building by conveyor are palletized for storage and/or shipping at J.M. Schneider, Inc. The company has a fully integrated ABC system.

grated ABC systems, such J.M. Schneider Inc., one of Canada's largest producers of premium quality food products, which switched to ABC for external reporting. Mark Hanley, controller at Schneider, remarked, "One of the key advantages of a fully integrated ABC system is the cost savings when dual systems are eliminated."

Reasons companies give for *not* using ABC for external reporting include the acceptability of traditional costing systems, such as standard costing, by auditors and the purported lack of impact on the bottom line of using more accurate but costly systems such as activity-based costing. The essence of the latter assertion is that although the more elaborate ABC system costs individual products in a different way from traditional systems, in aggregate, there is no difference on the bottom line or in valuation. *(If all the peanut butter gets spread, what does it matter how?)*

If a company experiences no material difference in its reported aggregate amounts for inventory and cost of sales when it changes to an activity-based accounting system, there is no justification for adopting ABC for external reporting. Practitioners appear to validate this position. Typical is the claim by the plant controller of Valmont/ALS, that "…the system (traditional cost) provides an accurate valuation of inventory for our financial reports."[4]

But is it true? What assumptions underlie such assertions? Do scenarios exist in which use of traditional costing compared to activity-based costing yields material differences in reported amounts for inventory and cost of sales? If so, the common practice of using traditional costing for external reporting is of dubious value to existing and potential investors and creditors. It follows that ABC systems should be adopted for all purposes, not only for economic decision making and motivation of managers.

GAAP FOR INVENTORY COSTING

Because the profession only recently has realized the benefits of more accurate costing systems for *internal* reporting purposes, there have been few, if any, expressions of the need for change in GAAP for *external* reporting.

Per GAAP, the key components of inventory valuation are:

■ The major objective of inventory valuation is the proper determination of income.
■ The basis of inventory accounting is cost—the sum of expenditures and charges, direct and indirect, to bring goods to existing condition for and location of sale.
■ Absorption costing is required.
■ Inventory should be valued at the lower of cost or designated market (LCM).
■ Valuation may be based on item by item, pools of similar items, or entire inventory. Any writedown should be reflected as a loss in the current period.
■ Standard costs may be used if they are adjusted at reasonable intervals to reflect actual costs.

I want to make several additional points. First, focus is on *accurate* income determination. Any costing system used should reflect periodic income *accurately*. Second, although allocation is required, no guidance is given as to the appropriate method(s). The only requirement is that cost of sales should reflect approximate "actual" costs—therefore the need for reasonably frequent adjustments to standard costs. Thus, activity-based systems can be used under current GAAP. Third, write-

downs of inventory resulting from the application of the "lower of cost or market" rule can be based on individual product costs, pools of similar items, or the entire inventory.

In summary, the allocation of production overhead for external reporting purposes should yield an accurate determination of income and provide for the valuation of inventory on an LCM basis. The common belief is that the use of a traditional costing system is adequate for these purposes. A simple illustration will show how traditional costing and activity-based costing yield significant differences in income and valuation.

ANNUAL INCOME AND INVENTORY VALUE: AN ILLUSTRATION OF ABC AND TRADITIONAL COSTING

Diversified Company has responded to increased competitive pressures by modifying its two major product lines. Product line A is characterized by large-volume orders and a rather simple production process. The newer product line B is characterized by small orders and a more complex production process involving frequent engineering changes. For many years the company has used a traditional costing system for cost allocation purposes. Under this system, which was developed to support a labor-paced manufacturing environment, production overhead costs are allocated to product on the basis of direct labor costs. With overall profits declining, management is considering policy options that will provide improved current-year financial results. Because of policy constraints, the annual production of both product lines is not subject to change until next year, so the primary options relate to product emphasis by the sales force.

Budgeted data for the current year are given in Table 1. Marketing indicates that results from the first three quarters of the current year show that projected annual sales for both product lines A and B will meet the budgeted levels of 50,000 and 10,000 units, respectively, unless a shift in emphasis is

TABLE 1/DIVERSIFIED COMPANY BUDGET DATA FOR 1993

		Product Line A	Product Line B
Predetermined Standard Overhead Rate:			
Estimated Annual Overhead	$10,500,000		
Estimated Anual Direct Labor Cost	$1,050,000		
Predetermined Standard Overhead Rate	1,000%		
Sales Price per Unit		$ 240	$ 900
Standard Production Costs per Unit:			
Direct Materials		$ 10	$ 170
Direct Labor		$ 15	$ 30
Overhead at 1,000% of Direct Labor		$ 150	$ 300
		$ 175	$ 500
Gross Margin per Unit		$ 65	$ 400
Gross Margin Percentage		27.1%	44.4%
Beginning Inventory [Units]		7,500	1,500
Production [Units]		50,000	10,000
Sales [Units]		50,000	10,000

◆ Net realizable value for all products is 90% of the sales price.
◆ Normal profit for all products is 30% of cost.

made. Production levels also are on schedule and are considered fixed because of contractual obligations. The gross margin percentages for product lines A and B are 27.1% and 44.4%, respectively. The overall gross margin percentage based on the entire inventory is 34.5%.

Policy options can result in sales volume varying as much as 10% from budgeted levels for each product line. The question has been raised concerning the impact of these policy changes on reported income and asset valuation. Diversified's external auditor assured management that under generally accepted accounting principles, Diversified can continue to use the existing traditional costing system for financial reporting. Based on this assurance, Diversified used traditional cost data to prepare an analysis of the impact of two scenarios on reported income and inventory valuation:

1. Emphasis on product line A, with sales volume increasing by 10%, resulting in a decrease of 10% in sales of product line B.
2. Emphasis on product line B, with sales increasing by 10%, resulting in a decrease of 10% in sales of product line A.

Table 2 gives results of the standard-cost-based analysis of both scenarios. Scenario 1 was to shift sales effort from product line B to product line A. For purposes of comparison, the application of lower of cost or market is shown based on similar pools and on entire inventory. Diversified consistently has used the similar pools basis, so I'll use it throughout this discussion.

The primary change in policy was pricing, with a $20 (average) reduction in the price of A's products (to $220) yielding a 10% increase in vol-

TABLE 2/STANDARD COST-BASED ANALYSIS

Scenario 1: Emphasize Product Line A

Inventory Valuation at LCM:	Pools A	B	Entire Inventory
Standard production cost per unit	$175	$500	$1,687,500
Designated market:			
Replacement cost (assumed equal to standard production cost)	175	500	1,687,500
Net realizable value (NRV)	198	878	2,688,750
Floor (NRV less normal profit)	146	728	2,182,500
Designated market value	175	728	2,182,500
Lower of cost or market	175	500	1,687,500
Write-down required per unit	0	0	
Total loss accrued	0	0	0

Gross Margin Under Standard Costing

	A	B	Total
Sales	$12,100,000	$8,775,000	$20,875,000
Cost of goods sold:			
Beginning inventory	1,312,500	750,000	2,062,500
Production	8,750,000	5,000,000	13,750,000
Cost of goods available	10,062,500	5,750,000	15,812,500
Less ending inventory	437,500	1,250,000	1,687,500
Cost of goods sold	9,625,000	4,500,000	14,125,000
Gross margin before write-down	2,475,000	4,275,000	6,750,000
Loss from write-down of inventory	0	0	0
Gross margin	$ 2,475,000	$4,275,000	$ 6,750,000
Gross margin percentage	20.5%	48.7%	32.3%

Scenario 2: Emphasize Product Line B

Inventory Valuation at LCM:	Pools A	B	Entire Inventory
Standard production cost per unit	$175	$500	$2,437,500
Designated market:			
Replacement cost (assumed equal to standard production cost)	175	500	2,437,500
Net realizable value (NRV)	234	765	3,307,500
Floor (NRV less normal profit)	182	615	2,576,250
Designated market value	182	615	2,576,250
Lower of cost or market	175	500	2,437,500
Write-down required per unit	0	0	
Total loss accrued	0	0	0

Gross Margin Under Standard Costing

	A	B	Total
Sales	$11,700,000	$9,350,000	$21,050,000
Cost of goods sold:			
Beginning inventory	1,312,500	750,000	2,062,500
Production	8,750,000	5,000,000	13,750,000
Cost of goods available	10,062,500	5,750,000	15,812,500
Less ending inventory	2,187,500	250,000	2,437,500
Cost of goods sold	7,875,000	5,500,000	13,375,000
Gross margin before write-down	3,825,000	3,850,000	7,675,000
Loss from write-down of inventory	0	0	0
Gross margin	$ 3,825,000	$3,850,000	$ 7,675,000
Gross margin percentage	32.7%	41.2%	36.5%

ume (5,000 units). Accompanying the changes in policy for product line A was a reduced sales force effort for product line B along with an increase in B's average price of $75 (to $975), yielding a volume of 9,000 units. This scenario results in a reduction in overall gross margin of 2.2% (34.5% - 32.3%) with no inventory writedown.

Scenario 2 was a shift in sales effort from product line A to product line B. The price of B was reduced by $50 (to $850), while the price of A was increased by $20 (to $260). The resulting volumes were 45,000 and 11,000 units for production lines A and B, respectively. The resulting increase in gross margin was 2% (36.5% - 34.5%) with no inventory writedown.

Based on the traditional cost-based gross margin analysis, Scenario 2 seemed the choice as it predicted the largest gross margin (36.5%). Management, however, is concerned about the accuracy of the traditional cost data and suggests using an activity-based costing study to recost both scenarios. The firm's controller argues that an ABC study is not necessary because, although the gross margins of individual product lines would differ when recosted, the aggregate gross margin as well as inventory valuation would not differ from the amounts generated via traditional cost-based analysis. Thus, the same overall margins would result, the decision would not be impacted, nor would the resulting reported financial reports be affected.

Should the ABC study be done? Management decided in favor of the study for

economic decision-making purposes. The combination of decreasing profitability and increasing diversity in both product line sales volume and process complexity—coupled with an increased overhead subject to allocation—prompted thede-

TABLE 3/ACTIVITY-BASED COST ANALYSIS

Scenario 1: Emphasize Product Line A

	Pools		Entire
Inventory Valuation at LCM:	A	B	Inventory
ABC production cost per unit	$75	$1,000	$2,687,500
Designated market:			
Replacement cost	75	1,000	2,687,500
Net realizable value (NRV)	198	878	2,688,750
Floor (NRV less normal profit)	176	578	1,882,500
Designated market value	176	878	2,687,500
Lower of cost or market	75	878	2,687,500
Write-down required per unit	0	123	
Total loss accrued	0	306,250	0

Gross Margin Under Activity-Based Costing

	A	B	Total
Sales	$12,100,000	$8,775,000	$20,875,000
Cost of goods sold:			
Beginning inventory	562,500	1,500,000	2,062,500
Production	3,750,000	10,000,000	13,750,000
Cost of goods available	4,312,500	11,500,000	15,812,500
Less ending inventory	187,500	2,500,000	2,687,500
Cost of goods sold	4,125,000	9,000,000	13,125,000
Gross margin before write-down	7,975,000	(225,000)	7,750,000
Loss from write-down of inventory	0	306,250	306,250
Gross margin	7,975,000	(531,250)	7,443,750
Gross margin percentage	65.9%	-6.1%	35.7%

Scenario 2: Emphasize Product Line B

	Pools		Entire
Inventory Valuation at LCM:	A	B	Inventory
ABC production cost per unit	$75	$1,000	$1,437,500
Designated market:			
Replacement cost	75	1,000	1,437,500
Net realizable value (NRV)	234	765	3,307,500
Floor (NRV less normal profit)	212	465	2,876,250
Designated market value	212	765	2,876,250
Lower of cost or market	75	765	1,437,500
Write-down required per unit	0	235	
Total loss accrued	0	117,500	0

Gross Margin Under Activity-Based Costing

	A	B	Total
Sales	$11,700,000	$9,350,000	$21,050,000
Cost of goods sold:			
Beginning inventory	562,500	1,500,000	2,062,500
Production	3,750,000	10,000,000	13,750,000
Cost of goods available	4,312,500	11,500,000	15,812,500
Less ending inventory	937,500	500,000	1,437,500
Cost of goods sold	3,375,000	11,000,000	14,375,000
Gross margin before write-down	8,325,000	(1,650,000)	6,675,000
Loss from write-down of inventory	0	117,500	117,500
Gross margin	8,325,000	(1,767,500)	6,557,500
Gross margin percentage	71.2%	-18.9%	31.2%

cision. The results of the recosting are shown in Table 3.

Product line A consists of high-volume and low-complexity products for which the demands of overhead activities upon resources are low. The resulting ABC allocation was reduced dramatically. Now, rather than $150 per unit (see Table 1), overhead is only $50, yielding a total unit production cost of $75. Product line B consists of low-volume and high-complexity products for which the demands of overhead activities upon resources are high. As a result, product line B now absorbs most of the production overhead —$800 per unit compared to $300 under traditional costing.

Table 3 presents Scenario 1 using ABC. Instead of the expected aggregate gross margin of 32.3% per the traditional cost system, the gross margin is 35.7%. Further, a substantial inventory writedown amounting to $306,250 (1.47% of sales) is necessary. An important issue is brought out here. *If the primary purpose of financial reporting is to provide useful information to potential and existing investors and creditors for their assessment of the firm's economic resources, then the avoidance of substantial loss (1.47% of sales) in the utility of inventory through application of GAAP is difficult to justify.* The net increase of 3.5% is reconciled as follows:

Gross Margin per Traditional Costing	32.34%
Less:	
Inventory Writedown	(1.47)
Add:	
Increase in B Inventory x Increase in B Cost	
[1,000 Units x ($1,000–$500)]/$20,875,000	2.40
Decrease in A Inventory x Decrease in A Cost	
[5,000 Units x ($175–$75)]/$20,875,000	2.40
Gross Margin per Activity-Based Costing	35.67%

The major increase in gross margin is due to the increased deferral of B's overhead costs, which are dramatically higher under ABC, coupled with the reduced costs of sales of A from beginning inventory, which are substantially lower under ABC. So, rather than a net reduction in overall gross margin of 2.2% as predicted under traditional costing, Scenario 1 actually results in a substantial increase in gross margin.

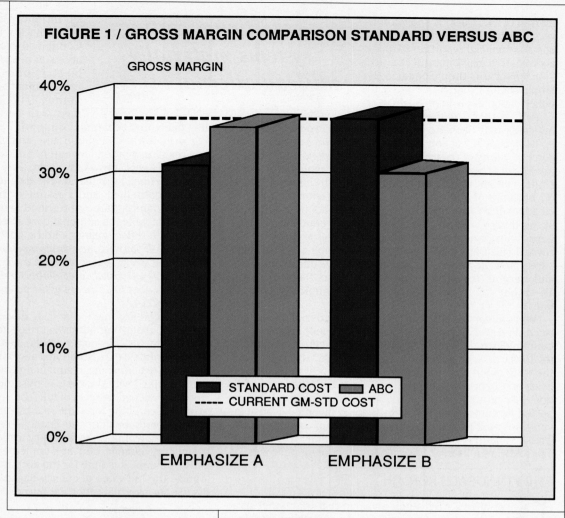

FIGURE 1 / GROSS MARGIN COMPARISON STANDARD VERSUS ABC

Table 3 also presents Scenario 2 results. From the above analysis of Scenario 1, it might be predicted that Scenario 2 under ABC will yield a dramatically lower gross margin than under traditional costing because Scenario 2 was to shift volume of sales from product line A to product line B—increasing the sales of the much-higher-cost product line. The reconciliation of the gross margins under the two costing systems is:

Gross Margin per Traditional Costing	36.46%
Less:	
Inventory Writedown	(.56)
Increase in B x Increase in Cost	
[[1,000 Units x ($1,000–$500)]/$21,050,000]	(2.38)
Decrease in A x Decrease in Cost	
[[5,000 Units x ($175—$75)]/$21,050,000]	(2.38)
Gross Margin per ABC	31.14%

As in Scenario 1, the impact of changes in inventory levels costed at significantly different amounts with an ABC system has a dramatic impact upon the reported income and inventory valuations. Instead of the expected aggregate gross margin of 36.5% per the traditional standard cost analysis, ABC analysis indicates the overall gross margin percentage will be 31.2%, or 5.3% less!

Figure 1 summarizes the differences between reported overall gross margin amounts for traditional costing compared to activity-based costing. The current overall gross margin of 34.5% also is shown. If Diversified continues to use traditional cost for financial reporting purposes and *reported* gross margin as a decision criterion, then Scenario 2—emphasizing Product line B—is the policy action likely to be taken.

ABC analysis, on the other hand, indicates that Scenario 1 —emphasizing Product line A— is the best policy action. *Which system should be used for purposes of financial reporting, economic decisions, and motivation of managers?* Imagine the dilemma management faces. Under current traditional costing, and with the wholehearted blessing of their external auditors, reported margins clearly will be maximized if Scenario 2 is adopted—emphasizing the low-volume, high-complexity product line B. Perhaps management performance evaluation and associated rewards also are contingent upon the same external measures. Now, however, management is aware that actual costs and margins, revealed via the ABC analyses, favor Scenario 1—emphasizing the high-volume, low-complexity product line A!

What about the financial reporting purpose of allocation? According to current GAAP the objectives of inventory accounting include "proper income determination, valuation at the lower of cost or market, and actual cost." It is clear from the illustration that the traditional costing system distorts costs and hence the reported results of operations. In addition, inaccurately costed products resulted in overstated reported inventories as well as overstated income because inventories aren't written down to the lower of cost-or-market. These violations of GAAP are avoided when ABC is used. Thus ABC results in improved allocation for *all* purposes.

THE FINAL SALE FOR ABC

Diversified's ABC study revealed that traditional standard costing not only distorted product line costs but resulted in material differences in aggregate amounts reported under GAAP. Further, because performance measures were tied to financial results, managers were motivated toward decisions that were dysfunctional from an overall company perspective. The new strategy Diversified adopted was to emphasize production as well as sales of product line A. Further, the company adopted a fully integrated ABC system for all allocation purposes including external reporting—in full compliance with GAAP.

My original assertion was that no differences are caused in reported aggregate amounts for income and inventory valuation when a company adopts an ABC system compared to a traditional cost system. From the development and analysis of the Diversified case however, we discovered that this assertion is true only under rather restrictive conditions: (1) No inventory writedowns are required under either system, and (2) production and sales are identical, so no changes in inventory exist. When either or both these conditions exist, significant differences will occur in both reported income and inventory valuation. As current GAAP requires a focus on accuracy of both income determination and valuation, activity-based costing should be considered a better approach. *In fact, it can be argued that traditional costing systems materially mislead external users and hence should not be considered acceptable.*

How typical is the environment of Diversified—pressure on profits from increasing competition, increasing diversity in products, and increased complexity of operating process-

...traditional costing systems materially mislead external users...

es? Inventory turns were 7.5 and 5.9 for Scenarios 1 and 2, respectively. Certainly it is possible for such variations to occur as a result of a combination of exogenous forces and management actions. Even in a just-in-time (JIT) production environment with low amounts of inventory, it is likely that accurate costing will reveal products requiring writedown. In addition, unpredictable economic factors can result in year-end inventory buildups that impact inventory levels over a two-year cycle, thus generating scenarios similar to ones I discussed. The data used in the illustration were hypothetical, and I assumed that the application of ABC was appropriate and resulted in more accurate product costs relative to a traditional cost system that had not been updated to reflect changes in the operating environment of the firm.[5] *If your business environment mirrors that of Diversified, and if you continue to use a traditional costing system based on its purported acceptability for financial reporting purposes, you need to be aware of the potential distortions and violations of GAAP.*

The aged argument that cost allocations of overhead are arbitrary, distorting otherwise reasonably accurate product cost estimates, no longer holds. ABC systems have overcome weaknesses in traditional allocation schemes. Further, the costs to companies maintaining two separate costing systems coupled with the costs of dysfunctional decisions most certainly exceed the cost of full ABC integration. Individuals who are searching for additional arguments in order to "sell" ABC should consider the financial reporting purpose.[6] Although some innovative industry leaders are not waiting for regulatory change and are implementing fully integrated ABC systems, it is time for the accounting profession to recognize the full value of activity-based accounting, including its use for external reporting purpose. ∎

William O. Stratton, CMA, is associate professor of accounting at the University of Michigan-Dearborn and holds a Ph.D. degree from the Claremont Graduate School. He has written several supplements for cost and management accounting texts, including the Instructors's Resource Manual *for the cost text by Charles Horngren and George Foster. He is a member-at-large. As of June 1993, Dr. Stratton can be reached at (719) 549-2142 at the University of Southern Colorado where he will be chair of the accounting program .*

---

[1] For an interesting and informative discussion of the various purposes of cost allocation, see Charles T. Horngren and George Foster, Cost *Accounting: A Managerial Emphasis,* 7th Edition, Prentice Hall, Englewood Cliffs, N.J., Chapter 14.
[2] Traditional cost systems are cost systems where little, if any, attempt is made to identify and link homogeneous cost pools with cost drivers. While a particular firm's standard cost system may be traditional, it is worthy of note that some firms incorporate both standard costing and activity-based costing.
[3] One of the few articles suggesting a change in GAAP is "Battle at the GAAP? It's Time for a Change," by Dennis Peavey, MANAGEMENT ACCOUNTING®, February 1990, pp. 31-35.
[4] David S. Koziol, "How the Constraint Theory Improved a Job-Shop Operation," MANAGEMENT ACCOUNTING®, May 1988, p. 45.
[5] For a discussion of the appropriate use of ABC, see "Are You Distorting Costs By Violating ABC Assumptions?" by Harold P. Roth and A. Faye Borthick, MANAGEMENT ACCOUNTING®, November 1991, pp. 39-42.
[6] For a discussion of the "art of selling ABC," see "Selling ABC," by John M. Brausch, MANAGEMENT ACCOUNTING®, February 1992, pp. 42-46.

Is this article of interest to you? If so, circle appropriate number on Reader Service Card.	**Yes** 60	**No** 61

Using ABC to Support Continuous Improvement

National Semiconductor applies a two-pronged approach.

BY PETER B.B. TURNEY AND ALAN J. STRATTON

In early 1991, National Semiconductor Corporation (NSC) embarked on its first implementation of activity-based costing (ABC). The goals of the pilot project were ambitious: to improve reported product costs *and* to provide information to guide improvement efforts—in several plants around the world.

In the first plant, the project team ran into immediate difficulty achieving these goals. To meet the improvement goal, NSC's managers wanted information that described the many facets of work in each area of the plant. But this required a detailed and complex model that was judged too costly and time-consuming to build.

As a result of these concerns, activity detail in the model was reduced to a summary level. This summary information was sufficient to report reasonably accurate product costs and thus meet the first goal. It was too aggregated, however, to provide insights about how and where to improve.

Results were disappointing. Despite a strong management commitment, and much attention to training, there was no evidence that ABC had any impact on improvement efforts.

In the second plant, NSC took a different approach to design. This second model included two different types of activities, micro and macro activities. Micro activities were detailed activities reflective of individual units of work and were intended to support activity improvement.[1]

Macro activities were summary activities. The costs of several related mi-cro activities were assigned to a single macro activity. Macro activities were used for product costing and for assigning the cost of internal suppliers to their internal customers.

Prior to the completion of the project, lists of costed micro activities were distributed to the managers who

In this National Semiconductor factory, 20 improvements were made in one month in response to one piece of information.

had been interviewed previously. The managers were asked to confirm the correctness of the information prior to the completion of the model.

This single communication was unintentionally responsible for accelerating the pace and impact of improvements in the plant. Within a one-month period, it was found that more than 20 improvements had been made in response to the micro activity information. In addition, the NSC model reported accurate product costs at a reasonably low cost. Macro activities simplified the task of product costing and reduced the overall complexity of the model.

In this article we show how to design an ABC model to support continuous improvement. Using actual examples from NSC, we explain how a two-dimensional ABC model using micro and macro activities supplies the required information in an economical manner. How this information is used in the continuous improvement process also is described.

Based on our experience at NSC and elsewhere, we believe that this approach to ABC is the most significant development in the design of ABC models in recent years. It is the fulcrum on which ABC has moved from a narrow focus on product costing to a broader activity-based management perspective.

TWO-DIMENSIONAL ABC

Modern ABC models contain two dimensions: a cost view, and a process view (Figure 1). The presence of two dimensions extends ABC beyond product costing to the world of continuous improvement.[2]

The process view of ABC contains information about why work is done and how well it is performed. This information is used to assess the performance of work within the organization. Information provided about each activity or process includes cost drivers, performance measures, and other information—such as cost of quality—used in the continuous improvement process.

Cost drivers determine the workload and effort required to perform an activity. They include factors relating to the performance of supplier activities as well as factors internal to the activity. Performance measures describe the work done and the results achieved in an activity. They include measures of cost, quality, and time.

The cost view of ABC contains information about the cost of resources, activities, and products and customers. This information is used in strategic and tactical analyses, such as evaluating customer profitability, prioritizing improvement projects, and setting cost targets.

ABC uses two types of driver to assign cost to activities, outputs, and customers. *Resource* drivers assign the cost of resources to activities. For example, the resource driver "percent of effort" might be used to assign the cost of people to the activities they perform.

Activity drivers assign the cost of activities to products and customers. For example, the activity driver "number of purchase orders" might be used to assign the cost of the activity "preparing purchase orders" to the parts that are purchased.

MICRO/MACRO ACTIVITIES

The use of micro and macro activities allows two types of activity to be incorporated into the ABC model and the serving of two distinct customers of ABC information. The micro, or detailed activities, are part of the process view of ABC. The macro, or summary activities, are part of the cost assignment view of ABC.

Micro activities are the focal point of improvement efforts. Detailed cost and noncost information, including cost drivers and performance measures, is attached to micro activities. Micro activities are not used to cost products—the cost of micro activities

is assigned to macro activities, not to products.

Macro activities are aggregations of related micro activities. Their primary purpose is to facilitate the reporting of accurate product costs, but they are too summarized to guide the improvement of individual activities.

The cost of a macro activity is assigned to products using a single activity driver, which reduces the cost and complexity of the ABC model because activity drivers are not attached to micro activities. It also maintains the accuracy of reported product costs because all micro activities within a macro activity are used in the same way by each product.

WAFER SORTING

The ABC design team at NSC built a micro/macro activity model for a wafer sorting process. This process took a thin slice of silicon (a wafer) and examined the dies on the wafer to see if any were defective. The team discovered seven micro activities within the process. They included writing die testing programs and handling batches of wafers before and after processing (Table 1). The team also discovered various micro activities in the support departments that sustained the sorting process. They included activities associated with providing materials to the process, such as placing purchase orders and bidding on new purchases.

No additional effort was required to identify these micro activities. Depart-

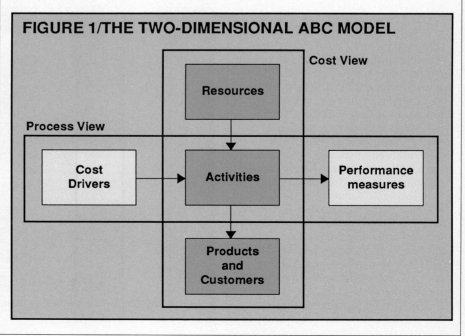

FIGURE 1/THE TWO-DIMENSIONAL ABC MODEL

Cost View

Process View

Resources

Cost Drivers → Activities → Performance measures

Products and Customers

TABLE 1/DESIGN OF THE ABC MODEL FOR THE SORTING PROCESS
NATIONAL SEMICONDUCTOR CORPORATION

Micro Activity	Rule 1: Level	Rule 2: Activity Driver	Rule 3: Purpose	Macro Activity
Direct activities:				
Developing test programs	Product	Number of products	Sort direct	Developing/testing products
Making probe cards	Product	Number of products	Sort direct	Developing/testing products
Setting up lots	Batch	Number of lots	Sort direct	Handling wafer lots
Maintaining probe cards	Batch	Number of lots	Sort direct	Handling wafer lots
Testing products	Unit	Number of dies tested	Sort direct	Testing dies
Collecting engineering data	Batch	Number of lots	Sort direct	Handling wafer lots
Handling wafer lots	Batch	Number of lots	Sort direct	Handling wafer lots
Supplier activities:				
Providing indirect materials	Process	Use of materials	Sort sustaining	Providing materials
Purchasing materials	Process	Use of materials	Sort sustaining	Providing materials
Providing utilities	Process	Space	Sort sustaining	Providing space
Providing space	Process	Space	Sort sustaining	Providing space

ment managers supplied the micro activity information during the data-gathering process. Micro activities were equivalent to individual units of work in each department, so their description was a natural response to the question, "what work do you do?"

Interestingly, equivalent micro activity information was obtained from interviews in the first plant but was "thrown away" as unwanted detail. This time, however, the detail was retained and built into the model.

Various pieces of nonfinancial information—called attributes—were attached to the micro activities. The purpose of these items of nonfinancial information was to illuminate the improvement process.

Attributes included cost drivers; performance measures, value-added or nonvalue-added; and cost of quality. For example, the micro activities in the sorting process detected errors and were therefore tagged with the attribute "internal appraisal." This tagging of information in the ABC database facilitated the preparation of reports about the plant's cost of quality.

The costs of the seven micro activities within the sorting process were combined to make three process macro activities: testing dies, handling batches of wafers, and developing the tooling needed to test each type of wafer (Table 1). The costs of micro activities performed by internal suppliers were assigned to two separate macro activities: unit-based support and batch-based support.

The team followed three criteria in preparing macro activities.[3] Micro activities that met all three criteria were combined into a macro activity:

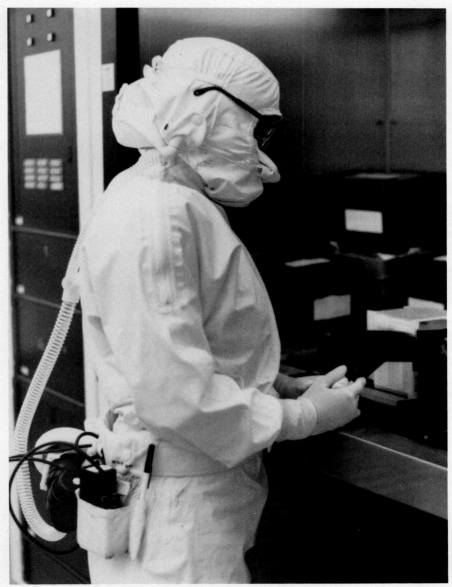

National Semiconductor worker tests silicon wafer as part of ABC.

- Only activities performed at the same level can be combined. Level relates to the output or customer of the activity. For example, testing an individual die (unit level), setting up the test equipment to test a batch of wafers (batch level), and developing a test program for a particular die (product level) could not be combined.[4]

It made sense to keep activities of different levels separate because the cost of activities at different levels varied in response to different factors. For example, the cost of the batch-level activity-testing wafers varied with the number of batches tested. By contrast, the cost of the product-level activity developing a test program varied with the number of different types of products tested.

- Activities that used the same activity driver could be combined without diminishing the reported accuracy of product costs. Activities that used different activity drivers could not be combined without dropping one or other of the drivers (only one activity driver per activity is possible in an ABC model[5]).

For example, the cost of setting up the test equipment and collecting test data was assigned using the activity driver "number of tests." These two activities therefore met rule 2.

The use of the testing dies activity was determined by the number of dies, not the number of tests. Its cost was therefore assigned to dies using the activity driver "number of dies" and could not be combined with the other activities that used different activity drivers.[6]

- Activities included in a macro activity had to be of common purpose or function. For example, some of the sorting activities, such as developing tests and maintaining probe cards, also were performed in other parts of the plant. These activities were part of a totally different process—and the responsibility of a different work team—and their cost was not assigned to a macro activity in the sorting process.

The costs of micro activities performed inside and outside the sorting process were assigned to separate macro activities because micro activities performed inside the process differed in level from those performed

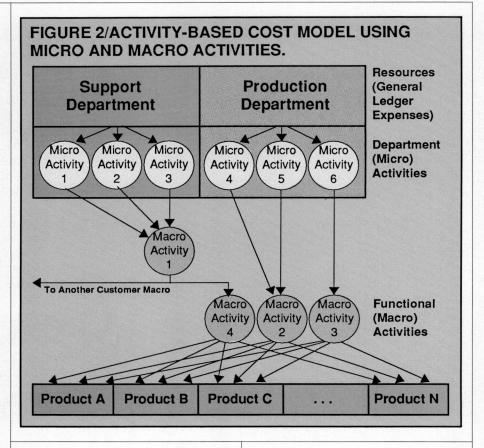

FIGURE 2/ACTIVITY-BASED COST MODEL USING MICRO AND MACRO ACTIVITIES.

outside (rule 1). Those within the process sustained products, while those performed outside the process (supplier activities) sustained the process itself. For example, the activity providing indirect materials, performed in the purchasing department, helps sustain the sorting process (Table 1).

TWO-DIMENSIONAL ABC AND MICRO/MACRO ACTIVITIES

The use of micro and macro activities changed the structure of the ABC model. The responsibility and economic aspects of the model were now kept separate, facilitating the model's dual product costing and performance improvement objectives. It also simplified the model, reducing the cost of system design and maintenance.

The Responsibility Model. The NSC model organized micro activities by department (Figure 2). The model assigned the cost of resources charged directly to a department to the micro activities within it. However, the model did not assign costs from other departments to these activities.

This micro activity structure paralleled the responsibility structure of the organization and supported process

improvements in each jurisdiction. The micro activities within a department also corresponded directly to the resources charged to that department in the general ledger.

The micro activities in each department were grouped into departmental macro activities (according to the rules described above). Each macro represented a summary of similar activities. Each department macro activity also provided a starting point for improvement prioritization.

The Economic Model. Once the macro activities were established, the next step was to assign the cost of supplier activities to the sorting process (Figure 2). This assignment was based on estimates of their use and reflected an internal supplier-customer relationship. This cost assignment added economic meaning and utility to the model. First, each set of macro activities for a process contained all work performed within the process *and* the cost of supplier activities consumed by it. It included the cost of all work used in or by the process.

The ABC model therefore revealed the total cost of the sorting process—including the "hidden costs" of the process located elsewhere in the organization. This information could be used, for example, in make-or-buy analyses on the sorting process or determinations of the cross-functional impact on cost of changes in the sorting process.

Second, it reduced the cost of reporting product costs because of the relative ease of assigning the cost of supplier activities to the processes that benefited. Usually, there was a clear supplier-customer relationship, and data measuring the use of supplier activities were readily available.

Once the cost was assigned to the customer process, the method of assignment to the products was easy. The cost of the support macro activity in each process was assigned using the primary activity driver in the process (such as the number of dies or the number of wafers).[7] The data for this driver already had been entered into the model to cost other activities in the process, so there was no additional data collection or data entry cost associated with the assignment.

In contrast, NSC previously had attempted to assign the cost of internal supplier activities directly to products. This was difficult because the relationship of the activity to products usually was not clear.

The benefits of this structure can be seen clearly when contrasted with the traditional two-stage cost assignment model (Figure 3).[8] The two-stage model, used in early ABC models, defined activities in only general terms. An activity was really a plant-wide cost pool reflecting a class of activity. Cost was assigned from any number of departments to a single cost pool. The cost of each cost pool was then assigned to products using an activity driver that best measured the consumption of

that cost pool by the products.

The two-stage model reported more accurate product costs than traditional volume-based approaches. But its value for activity management and performance improvement was limited. One difficulty was the lack of detailed cost information about activities and the total lack of nonfinancial information. Another difficulty was the lack of responsibility of any one manager or department for a cost pool.

Two-stage models also were quite complex. The criss-crossing of cost assignment paths from departments to cost pools created a challenge when tracing cost from cost pools back to the originating departments.

MAJOR ADVANCE FOR COST MANAGEMENT

Two-dimensional activity-based costing is a major advance for cost management. It turns ABC into a true cost management system that supports product costing *and* performance improvement.

The key to building a two-dimensional ABC model is to use micro and macro activities. Micro activities are the units of work in a department that are managed on a day-by-day basis. Macro activities are summaries of work that facilitate reporting accurate product costs and yield the cost of internal supplier-customer relationships.

NSC's ABC model is a good example of two-dimensional design. It shows how micro activities are combined into macro activities using three rules. It reveals a two-level model structure that includes both responsibility and economic information.

The NSC model does not illustrate

all possible design alternatives. For example, the micro activities in the NSC model are organized by department. Some firms, however, choose to organize micro activities by cross-functional process.

An apparently simple design innovation, the two-dimensional model with micro and macro activities is a boon for ABC system designers. In addition to improving the quality and flexibility of ABC information, it reduces the cost and complexity of ABC models. ∎

Peter B.B. Turney is chief executive officer, Cost Technology, Inc., Portland, Ore., and the author of Common Cents: The ABC Performance Breakthrough. *He can be reached at (503) 292-5690.*

Alan J. Stratton, CMA, CPA, is worldwide activity-based management coordinator and former controller at National Semiconductor Corporation, Arlington, Tex. He is a member of the Fort Worth Chapter.

[1]Information about the tasks that underlay each activity was not included in the model. It was expected that this information would be developed by the users in response to their need for detailed activity information.
[2]See Chapters 4, 5, and 6 of Peter B.B. Turney, *Common Cents: The ABC Performance Breakthrough,* (Portland: Cost Technology, 1992) for an extended discussion of two-dimensional ABC.
[3]These criteria were based on the rules for the design of macro activities in *Common Cents: The ABC Performance Breakthrough,* p. 126.
[4]Unit, batch, product, and process activity levels were first described by Robin Cooper in "Cost Classification in Unit-Based and Activity-Based Manufacturing Cost Systems," *Journal of Cost Management,* Fall 1990, pp. 4-14. See *Common Cents: The ABC Performance Breakthrough,* pp. 146-150, for a complete discussion of activity levels.
[5]See *Common Cents: The ABC Performance Breakthrough,* pp. 281-284, for a discussion of the rules of selecting activity drivers.
[6]Testing dies is also a unit level activity, so it also fails rule 1 as a candidate for combining with the other two testing activities.
[7]Assigning the cost of an activity such as "providing facilities space" to products using the "number of dies" as the activity driver is not theoretically correct. (The activity is processing sustaining, and the activity driver is unit-level). However, from a practical standpoint it makes sense. First, space is clearly consumed by the process. Second, the amount of space required by the sorting process is determined primarily by the volume of dies. Third, there is no theoretically correct answer.
[8]See, for example, Robin Cooper, "The Two-Stage Procedure in Cost Accounting: Part One," *Journal of Cost Management,* Vol. 1, No. 2, Summer 1987, pp. 43-51.

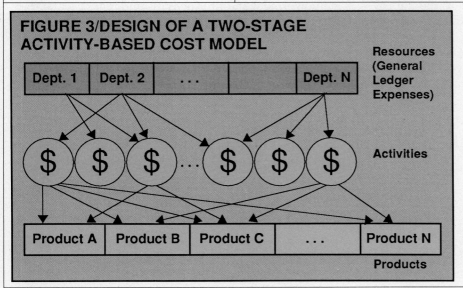

FIGURE 3/DESIGN OF A TWO-STAGE ACTIVITY-BASED COST MODEL

Resources (General Ledger Expenses)

Dept. 1 Dept. 2 . . . Dept. N

Activities

$ $ $ . . . $ $ $

Products

Product A Product B Product C . . . Product N

Looking to the Future

While this anthology portrays the development, unfolding, and progression of ABC management systems—systems that provide significant insight into the consumption of resources by activities and processes—another view, an organizational view, indicates that a major shift appears to be taking place in the worker/management relationships. As the roles and responsibilities of workers and managers are changed so, too, will the organization be changed.

Initially, ABC focused on improving costing of products and markets. A new focus, activity-based management, encompasses the management of activities and processes as the route to continuous improvement. ABC management systems appear to be unfolding and progressing to support all the firm's business processes better. These systems mirror the manufacturing process and evolve continually. In addition, it appears that cost concepts of the past are being incorporated in new ABC systems to enhance managerial decision making.

A new, more participative role is envisioned for the financial manager. The new financial manager will use the computer to model the firm's business activities and processes and will be part of the cross-functional team providing information to process owners to support the firm's activities and processes. The financial manager's dedication to the improvement of financial management processes will not go unnoticed.

As firms focus on business process reengineering, workers or process owners will develop the cost information. With accountants as partners on these workteams, workers can accept responsibility and participate in decision making so that decisions are made at levels below management. Managers are freed to act as coaches or facilitators in the workforce because everyone has bottom line responsibility and knowledge of how to improve profitability. This approach militates against decisions being made the "old way"—by the numbers—usually based on an inadequate knowledge of the firm's business processes. These customer-focused, process-driven organizations will be far different from those that preceded them.

Will this shift toward the people-oriented paradigm corporation cause a change in the management of human resources? For those people who do not have a natural job fit with the new job specifications, will corporations continue to believe that they can overcome shortcomings with training? More money for training and education will not necessarily improve productivity.

Next-generation people assessment tools should be developed to measure the company workforce to ascertain fit to the changed corporate culture and changed business processes. These new assessment tools, benchmarked (validated) against a diverse group of employed people, will serve to reduce waste in the employee selection process, increase worker empowerment and productivity, and reduce a major but real "hidden" business cost—turnover cost. In this larger context, the entire subject of human resource process management should be challenged and reexamined to support the people-oriented paradigm corporations of the future. ∎

Bibliography

Beaujon, George J., and Vinod R. Singhal. "Understanding the Activity Costs in an Activity-Based Cost System." *Journal of Cost Management,* Spring 1990, pp. 51-72.

Borden, James P. "Software for Activity-Based Management." *Journal of Cost Management,* Fall 1991, pp. 7-37.

Brimson, James A. *Activity Accounting: An Activity-Based Costing Approach.* New York, John Wiley & Sons, 1991.

Brinker, Barry J., ed. *Emerging Practices in Cost Management* [a compilation of 50 articles from the *Journal of Cost Management,* Spring 1987 to Fall 1990]. Boston, Warren, Gorham & Lamont, 1990.

Cokins, Gary, Alan Stratton, and Jack Helbling. *An ABC Manager's Primer.* Montvale, NJ, Institute of Management Accountants, 1993.

Cooper, Robin. "Cost Classification in Unit-Based and Activity-Based Manufacturing Cost Systems." *Journal of Cost Management,* Fall 1990, pp. 4-14.

___. "Implementing an Activity-Based Cost System." *Journal of Cost Management,* Spring 1990, pp. 33-42.

___. "The Rise of Activity-Based Costing — Part One: What Is an Activity-Based Cost System?" *Journal of Cost Management,* Summer 1988, pp. 45-54.

___. "The Rise of Activity-Based Costing — Part Two: When Do I Need an Activity-Based Cost System?" *Journal of Cost Management,* Fall 1988, pp. 41-48.

___. "The Rise of Activity-Based Costing — Part Three: How Many Cost Drivers Do You Need, and How Do You Select Them?" *Journal of Cost Management,* Winter 1989, pp. 34-46.

___. "The Rise of Activity-Based Costing — Part Four: What Do Activity-Based Cost Systems Look Like?" *Journal of Cost Management,* Spring 1989, pp. 38-49.

Fisher, Steven A. et al. "Implementing Activity-Based Costing: Lessons from the Gencorp Experience." *Corporate Controller,* September/October 1990, pp. 15-20.

Johnson, H. Thomas. *Relevance Regained: From Top-Down Control to Bottom-Up Empowerment.* New York, The Free Press, 1992.

Kaplan, Robert S., Robin Cooper, Lawrence Maisel, Eileen Morrissey, and Ronald Oehm. *Implementing Activity-Based Cost Management: Moving from Analysis to Action.* Montvale, NJ, Institute of Management Accountants, 1992.

O'Guin, Michael C. *The Complete Guide to Activity-Based Costing.* Englewood Cliffs, NJ, Prentice-Hall, 1991.

Ostrenga, Michael R. et al. *The Ernst & Young Guide to Total Cost Management.* New York, John Wiley & Sons, 1992.

Rotch, William. "Activity-Based Costing in Service Industries." *Journal of Cost Management,* Summer 1990, pp. 4-14.

Sakurai, Michiharu. "Target Costing and How to Use It." *Journal of Cost Management,* Summer 1989, pp. 39-50.

Turney, Peter B.B. *Common Cents: The ABC Performance Breakthrough.* Hillsboro, OR, Cost Technology, 1991.

Institute of Management Accountants (IMA)
IMA's Continuous Improvement Center

Improving the contribution of financial management to an organization's success

IMA's Continuous Improvement Center (CIC) will assist organizations to measure how well they are doing, to learn what others are doing, and to identify the best practices in financial management.

ASSESSMENT ASSISTANCE AND BENCHMARK DATABASE

Participating organizations will use an assessment manual to evaluate their financial management functions. An associated survey document will feed a computerized benchmark database managed by IMA. This database will represent a critical mass of comparable measurements from a cross-section of organizations.

PERFORMANCE IMPROVEMENT AND RECOGNITION

The participating organizations will develop an internal improvement plan by comparing the results of their assessment activities with equivalent information from the benchmark database. These comparisons would help identify those areas that would provide meaningful bottom line results. If the plan is adopted internally and the participating organization views recognition as a positive motivator, the CIC will offer a national recognition program for those who achieve the objectives of their improvement plan.

BEST PRACTICES

IMA will offer training, forums, and focused research studies to support the center. Over time, best practices should evolve that could be considered models for good performance in financial management. As an independent and objective repository, CIC will facilitate the collection and dissemination of information. IMA will not engage in analysis and consulting relating to a particular organization's results. CIC will ensure confidentiality and interpret the data received for comparability.

CIC BENEFITS

This IMA initiative will be an important factor in organizations' efforts to become more competitive. By knowing what others do and how well financial processes can and are being performed, management can focus on changes that can make a real difference in their organizations—reducing head count, decreasing cycle time, lowering defect rates, reducing process costs, improving financial management contributions to organization management, and enhancing the image of financial management.

PARTICIPANTS

Meetings with Fortune 500 and other entities to present IMA's CIC confirm the value of this Center. One of the most important values is the sharing of information and best practices with other organizations. IMA is committed to assisting our members' employers to improve their financial processes. Organizations interested in becoming a part of the CIC and participating in its programs should contact William McMahon at (201) 573-6266 or fax (201) 573-0639.

■

THREE BOOKS ~~ON ABC/~~ CM from IMA

IMPLEMENTING ACTIVITY-BASED COST MANAGEMENT:
Moving from Analysis to Action gives a state-of-the-art view of the ABC principles and implementation experiences of eight companies. The findings will help you to understand the design decisions and pitfalls and the organizational dynamics that can directly affect the success of an ABC system.

AN ABC MANAGER'S PRIMER:
Straight Talk on Activity-Ba~~sed~~ ~~takes the mystique~~ out of ABC. The primer, initiated by CA~~M-I~~ ~~and written in simple, clear~~ language, gives a head start for imple~~menting~~ ~~project.~~

IMPLEMENTING A~~CTIVITY-BASED COSTING~~
(Statement on Man~~agement Accounting No. 4T)~~ helps ~~management~~ accountants under~~stand their role and responsibilities in ABC~~ projects. It gives a practical m~~ethod of designing ABC systems, alternative~~ approaches for ABC ~~implementation, and suggestions for ensuring that~~ the benefits of ABC a~~ctually are realized. The statement was developed~~ and first published by ~~The Society of Management Accountants~~ of Canada.

Mail to:
Institute of Management Accountants
Special Orders Department
10 Paragon Drive
Montvale, NJ 07645-1760

Phone: 1-800-638-4427,
or: 1-201-573-62~~~~
FAX: 1-201-573-95~~~~

Please send me:

- [ ] IMPLEMENTING ACTIVITY-BASED COST MANAGEMENT: Moving from Analysis to Action   #92268/$35.00
- [ ] AN ABC MANAGER'S PRIMER: Straight Talk on Activity-Based Costing   #93282/$15.00
- [ ] IMPLEMENTING ACTIVITY-BASED COSTING SMA 4T   #94290/$7.50 each

Total books: _____ Total price:_____
Less 20% (if applicable)*:_____
N.J. residents, please add 6% sales tax: _____
Shipping & handling charge:_____
TOTAL:_____

*IMA members are entitled to a 20% discount.
Member # : _____

- [ ] Nonmember; please send me membership info.
- [ ] Send the 1994 IMA Catalog of Publications.

SHIPPING AND HANDLING   All orders within the continental United States are sent by United Parcel Service (UPS) or first-class mail. You should receive delivery within two weeks. Minimum shipping & handling charge per shipment is $6.00 for 1-3 items; $9.00 for 4-10 items; $12.00 for 11-20 items; and $20 for 21 or more items. Overnight via Airborne Express or 2nd Day Delivery (Blue Label) via UPS is available at your expense. Please call for more information. Orders to Canada, Alaska, and Hawaii will be charged 20% of total order; minimum is $10.00. All other destinations outside the U.S. add 40% for shipping and handling; minimum is $20.00.

~~the report must be included~~ d.
~~Payments must be drawn on a U.S. bank. All orders~~ must be prepaid.

_____
~~(Name (please print or type)~~

_____
~~(Title if part of mailing address)~~

Address (do not use P.O. box number)
_____

City, State, Zip
_____

Please make check payable to :

Institute of Management Accountants

- [ ] Check enclosed
- [ ] American Express (15 digits)
- [ ] MasterCard (16 digits)
- [ ] Visa (13 or 16 digits)

1	2	3	4	5	6	7	8	9	10	11	12	13	14	15	16

_____   _____
Expiration Date   Signature

ABC/AMB11/93

MEMBERSHIP APPLICATION

INSTITUTE OF MANAGEMENT ACCOUNTANTS, INC.

10 PARAGON DRIVE, MONTVALE, NEW JERSEY 07645-1760 · 201-573-9000 · 1-800-638-4427

Check One. (✓) ☐ INITIAL APPLICATION ☐ REINSTATEMENT

FOR OFFICE USE ONLY

BATCH NUMBER	PAYMT. BY CK.	AMOUNT	VOL	ELECTION DATE
	☐ PERSONAL ☐ COMPANY			

PERSONAL INFORMATION:
(Print Legibly or Type) Use Black or Blue Ink

Mr.	Ms.	Miss	Mrs.	Dr.	Male	Female	Social Security Number	Professional Designations
☐	☐	☐	☐	☐	☐	☐	- -	☐ CMA ☐ CPA ☐ CIA ☐ CFA Other:

First Name — Middle Name — Last Name — Suffix

First Name or Nickname for IMA Badges (Optional)

Home Street Address — Street

Date of Birth

City — State — Zip Code (9 Digit)

Marital Status (Optional) / Number of Children (Optional) — Year of Birth of Each Child (Optional)

Part Time/School Address — Street — City — State — Zip Code (9 Digit)

Telephone Number at Part Time Address ( )

Effective Date (Month to Month)

Spouse's First Name — Middle Name — Last Name

Nickname for IMA Badges — Spouse's Professional Designation

Send IMA Mail
☐ Home ☐ Busines

Telephone Preference
☐ Home ☐ Business

COMPANY NAME: (Please Print or Type)

Hire Date

Street Address (include suite, room and/or mail stop)

Home Telephone Number ( )

Business Telephone ( ) — Extension

City — State — Zip Code (9 Digit)

Fax Number ( )

SIC Code (See Reverse Side)	Job Title Code (See Reverse Side)	Responsibility Code (See Reverse Side)

Company Size (Check One)
☐ Under $50 Million
☐ $50 - 500 Million
☐ $501 Million - $5 Billion
☐ Over $5 Billion

CHAPTER AFFILIATION: (Name of Chapter/Student Chapter - Your Choice)

Chapter Number

☐ Member-At-Large ☐ Check here if no chapter affiliation desired

EDUCATION - College, Business, Graduate School(s)
(Fill In All Applicable Information)

MAJOR	DATE(S)	DEGREE(S)

MEMBERSHIP - FILL IN AS APPROPRIATE - ALL PAYMENTS MUST BE IN U.S. DOLLARS

DUES · **REGULAR:** U.S.A. AND CANADA
☐ 1Yr. $125 ☐ 2Yr. $240 ☐ 3Yr. $345 $_____

· **INTERNATIONAL MEMBER-AT-LARGE** $125
You must reside outside the U.S.A. and CANADA

· **ACADEMIC:** U.S.A. AND CANADA   Must be a full-time faculty member $ 62.50

· **ASSOCIATE:** U.S.A. AND CANADA   Must apply within 2 years of completing full-time studies   1st Year $ 42 / 2nd Year $ 83

· **STUDENT MEMBERSHIP:** Not less than 6 equivalent hours per semester. $ 25
U.S.A. AND CANADA   *Fill in school name below.
*Name of School _____ Expected Date of Degree

OPTIONAL SERVICES**
**IMA Membership Required
☐ Controllers Council $ 75
☐ Cost Management Group $ 75
☐ Research Publications Service $ 50

$_____

REGISTRATION / REINSTATEMENT FEE
NOTE: Regular, Academic & International Members ONLY $ 15:00

☐ I am enclosing a check payable to : INSTITUTE OF MANAGEMENT ACCOUNTANTS, INC.
☐ Charge my credit card: ☐ VISA ☐ MASTERCARD ☐ AMEX
CREDIT CARD NUMBER _____ EXPIRATION DATE ←

TOTAL $_____

I affirm the statements on this application are correct and agree to abide by the Standards of Ethical Conduct for Management Accountants.

SIGNATURE X _____

Sponsor's Name (if applicable), or Signature of Professor or Registrar (for student)

DATE _____   Sponsor's Member No. (if applicable) _____

ADMISSION CRITERIA FOR MEMBERSHIP: INSTITUTE OF MANAGEMENT ACCOUNTANTS, INC. I affirm that I meet the criteria for membership (on reverse side) which I have circled.
Please circle only one.   b: 1, 2, 3, 4, 5, 6, 7

CPA Certificate Number _____ State _____ Year _____

Are you required to report CPE hours annually? ☐ No ☐ Yes (See Reverse Side)

Have you ever been convicted of a felony? ☐ No ☐ Yes (See Reverse Side)

CMA Certified Management Accountant Program
☐ Check Here to receive information about IMA's prestigious certification program

☐ No ☐ Yes

PLEASE READ BOTH SIDES

NOTE: PAYMENT IN FULL MUST ACCOMPANY APPLICATION - FEES SUBJECT TO CHANGE

EFFECTIVE SEPTEMBER 1, 1993

INSTITUTE OF MANAGEMENT ACCOUNTANTS, INC.

Admission Criteria for Membership - All persons residing within the United States, its possessions, or Canada, and who are otherwise qualified for membership under the Bylaws, are eligible for membership as Regular Members, Associate Members or Student Members as defined in Article II, Section 2 of the Bylaws, provided they meet the following minimum criteria:

(b)

(1) Have a full four-year degree, with a major in accounting or a minimum of 21 semester hours in accounting, or an advanced degree with 15 semester hours in accounting, or

(2) Have a full four-year college degree and hold either a management accounting position or management accounting teaching position or be admitted to the CMA program at the time of admission, or

(3) Have a two-year degree with a minimum of 15 semester hours in accounting plus four years of experience in a management accounting position at the time of admission, or

(4) Hold a CPA certificate, or an international certificate comparable to a CPA or CMA certificate

(5) Have six years of experience in management accounting, or

(6) Agree to complete 18 Continuing Professional Education (CPE) hours in IMA-approved programs (local or national) in each of the five consecutive years from the date of admission. A member not fulfilling the commitment will automatically be dropped from membership, or

(7) Be a college student carrying a minimum of six undergraduate or graduate hours (or equivalent) per semester within a school, college or university in the United States.

NOTE: Prior felony conviction - This application, with a brief explanation of circumstances, should be sent directly to the Executive Director of IMA at the address on the reverse side of this form in an envelope marked "Confidential".

STANDARD INDUSTRY CLASSIFICATIONS (SIC)

AGRICULTURE, FORESTRY, FISHERIES
01 AGRICULTURAL PRODUCTION
07 AGRICULTURAL SVCS / HUNTING / TRAPPING
08 FORESTRY
09 FISHERIES

MINING
10 METAL MINING
11 ANTHRACITE MINING
12 BITUMINOUS COAL / LIGNITE MINING
13 CRUDE OIL / LIGNITE MINING
14 MINING / QUARRY NONMETALLICS

CONTRACT CONSTRUCTION
15 BLDG. CONSTRUCTION - GENERAL CONTRACTORS
16 CONSTRUCTION - OTHER
17 CONSTRUCTION - SPECIAL TRADE CONTRACTORS

MANUFACTURING
19 ORDINANCE / ACCESSORIES
20 FOOD / KINDRED PRODUCTS
21 TOBACCO MANUFACTURERS
22 TEXTILE MILL PRODUCTS
23 APPAREL / FINISHED FABRICS
24 LUMBER / WOOD PRODUCTS

MANUFACTURING CONTINUED
25 FURNITURE / FIXTURES
26 PAPER / ALLIED PRODUCTS
27 PRINTING / PUBLISHING
28 CHEMICALS / ALLIED PRODUCTS
29 OIL REFINING / RELATED INDUSTRIES
30 RUBBER / MISC. PLASTICS PRODUCTS
31 LEATHER PRODUCTS
32 STONE, CLAY, GLASS / CONCRETE PRODUCTS
33 PRIMARY METAL INDUSTRIES
34 FABRICATED METAL PRODUCTS
35 MACHINERY, NONELECTRICAL
36 ELECTRICAL MACHINERY
37 TRANSPORTATION
38 PROFESSIONAL, SCIENTIFIC, CONTROL INSTRUMENTS
39 MISC. MANUFACTURING INDUSTRIES

TRANSPORTATION, COMMUNICATION & UTILITY SERVICES
40 RAILROAD TRANSPORTATION
41 LOCAL AND SUBURBAN TRANSPORTATION
42 MOTOR FREIGHT / WAREHOUSING
44 WATER TRANSPORTATION
46 PIPE LINE TRANSPORTATION
47 TRANSPORTATION SERVICES
48 COMMUNICATION
49 ELECTRIC, GAS / SANITARY SERVICES

WHOLESALE & RETAIL TRADE
50 WHOLESALE TRADE
52 BUILDING / HARDWARE / FARM EQUIP DEALERS
53 RETAIL TRADE - GENERAL
54 FOOD STORES
55 AUTO DEALERS / SERVICE STATIONS
56 APPAREL / ACCESSORY STORES
57 FURNITURE / FURNISHINGS / STORES
58 EATING / DRINKING PLACES
59 MISC. RETAIL STORES

FINANCE, INSURANCE & REAL ESTATE
60 BANKING
61 CREDIT AGENCIES NOT BANKS
62 SECURITY / COMMODITY BROKERS, AND SERVICES
63 INSURANCE CARRIERS
64 INSURANCE AGENTS, BROKERS
65 REAL ESTATE
66 COMBINATIONS OF REAL ESTATE, INSURANCE, LOANS
67 LAW OFFICES
67 HOLDING, INVESTMENT COMPANIES

SERVICES
70 HOTELS / ROOMING HOUSES / CAMPS, ETC.
72 PERSONAL SERVICES
73 MISC. BUSINESS SERVICES
75 AUTO REPAIR, AUTO SERVICES / GARAGES
76 MOTION PICTURES
79 AMUSEMENT / RECREATION SERVICES
80 MEDICAL / HEALTH SERVICES
81 LEGAL SERVICES
82 EDUCATIONAL SERVICES
84 MUSEUM / ART GALLERIES / GARDENS
86 NONPROFIT MEMBERSHIP ORGANIZATIONS
88 PRIVATE HOUSEHOLDS
89 PUBLIC ACCOUNTING

GOVERNMENT
91 FEDERAL GOVERNMENT
92 STATE GOVERNMENT
93 LOCAL GOVERNMENT
94 INTERNATIONAL GOVERNMENT

JOB TITLE

01 OWNER
03 CHAIRMAN OF THE BOARD
05 CHIEF FINANCIAL OFFICER
15 CHIEF EXECUTIVE OFFICER
07 PRESIDENT
09 GROUP PRESIDENT
11 CORPORATE SECRETARY
13 CORPORATE TREASURER
15 EXECUTIVE VICE PRESIDENT
17 SENIOR VICE PRESIDENT
19 VICE PRESIDENT
21 ASSISTANT VICE PRESIDENT
23 GROUP VICE PRESIDENT
25 DIVISIONAL VICE PRESIDENT

27 CORPORATE CONTROLLER
29 ASST. CORPORATE CONTROLLER
31 DIVISIONAL CONTROLLER
33 PLANT CONTROLLER
35 DIRECTOR
37 GENERAL MANAGER
39 MANAGER
41 GENERAL SUPERVISOR
43 SUPERVISOR
45 CHIEF ACCOUNTANT
47 ACCOUNTANT
49 ECONOMIST
51 ANALYST
53 SYSTEMS ANALYST

55 PROGRAMMER
57 ADMINISTRATOR
59 AUDITOR
61 BOOKKEEPER
63 ACCOUNTING CLERK
65 DEAN
67 PROFESSOR
69 ASSOCIATE PROFESSOR
71 ASSISTANT PROFESSOR
73 INSTRUCTOR
75 CONSULTANT
77 PRINCIPAL
79 PARTNER
99 OTHER

RESPONSIBILITY AREA

01 GENERAL MANAGEMENT
05 CORPORATE MANAGEMENT
10 PUBLIC ACCOUNTING
15 GENERAL ACCOUNTING
20 PERSONNEL ACCOUNTING
25 COST ACCOUNTING

30 GOVERNMENTAL ACCOUNTING
35 FINANCE
40 RISK MANAGEMENT
45 BUDGET AND PLANNING
50 TAXATION
55 INTERNAL AUDITING

60 EDUCATION
65 INFORMATION SYSTEMS
70 STUDENT
75 RETIRED
80 OTHER

Management Accounting subscription rates per year:

- Members $20.00 (included in dues, nondeductible)
- Student members: $12.50 (included in dues, nondeductible)
- Nonmembers: $125.00
- Nonprofit Libraries: $62.50

PD 11/92